A Wedding to Die For

Heather Haven

The Wives of Bath Press

A Wedding to Die For © 2010 by Heather Haven

The Wives of Bath Press
5512 Cribari Bend
San Jose, CA 95135

http://www.heatherhavenstories.com

Print ISBN-978-0-9892265-1-6
eBook ISBN-13: 978-0-9892265-2-3

First eBook edition May 1, 2011

Testimonials

♥ "Heather Haven makes a stellar debut in *Murder is a Family Business*. With an engaging protagonist and a colorful cast, Haven provides a fresh voice in a crowded genre. We will be hearing more from this talented newcomer. Highly recommended." **Sheldon Siegel. New York Times Best Selling Author of** *Perfect Alibi.*

♥ *A Wedding to Die For* "Wonderfully fresh and funny!" - **Meg Waite Clayton, Author of** *The Race For Paris*

♥ *Death Runs in the Family* "I loved the mystery. I loved the characters and the way the author developed their relationships, I thought the pacing of the story was perfect, and I even learned some Spanish! The author ties all the plot lines together nicely at the end, so I put the book down feeling satisfied and ready to pick up some of her other novels. I hope you'll give Heather Haven's books a look and let me know what you think!" **Amy M. Reade,** Reade and Write

♥ *DEAD....If Only* "There is so much action packed into this book. The characters are terrific. I loved all of them. I will definitely be going back to start at the beginning!" **Linda Strong, Mystery Readers Book Club**

♥ *The CEO Came DOA* "This is a strong work in the genre of the mystery/thriller!" **San Francisco Book Review**

♥ *The Culinary Art of Murder* "This latest installment of Haven's murder mystery series offers a twisty whodunit laced with a healthy dose of suspense. A solidly entertaining mystery." **Kirkus Reviews** ~

Acknowledgments

To our wonderful neighbor, Mexico, and all its inhabitants.

Dedication

I would like to dedicate this book to my Café Bee writing buddies, to Ellen Sussman and my fellow participants in her writing classes, especially Baird Nuckolls, friend and editor, to my supportive husband, Norman Meister, to families everywhere, and to my mother, Mary Lee, who is more like daughter, Lee, than Lila, just in case anyone asks.

A Wedding to Die For

Book Two
in
The Alvarez Family
Murder Mystery Series

Heather Haven

Table of Contents

Chapter One

I Love to Cry at Weddings

Mira McFadden was getting married. And I was the thirty-four-year-old divorcee who had introduced her best friend to one of her brother's best friends, who also happens to be my mother's godson. For the record, I can't keep up with any of it.

What I have learned is when Cupid's wings start flapping, take cover. And when the groom gets arrested for murder, please don't call me, Lee Alvarez. I may be a private investigator, but I am a reluctant one. Especially these days.

This all started three months ago. Carlos Garcia, groom and suspect, ran into Mira and me in a Chinese restaurant at Fisherman's Wharf, we having ordered too much lobster moo goo gai pan and chicken lettuce rolls, and he looking as if he could use a good meal. I asked him to join us. It was as simple as that.

For the record, it never occurred to me for one minute these two might fall in love. It also never crossed my mind they would wind up getting engaged, let alone plan a big in-your-face wedding. Jeesh, it was just lunch.

Who would have thought this Latino playboy, whom I have known since he was gnawing on pacifiers, would become besotted by a shy, soft-spoken female three years his senior, whose idea of a good time consisted of analyzing the contents of a mound of rocks found in the backyard? Not me, for one.

True, she was drop-dead gorgeous, with one of the sweetest, most generous natures in the world. The daughter of two tall Irish-Americans, she had honey-red hair, turquoise eyes, and a glorious ivory complexion covering her nearly six-foot-high frame. Even at my own five foot eight, when standing next to her, I looked like I was parked in a hole. We were a study in contrasts, we two best buds, me with wavy, brunette hair, dark blue eyes, and a slightly olive complexion, more exotic than not, and Mira looking like a larger-than-life water nymph.

Her beauty aside, Mira was also one of the planet's major klutzes. It wasn't at all unusual for her to trip over her own feet in the middle of a room, hurtling her elongated frame to the floor, taking several objects or people with her.

There is even photographic evidence of just such an event where, on her eighteenth birthday, she fell into her five-tiered birthday cake in front of two thousand people at a fashion show. It was right around the time her father, head of the McFadden Fashion Empire, got rid of the illusion his little girl would become a top model. Yes, she had the physical attributes, as well as being heir to the throne, but when destiny covers you in buttercream icing at the end of a runway, and the occasion has been frozen in time by every major newspaper, it's probably better to make other plans. Mira enrolled at Stanford University, obtaining a PhD in geophysics. Good girl.

A few years later, enter Carlos, "One of the ten most eligible bachelors in Latin America," as the *San Francisco Chronicle* liked to say. A scant two months later, early May, to be exact, he threw away his little black book and begged Mira on bended knee to be his bride. I was there. I saw the bending and the begging. Between his hot looks, gentle humor, devotion to her, and ability to sing any love song in Spanish, she would have been a fool to let him get away. In fact, in her excitement to say yes, Mira knocked a chocolate vodka martini onto his pristine, white-linen lap. He didn't even care. That's love.

This was all happening while I was on a demanding twenty-four-seven undercover assignment, buoying up my own sagging relationship with the man in my life, John Savarese, and raising Rum Tum Tugger, an adolescent feline, better known as My Son the Cat. Not that raising a cat is all that tough, but I was feeling stretched pretty thin. All I needed was a wedding.

Between being maid of honor, sister of the groom's best man, and daughter of the godmother of the groom, I became enmeshed in the upcoming nuptials like nobody's business. Everything except the romance seemed to revolve around me. I've said it before, and I'll say it again: Cupid has a lot to answer for.

Then Mira came down with the flu during the wedding preparations. High on love, she kept running, jumping, and leaping until she collapsed with pneumonia. She was going to be fine but needed complete bed rest for the next two or three weeks. This made it all pretty intense, as her dream wedding was being thrown together at the last minute due to a sudden cancelation at Stanford Memorial Church, Mem Chu, for one of the Saturdays mid-June. It was now pushing the end of May. Usually there's a two-year wait for such openings at what some people call "the closest thing you can get to a cathedral this side of Manhattan's East River."

My stubborn friend had her heart set on being married in this spectacular church ever since she saw it our freshman year. Postponing the festivities was out of the question. If Mira had to wobble down the aisle in three weeks' time filled to the gills with antibiotics, then wobble she would.

Carlos was to graduate from the MBA Program at Stanford's Graduate School of Business one week before the nuptials. Directly after the wedding, he had to head back to San Miguel de Allende, Mexico, bride in tow, to take over running the four-thousand-acre cattle ranch, Los Pocitos de Oros, being temporarily managed by his adoptive mother, Virginia Garcia, who's also my mother's longtime friend.

So in less time than it takes to grow out your nails, a formal wedding with two hundred guests from the varying worlds of fashion, politics, theater, and society was being thrown together. I hold moo goo gai pan personally responsible.

One recent Saturday morning, I sat at the ancestral dining room table across from my beautiful, ice-blonde, and very put-together mother, Lila Hamilton-Alvarez. As for me, I was puffy eyed, exhausted, and looking like something my cat had left in his litter pan.

"We should have hired somebody to stuff these stupid things, Mom," I groaned, filling envelopes with yea or nay response cards and a sheet of driving instructions to the upcoming shindig. "There must be a million of them."

"There are only two hundred, Liana, but I want Mira Louise to know we did this *ourselves*, and we didn't hire anybody." Mom has a habit of stressing certain words in every sentence she utters, like the word "ourselves," which makes me crazy.

"After all," she continued, stressing away, we're all she has. Her mother is dead, and her father is nowhere to be seen, *as usual*."

"Mr. McFadden did *design* and *build* the gowns for the bride *and* attendants, Mom," I said but paused, realizing I had imitated her vocal pattern. I mentally slapped myself across the face and went on, "And I think he's still planning on giving her away."

"At least," Mom countered, "he hasn't reneged on *that* yet."

"True. Maybe this time he'll be there for her. We can only hope."

"Mateo is standing by, just in case," she sniffed.

She was referring to my wonderful Tio, more of a grandfather to me than an uncle. Through the years, he's filled in for Mira's father on more than one occasion ever since I brought her home. His has a large heart, with room for us all.

I sat for a moment, sifting through sad thoughts about my friend's childhood. There had been the early divorce, followed by the shuffling between two warring parents, the death of her mother when she was thirteen, and then living with an uncaring, narcissistic father. Mira's family experience was so different from mine. Now that my dad was gone, my family was even closer, especially with our having to run the family business, Discretionary Inquiries, a Silicon Valley-based software investigation service.

"You're right," I said. "We are all she has. Don't pay any attention to me, Mom. I'm just tired."

For the past few weeks, I'd been driving back to my pretend day job around midnight. That was after the last workaholic cleared the building but before the scheduled 4:00 a.m. trash pickup. I'd ransacked our client's latest piles of garbage in hopes of finding some evidence of which employee was stealing top-secret encoding. A couple of hours later, I'd drag myself home, shower off bits of pizza and po' boys, and get a little sleep.

At 5:00 a.m. the alarm would go off, and it would be time to start my day all over again. I could have slept an extra forty-five minutes each day by eliminating my daily ballet barre, but that will never happen. Dance centers me. Even though I've had to face that I am, at best, a mediocre dancer and could never make a living at it, I still need ballet in my life. It's the necessary food for my soul, my own pizza and po' boys.

Born Liana but known as "Lee" to everyone in the world, save a mother who would rather eat broken glass than utter a nickname, slang word, or abbreviation. I am half Latina, half WASP, and 100 percent private investigator for Discretionary Inquiries Inc. That's the family-run business left to my mother, brother, and me by my dad, Roberto Alvarez, a Mexican immigrant who made good and died unexpectedly and too young of an aneurysm a little over two years ago. I mourn his loss every day. The family now consists of Lila Hamilton-Alvarez, mother; Richard Alvarez, brother; Vicki, sis-in-law; Mateo "Tío" Alvarez, uncle; and yours truly.

When Mom's not around, we refer to Discretionary Inquiries as DI. It's one classy operation. That's probably because Lila Alvarez, the driving force behind it, is one classy lady. She believes what really separates us from the rest of the animal kingdom is our ability to accessorize.

If DI were a car, it would be a Rolls-Royce. I own a Chevy, so I needn't go on. I always get the job done, but I get it done a little differently than anyone else. It's a blessing; it's a curse.

With the help of about twenty employees, we deal with the theft of intellectual property, hardware, and software programming in Silicon

Valley, often worth millions of dollars. Computer thievery is frowned upon here, especially by the injured company, so this type of skullduggery usually winds up on our doorstep. I am proud to say that DI has a recovery/prosecution rate of over 94 percent. "We Are Smokin'" should be our motto, but I'm sure Lila Hamilton-Alvarez would never put that on a business card.

"I've always *sworn* by cucumbers, Liana," Mom said, interrupting my reverie. "Use those, and you'll be fine."

Frankly, I had no idea what she was talking about, having lost myself earlier in my mental wanderings. I fought to remember what I'd said a good five minutes before. Was it something about me looking like cat scat, and my mother looking like something out of *Vogue*. No, no. I was just thinking that; I hadn't said it. Then the thread came back. Pooped, tired, and exhausted. That was me.

"Okay, I'll do that. Cucumbers," I echoed and changed the subject. "Mom, the gowns arrive this afternoon by special delivery. I hope I make it back from the florist's in time to sign for them."

"Why don't we have Mateo keep an eye out for the delivery truck?"

That's the upside of living on the family property in an apartment over the garage. The downside is you live on the family property in an apartment over the garage. Tugger and I share a two-bedroom, one-bath abode originally used by the live-in chauffeur back in the days when people in Palo Alto had such things. Four years ago, Mom and Dad renovated it as an inducement to my coming home after my marriage broke up.

"Good idea. I'll give him a call later." Just thinking about my uncle brightened my mood. "Speaking of Tío, the bridesmaids' fittings are at four o'clock. We're going to have a small party afterward, sans Mira, and Tío made the food." Apart from being wonderful, Tío is a retired chef. Recently, he's been trying to teach me how to cook. So far, what I have mastered is eating. "Try to stop by for it," I added.

"If I can. What's on the agenda for next week, Liana?" she asked, stacking envelopes alphabetically.

"Mainly, I'll be at my exciting job, delivering mail, emptying trash cans, refilling supplies, and being a general factotum."

I was distracted by a slight smile on Lila's face, and one of the flaps of an envelope sliced my finger. Sticking it in my mouth, I muttered, "Crap!"

"Liana!"

"Sorry."

"Regarding the job, are you making any headway?"

"Not really."

"That's too bad," Mom said. "And please stop making those sucking noises."

"Sorry." I pulled the offending digit out of my mouth.

"One hundred forty-three. If we can get these out in this morning's mail, the guests will have almost two weeks to respond in writing. The caterers will like that."

"The caterers told me yesterday that with this short notice, we were going to get one-hundred fifty-two chicken supremes and fifty beef Wellingtons and like it."

Mom smiled, saying, "That was before I spoke with them. They understand now that for the type of guests we are expecting, *salmon braconne, canard á l'orange, et de l'aubergine français seront plus convenables*" — she rattled off in flawless French — "is more appropriate."

"Okay, Mom, you're saying poached salmon, orange duck, and boiled eggplant are preferable to the chicken and beef? Just making sure I'm still up on my French."

"The eggplant has a few more ingredients than just boiling water," she said, "but essentially, that's what I'm saying."

My finger hurt from the effort, so I stopped stuffing the envelopes.

"Keep working," Mom said, nodding at the cellophane tape nearby on the table. "I think you can wrap some tape around your finger as a makeshift bandage."

She continued sealing the envelopes and adding postage, while I did as she told me and pressed on, like a good little soldier.

"Are you finished with that stack yet?" Lila said and brushed at the sleeves of the soft silk of her lemon-yellow jacket. No one wears lemon yellow like my mom. Absolutely radiates in it. When I wear anything in the citrus family, I look like I've got a bad case of jaundice. That's the difference between my mother's Nordic, cool beauty and my Latina coloring.

"Just about. By the way, were you going to meet me at the church at eleven thirty for the conference with the florist?"

"I don't think so. I need to get back to the office and finish up a few things. Then I'm meeting a client for lunch."

"On a Saturday?"

"Necessary, my dear. As for the flowers," Mom said, "keep it simple but elegant. For the church pews and altar, try white roses, open and budding, a little baby's breath, with a touch of lily of the valley, for interest. For Mira's bouquet, eight or ten cascading gardenias wrapped in white ribbons. And the attendants might have white rosebuds with colored ribbons that match each dress. Rosebud boutonnières for the men, as well, with Carlos's rose in a sterling silver holder. Virginia is wearing a Givenchy lavender suede-and-beaded gown. A single purple orchid might do nicely."

Everyone else in the world, except Mom, knew Virginia Garcia as "Tex," due to her love and devotion to the state. The two women had met outside Saks Fifth Avenue in Manhattan when Mom was six months pregnant with me. Tex had been pregnant, too, so a bond was formed faster than usual. Tex lost the baby — hence, adopting Carlos from a Mexican orphanage a few years later. The two women's friendship has endured over three decades even though they are as different as a bottle of Dom Perignon and a tall-necked Lone Star. Whatever void lives inside each of them, the other seems to fill. It's a mystery to the rest of us but makes perfect sense to them.

Mom went on. "As you know, Mira Louise has asked me to stand in for her deceased mother, and I have accepted the honor, so I, too, will need an orchid. I will be wearing ice blue, so something in a pale apricot shade should do."

I was writing furiously as my mother talked and would no doubt follow her suggestions to the letter. Neither Mira nor I had a clue about what flowers to order.

I'm not a wedding kind of person, having eloped at twenty-two with the Biggest Mistake of My Life. After eight years of trying to make a faithless marriage work, I finally had the courage to get out. As for Mira, she's more interested in boulders than flowers. If she had to, she could combine some pretty nifty rock formations for the occasion, but that might look a little odd, a granite bridal bouquet.

"Thanks, Mom," I said. "This is a big help. Hopefully, Mira's marriage will last longer than mine." I let out a dry chortle. Mom reached over and patted my hand, saying nothing. "I'm sorry. I shouldn't have brought up my own failure in the wedded-bliss department. Casts a pall over everything."

"You can't help but think of your own marriage at a time like this, good or bad. I know I've been thinking of your father even more the last few weeks." Mom smiled at me.

"Have you? In your case, Mom, that's nice."

"Do you keep in touch with Nicholas?"

"You must be kidding, right?" I said, before remembering I had never told my family the details about the night I left. It wasn't just the other women, who could hold reunions once a year in Yankee Stadium. It was that when I finally confronted him about them, he hit me. Once to knock me down and then once more to make sure I stayed there. I left him and our marriage as soon as I could get out.

"Nick and I have nothing to do with each other, Mom. I thought you knew he remarried a few months ago in Vegas. That part of my life is over."

"That's good." She smiled and changed the subject. "What more do you have to do? Possibly I can help," she offered.

"Thanks. Let's see." Dragging out a dog-eared, worn sheet of legal-sized yellow paper, I read it carefully. "Wow! I don't think there's much more." I giggled with relief. "I signed the contract with the two bands yesterday. One is an eleven-piece mariachi band that our very own Richard plays guitar with now and then. He's agreed to play a set with them. I thought that was a nice touch. The alternating band is a three-piece jazz combo. Something for everyone."

"Indeed," Mom responded.

"Allied Arts is renting us the restaurant for the reception, including the outside patios, from five thirty to eleven thirty p.m. Do you think ten cases of champagne, plus five cases each of Chardonnay and a Napa cabernet are enough?"

"That sounds more than sufficient. What else?"

I started counting off items on my fingers. "Bridal shower, next week. Richard is in charge of the bachelor party. The tuxes are ordered. The gowns arrive this afternoon, and I have two seamstresses set up for the fittings. I haven't seen a picture or rendering of the designs yet, but I'll bet they're incredible. Mr. McFadden designed them himself, something he hasn't done for years. He said he chose a 'theme,' which reminds me, I'll have to get samples of the fabric to the florist. Don't you own one or two of Warren McFadden's dresses?"

"No. I find him a little avant-garde, Liana," Mom said.

"I think they call it cutting edge now, Mom," I corrected.

"If you say so." She smiled and changed the subject. "Did you find a photographer?"

"Yes, finally. I thought I was going to have to buy a camera and take pictures myself."

"Who is it?"

"Did you know the reason the wedding that was supposed to take place at Mem Chu got canceled was because the bride came out of the closet and is now living in San Francisco with her lover, Charlene?"

"Get to the point, dear."

"I thought you might be interested in hearing the lead-in."

"No."

"Oh. Well, anyway, this guy was supposed to be their photographer, so he was available. I've seen his portfolio. He's good."

"That sounds *fine*," Lila said, somewhat mollified. "What about the rehearsal dinner? Didn't John offer to take care of that part of the festivities?"

"Originally, but he had to bow out due to a heavy work schedule."

"That's too bad."

"Yes," I said and nothing more. My latest love had been pulling back big-time on a lot of things, but I didn't want to admit it or deal with it yet. "However, Carlos took over and got us a private room at the new Japanese steakhouse for after we go through our paces." I looked at the tattered list again with all the check marks indicating completion and would have done cartwheels around the room if I hadn't been so tired.

"Mom, I think I've done it. After I order the flowers and take care of the fittings, I'm done," I said with pride. "This wedding is completely done and good to go."

Five hours later, I stood in front of a mirror, enveloped in what felt like eighty yards of a chartreuse moiré taffeta laughingly called "Whipped Lime." Between the starched crinoline underskirt, ruffled hem of the overskirt, and tufted bodice, all in a hideous yellow-green, I looked like a New Year's Eve float depicting baby poo.

I ripped open the other boxes to find matching gowns in different odious colors sporting the names of "Pineapple Fizz, Mango Madness, Orange Frappé, and Passion Fruit Frazzle." Mr. McFadden had created a theme, all right.

Jamba Juice Rejects. And in moiré taffeta. When Mom called his work avant-garde, she was being kind.

The phone rang, but I was afraid to move. On top of how I looked, any movement sounded like leaves trapped in a wind tunnel. *No wonder no one wore taffeta anymore,* I thought. Noise pollution. One of the seamstresses answered the phone and slapped it into my frozen hand.

"Hello?" I said.

"Lee, it's me. We need your help," Mira said. Her voice sounded frantic and as if she'd been crying.

"Mira? Are you all right?"

"No I'm not," she sobbed. "Carlos is being arrested for murder."

"What?" I said, sinking straight to the floor, buried in a mound of taffeta. "Carlos is being arrested for murder?"

"Yes, they say he murdered the thief who broke into our apartment last night. They're taking him away," she wailed.

"Wait a minute. What thief? What murder? Mira, what's going on?" She tried to tell me, but between the hysteria, coughing, and wheezing, I couldn't understand her.

"Never mind," I interrupted. "Hold tight. I'll be right there." I struggled to my feet and thought, *With the groom arrested for murder, maybe this good-to-go wedding just got up and went.*

Chapter Two

A Thief, a Dog and a Warrant

I ripped off the gown, threw on some clothes, flew out the door, and took the stairs two at a time down to my car. I'd shouted back to the two astonished seamstresses that they needed to let the bridesmaids know upon their arrival that I had an "urgent matter to attend to and would be back as soon as I could." I was just as glad not to have to see those women's faces when they got a load of the gowns they'd be wearing at Mira's wedding. Should there be a wedding.

While backing the car out of the garage, I spied Tío watering the yard. Updating my uncle, I asked him to keep an eye on the four friends who should be arriving shortly.

Carlos and the police were long gone by the time I got there, and Mira was borderline hysterical. Dressed in pajamas and robe and camped out on the sofa, she wheezed between sobs and hiccups. Having pneumonia is bad enough, but when your fiancé is arrested for murder, it could be a killer. Literally.

Scared Mira might have a relapse, I phoned my mother and was relieved when she said she'd be right over. Lila may wear four-and-a-half-inch stilettos, but she can move when she has to. She arrived in less than ten minutes, gathered Mira in her arms, and rocked her soothingly. Mom's only five foot four, and Mira towers over her. But in this case, motherhood was in the dominant position, and we knew it.

"Liana, why don't you make us some tea?" Mom asked after a moment and then turned to Mira. "You'd like some tea, wouldn't you, dear?" Mira nodded. "Good. And then we can do something about your hair," she added. Mira's hand fluttered up to her head, and she began combing at her hair with her fingers.

Mom was brushing Mira's tawny mane with long, soothing strokes by the time I returned from the kitchen. I knew the power of those brush strokes. They had been used on my own dark curls when I was a frightened or distraught child. Mira was calmer, and her flushed face was returning to its normal color. She even gave me a half smile when I set down the tray of tea, cookies, and sliced fruit.

"Excellent idea, Liana," said Mom, when she saw the food. She put down the brush and asked, "When was the last time you ate, Mira Louise?" Mira shrugged. "You must eat something, but first, take a deep breath and tell us exactly what happened. No histrionics or tears now," she warned, pouring tea into a cup and thrusting it into

Mira's hand. "There's time for that later. Right now we need the facts, so Liana can help you."

I arched an eyebrow at that last bit but sat in the chair across from Mom and Mira on the couch. "Okay," I said to my friend, "what happened?"

Sucking in air, Mira said, "Last night a man climbed in through the window over there. At least, that's how I saw him leave." She pointed in the direction of a series of four tall windows, one of which was next to an antiquated fire escape. "I guess he didn't think anyone was here. We were asleep in the bedroom, even though it was before seven."

"Did you report it?"

"Oh yes. The police were here and everything."

"Why didn't you call and tell us, dear?" Mom asked.

Mira looked at me guiltily before turning away with a coughing fit. Finally, she was able to say, "I didn't want to bother you. I know how much you've been doing for me already. I didn't think it was necessary. I thought we'd handled it." Mira gulped at the tea. Then she put the cup down on the tray and covered her face with shaking hands.

"It's okay. It's okay," I said, patting her knee. "We understand. You don't have to tell us everything that goes on in your life. That's just some 'mommy guilt' offered up for your amusement," I joked. Mira smiled. Mom glared. "Go ahead," I said to my friend.

"I heard him before Carlos did," Mira said. "I was half asleep, and I heard sounds coming from the living room. I thought it was a bird that flew inside. The windows don't have screens on them, and when it's warm, Carlos leaves them wide open for ventilation. A few times birds have flown in, like sparrows or pigeons. We leave them alone, and they always find their way back out again. It's not really a problem. The last time, it was a white dove. I wanted to see if it came back. I like birds."

"Let's move *past* the birds, dear," Mom suggested. "Tell us about the burglar."

"Yes. Well, I got up and went to see, not expecting it to be anything but one of them. You know, one of the birds." She paused, and I could see in her eyes she didn't want to talk about what happened next. Mom noticed it, too, so we sat and waited. Mira coughed again, unscrewed the cap of a cough medicine bottle, and took a swig. I noticed the label contained a warning about codeine and saw Mom noticed Mira didn't use a spoon. There was a lot of noticing going on here, but still we were silent waiting for Mira to go on.

She cleared her throat and said, "It wasn't even dark out yet. Anyway, I surprised him, the man." She shuddered. "He had a nasty look on his face, and then he started coming toward me. I was terrified. I didn't know what he was going to do. I screamed, and I must have stepped backward, because I tripped and fell into the wall unit. You know how I'm always falling over things. It made a lot of noise."

"Were you hurt?" Mom asked.

"A little, but more frightened than anything else. I screamed again, and by this time, Carlos was running out of the bedroom. It wasn't me the man was coming for, I realized later. I had been standing in front of the dog. When the man saw Carlos, he grabbed it and went out the window."

"Dog? You don't have a dog," I said, but Mira didn't hear me.

"Carlos started to go after him, but when he saw me lying there, he came back. I was a little dazed. One of the speakers had fallen on my head. Carlos thought the man hit me. He wouldn't listen. I kept telling him I fell, but he wouldn't listen."

Mom gasped. "A speaker fell on your head?"

"Yes, a small one," said Mira. "See? It's over there now." She pointed to a five- or six-inch silver speaker sitting on a square teak end table in a living room decorated in what Mom calls Scandinavian Contemporary. I think that means wood, leather, and chrome done in clean lines. Lush greenery, shelves of books, plus the findings from Mira's digs and Carlos's Mexican heritage made for an interesting, light, and airy room.

"I hope you went to the hospital to get checked out," Mom said.

"Yes, we went to the emergency room. I'm all right. It's just a little bump but..." She stopped speaking and picked up a cloth napkin from the tray, twisting and turning it.

"But what?" I said after watching her for a moment. There was something else frightening Mira besides the intruder.

"Lee, when you go to see Carlos, can you talk to him?"

"Talk to him? About what?"

She hesitated before speaking. "About the way he's been acting. Like at the hospital. He started saying the most awful things with the police there and everything. Nobody could calm him down."

"What did he say?" Mom asked.

"What he was going to do to the robber when he caught him. It wasn't the man's fault I got the bump on the head."

"Of course it was his fault, Mira Louise," Mom interjected, pouring more tea into Mira's cup. "You wouldn't have fallen if he hadn't broken into your home."

"Well, yes, but still..." She stopped speaking but continued to fold and unfold the napkin.

"What is it, Mira?" I asked. "Talk to me."

She hesitated again and finally blurted out, "Carlos was acting like a crazy man, Lee. I mean it. He was out of control. I've never seen him like that before."

"Listen," I said, "he was probably overwrought at the time. When someone you love gets hurt, sometimes you react strongly."

"Really?" She seemed to clutch at the possibility. "Because he scared me. He was shouting threats and banging chairs around. I couldn't get him to stop. Nobody could. It was like I didn't know him."

Mom took the napkin out of Mira's hand, replacing it with the tea. "Drink this down," she ordered. "I don't want you getting dehydrated." Mira obeyed, while Mom and I stared at one another.

The Alvarez family had known Carlos since Tex adopted him at four years of age. From the beginning, he'd been a thoughtful, sweet-natured child, bringing home stray animals and friends, treating the whole world like his extended family. This didn't sound like him at all. But the lesson I'd learned from my ex-husband, Nick, is you never really know what goes on behind closed doors.

"Mira…" I said, for the first time thinking the unthinkable. "Carlos has never hit you or anything like that, has he?"

"No, no! Never." She banged the empty cup down on the tray in her haste to defend Carlos. "You know I'd never take that. He's been nothing but kind and gentle."

"Except for now," I added. Mira nodded in agreement but didn't say anything.

"Well then, maybe it was a lot of sound and fury signifying nothing."

Mira shook her head. "No, he meant it. I could tell. I don't understand him going off like that. It didn't scare me for me," she clarified. "It scared me for what he might do to the man if he found him. That's why —" She broke off and took another swig of the cough syrup.

Mom took the bottle from Mira's hand and set it out of reach, saying, "How much of this have you had?"

"Only this," Mira responded. "I opened the bottle a minute ago."

"All right, that takes care of yesterday," I said. "Tell me about today."

"Carlos got a phone call around noon and went out right afterward." Mira leaned back, closing her eyes. "When I asked him where he was going, he said he would be back soon and for me not to worry. It was so unlike him not to tell me. We tell each other everything. At least I thought we did," she added through pinched lips.

Mom and I exchanged another look. I could tell she found this even more puzzling than I did.

"He went crazy again though," Mira continued. "The same as yesterday at the clinic. He kept saying nobody could do what that man did to me and get away with it. Then he left. A little over an hour later, he came home, and his face was all white and drawn, like he had seen or done something horrible and…" She paused.

"And what?" I prompted.

"He had blood on one of his sleeves." Her voice was small and sad. "I noticed it right away and asked him if he cut himself, but he said it wasn't his blood." Mira drew her knees up to her chest and buried her face in her folded arms. "I had to tell the police when they asked me. I had to."

"Of course you did," Mom soothed, caressing Mira's shoulders.

"What I don't understand," I mused, "is what brought the police here so fast. Didn't you say they showed up an hour or two after Carlos got back?"

"Yes. They said they got an anonymous phone call. Somebody claimed they recognized Carlos in a downtown garage and knew where he lived. Carlos had taken a shower and was lying down in the bedroom. He said he wanted to be by himself. I left him alone and was out here on the sofa trying to read. When I answered the door, the police barged in and began searching the place. I didn't think they could do that, but they showed us a search warrant."

I looked at Mom. "A search warrant? On a Saturday?"

"A phoned-in 'probable cause'?" Mom offered. I shrugged and nodded.

Mira looked up and asked, "What does that mean?"

"Never mind, Mira," I said. "Is there anything else you should tell me?"

"They found the bloody shirt in the hamper. They told me they were taking it as evidence." Mira buried her face in her crossed arms again. "Evidence of Carlos killing someone. I just can't believe it."

I wanted to know more but could tell she was exhausted, and the tears she'd bottled up were about to break through. "Okay, you've told me enough. Rest now, Mira. I'm going to make a few phone calls and try to see Carlos. I'm not sure what can be done over the weekend, but I'll do what I can." Mira lifted her head, smiled her thanks, and momentarily grasped my hand.

"Meanwhile," Mom said, "I want you to come and stay with Mateo and me until this gets settled. I don't want you here by yourself."

"Oh, no I couldn't," Mira protested and then leaned back, closing her eyes.

"I'm going to pack you a small bag," Mom said, turning away. "I assume the suitcases are still kept under the bed in the guest bedroom," she added, heels clicking on the wood floor as she strode down the hall and toward the bedrooms.

Standing up, I looked down at my friend. "You listen to Mom, Mira. You need to take care of yourself."

"You know, I don't understand why he took the dog," Mira whispered. "It wasn't worth anything."

"You mentioned a dog earlier. What dog?" I touched her on the shoulder, and she looked up at me with glazed and half-closed eyes. I guessed the codeine kicked in.

"Why, the little stone dog, the bluish statue Carlos found on the ranch a week or so ago. I don't think you ever saw it. It sat right over there," She pointed to an empty space in the wall unit.

I studied the living room of the three-bedroom apartment I had visited on and off much of my life with a new perspective. The condo was purchased by Tex and her late husband, Bart, in the '80s and used for their frequent visits to us and the Bay Area. The visits became even more frequent once they adopted Carlos, who was the same age as my brother, Richard. I remember Tex telling us, with Carlos in her life, her joy was boundless. Her love for her new son helped her through the difficult time of Bart's loss shortly after when he was thrown from a horse and killed.

Carlos enrolled in the MBA program at Stanford twenty-five years later and had been living full-time in this family pied-à-terre for the past two years. He and Richard saw each other often and became even closer friends than they had been as children. Then Mira came on the scene, and our two families were more intertwined. I assumed — we all did — that Carlos and Mira would be bringing yet another generation into these rooms and into our lives. I swallowed hard when I thought it might no longer be true.

I focused my attention back on Mira's drowsy voice. "The appraiser told us it wasn't worth anything just the other day." She faltered but went on, "I don't know why the man took it. Gosh, you have such pretty blue eyes, Lee," she murmured. "They're the color of twilight."

"What appraiser was this? What's his name?"

"The man at Mesoamerican Galleries. Can't remember his name, but it was the man with the silver hair who told us the blue dog was worth nothing." She giggled.

"Shhhhh," I said. "The codeine's kicked in, and you need to rest now. No more talk."

She nodded, curled up in a corner of the sofa, and I covered her with the mohair throw I'd given her for her birthday one year. Soon her breathing became deep and regular.

Walking down the hallway, I headed for the master bedroom to talk to Mom. I closed the door behind me so as not to disturb Mira.

"Mom, I'm going to go to the police station to see for myself what's going on. Maybe I can learn more there."

"Good." She glanced up from her packing. "I don't care how this looks, Liana. Carlos would never kill anybody."

I watched her fold a nightgown and place it into the small suitcase before I said, "You never know, Mom. We're all capable of doing a lot of things, given the right circumstances. You heard the doubt in Mira's voice."

"Mira Louise is sick and filled with drugs," replied Mom, crossing to the chest of drawers. "She doesn't know what she's saying. And as for you, you need to have more faith. You can't let what Nicholas did to you color your life forever."

I felt as if I'd been struck across the face, not by someone's hand, but by the truth. Did she know the whole story about my marriage but out of respect for me never said anything?

Whether she was avoiding how her words affected me or hadn't noticed, Mom stood back, focusing on my midsection. "Where did that come from?" she asked, pointing to my waist. "That belt doesn't go with that dress. Why, it's not even the same color."

Sure enough, in getting dressed after Mira's phone call, I'd grabbed a navy blue, wide leather belt instead of the black suede one that went with the black-and-red Vera Wang shirtwaist dress.

"Take it off immediately," she ordered. "It's better to have on no belt at all than the wrong one. Navy with black is completely unacceptable, I don't care what anyone says," she muttered, reaching out and drawing me near.

Standing on tippy toes, she placed a light kiss on my forehead that made me nervous. Mom doesn't usually display her emotions unless she knows I'm in over my head on something. When she gets all-out affectionate, it usually means I'm in deep doo-doo and don't know it yet. This time, however, I could feel it sloshing around my ankles.

Wordlessly, Mom returned to her packing, and I went out to the living room chewing on my lower lip. Just as I reached the front door, my cell phone rang, and I fumbled it out of my purse just before the call went into voice mail. I glanced at the number and felt my heart leap inside my chest. It was Carlos.

Chapter Three

The Butcher, the Baker, the Candlestick Maker

"Carlos?" I whispered, looking back inside the apartment to see if the ringing had awakened Mira. She was sleeping soundly.

"Yes. Lee, I'm in trouble, serious trouble."

"No kidding." I shut the door quietly and headed for the elevator. I wasn't sure how I should react to him. Was this an old childhood friend? A cold-blooded killer? Or both?

"Oh God, Lee, I've made such a mess of things."

"What does that mean? Did you kill that man?"

"No, no!" he said in a horrified tone. "It's all a mistake."

"Glad to hear it." The elevator door closed, and I pressed the button for the ground floor, wondering if the phone would continue to work. It did.

"Lee, I don't know what's going to happen. The police think I killed him!"

"Why did you go to the garage?"

"To buy the statue back. When I got there, I found him stabbed. I tried to help, I swear, but then I panicked and ran," he said.

"You're at the Palo Alto Police Department, right?"

"Yes, but they're taking me down to the hall of justice in San Jose soon."

"Is Frank there?" I asked. If he was, that was good news. Maybe for old times' sake, he'd give me some straight answers.

"Yes, I saw him earlier," he whispered.

"All right, Carlos. I'm on my way."

The Palo Alto Police Department is in the heart of downtown and minutes away from Mira and Carlos's apartment, so I was there before I got all my thoughts together. Standing outside, I stared at the building that's been almost a second home to me most of my life. Since I can remember, I'd been visiting either my father — before he left and started DI — or Frank Thompson, now the head of the Palo Alto Police Department, my godfather and close family friend.

When I was small, the officers on duty would give me day-old jelly donuts and sodas from the vending machine. As an adult, I am often here on official business. I've worked with many of the officers, and some I am proud to call friends, but I'd never walked inside these doors to try to help clear a friend of murder charges. It was an eerie feeling.

I went inside and headed to Frank's office. I knew I was expected because upon seeing me, the sergeant at the front desk shook her head, pointing in that direction. I would have asked her about her daughter's sixteenth birthday party, something she'd been working on for months, but this was not the time.

I knocked on Frank's door and heard his gruff voice ordering me to enter.

"Want to bring me up to speed on Carlos, Frank?" I asked, skipping normal greetings and throwing myself down in the closest chair.

He'd been sitting when I entered. When he saw me, he rose, tall and elegant, throwing the stack of papers he held in his hand on the desk. Then he decided to sit his six-foot frame back down again. In all my life, I'd never seen him so antsy. This was not a good sign.

Frank and my dad met in their freshman year at Stanford University, back in the '70s. Both were minorities, Dad a Latino and Frank an African American, and they were on scholarship to a pretty ivy league school during what is called "a period of social unrest." That wasn't what bound them together though. They were heart brothers. They thought and felt the same way about nearly everything even down to having the same sense of humor. After college, they joined the San Mateo Police Academy, graduated with honors, and went to work at PAPD together. Even when Dad left to start DI, their regard for one another never waned. They were proud of one another's achievements. When DI became successful, Frank used to say to everyone, "Roberto's the visionary. I just do grunt work." As for Dad, he threw a two-day block party when Frank got promoted to chief of police. My father's death, so sudden and without warning, almost killed Frank. I don't think he has ever recovered. But neither have I.

Rubbing his neck, he began talking in a tight voice. "A nine-one-one came in around twelve thirty this afternoon from an unidentified male. He said he was at the university garage and heard a man screaming on the floor above him. When the caller went to see what was going on, he said he recognized a Stanford student, Carlos Garcia, standing over a man who was lying near the staircase. The caller fled the scene but phoned 9-1-1 as soon as he could.

"When my men got to the garage, they found the body where the caller said it would be, along with the murder weapon. Carlos was gone. We did a quick run on the fingerprints on the weapon, and the prints matched Carlos."

"*Dios mio!*" I said and threw my hands up in the air. "This just gets worse and worse."

"Yes, it does," he said, rising and crossing to a small table in the corner. Frank turned back to me. "Want some coffee? I made it, so you stand forewarned."

"The usual paint thinner?"

"Yeah. Sometimes I take the leftovers home when Abby needs to clean the garage floor." He forced a smile.

I watched him pour two cups before I asked, "How'd you get such a quick match on the fingerprints?"

"Did you know Carlos is registered as a foreign student even though he has dual citizenship?"

"He mentioned that once. Something about the GSB's unofficial quota on US students being full that year, but if he came in as a foreign student, he could get in right away."

"And all foreign students have to be fingerprinted." Frank handed me a bright red mug with a holly wreath on it.

I took a sip and grimaced. The coffee was lukewarm and bitter. I would have asked for some sugar, but all the sweetener in the world couldn't fix this. "And who is this caller? Did you identify him?"

"No, but sometimes people don't like to get involved. The call came from one of the few pay phones left in town, so I don't think we can trace him."

"Well, how convenient." Frank ignored my comment, so I went on. "What about the victim? Who's he?"

"We don't know yet. He didn't have any papers on him other than an address in Mexico City. We sent his fingerprints off to Mexico in case they can help us," Frank said. "Lee, whatever his name is, it was the same man Carlos threatened to kill the night before in front of everyone at the hospital, including me. When I showed him the body, Carlos admitted it was the burglar. I had to arrest him. I had to."

"Mira mentioned his behavior at the hospital and said you were there. What happened?"

Frank put down his coffee and started straightening the top of his desk, something he does when he's frustrated. He looked up. "Last

34

night, when I found out who was reporting a robbery, I went to the hospital myself, with two of my men.

"When I got there, Mira was in seeing a doctor. I found Carlos in an extremely agitated state. He said to me, 'You should see what he did to Mira, Frank! If I ever find that bastard, I'll kill him. I'll kill him, I swear.' Now, this is not what you should be saying to a police officer."

"No, it isn't," I agreed.

"I tried to calm him down," Frank continued, shoving pens and pencils into a large, cracked jar to the right of him. "I said to him, 'Take it easy, man. It doesn't help to be talking like this. You just take care of Mira. Let me and my men take care of finding who did this.'"

Frank stopped speaking and stared directly into my eyes before he went on. "Lee, he shrugged me off, walked over and punched a nearby wall so hard it rattled the hanging pictures. I finally had to take him outside. I told him if he didn't stop the macho crap, I would arrest him for disturbing the peace and making threats against a citizen."

"How was he after that?" I asked.

"A little better. He said I was right. He didn't know what got into him. Not that the damage wasn't already done. There are about eight witnesses, including two of my own men, who heard him say he would kill the guy. Did I mention his fingerprints were on the murder weapon?" Frank said, shaking his head.

"What did Carlos say about that?"

"When I asked him, he said he found the man dying and tried to help by pulling the knife out, the idiot."

"So it was a knife. Sounds messy."

Frank nodded and resumed collecting and storing writing paraphernalia from the top of his cluttered desk. "Twelve-inch butcher knife. One of those fancy, professional jobs."

"What's a 'fancy professional job?' Keep in mind that I use a Swiss Army knife, even to chop vegetables."

"You're kidding."

"You wish."

"Instead of steel, the blade's made out of ceramic. One of those chefs on the Food Channel uses one, so they're hot right now. You get them at upscale stores, like Williams-Sonoma."

"Upscale?"

"They cost a fortune. Believe me, I know. I gave one to Abby for Christmas. The knife in question sells for around two hundred and fifty dollars. It's surprising to have it used as a murder weapon."

"Why is that?"

"The appeal of a ceramic knife is that it never needs to be sharpened, but it's easily broken if you're not careful. In fact, that's what happened here. Most of the knife is still inside the victim. Broken off near the handle."

"Lovely," I commented.

"Carlos admitted he did that when he tried to pull it out. And it's just the kind of knife a fancy, privileged boy might have on hand and use."

"We're back to the word, 'fancy.' Is that as opposed to the unfancy, underprivileged killer, who would probably use something cheaper and more reliable?"

"That's right."

"But possibly not," I argued. "A knife is a knife. Anyone could have used it, and it seems to have done the job. The man's dead."

"Statistically, most knife wounds come from blades made of stainless steel that cost fifteen or twenty bucks," he retorted. "Ceramic ones can break at an inopportune time, are expensive, and harder to come by. I'm not telling you anything the prosecution isn't going to glom on to. It's an unusual knife for the average man to get his hands on. Save the theatrics for the courtroom."

"Sorry."

"No, I am, Liana," he said after a moment. "I didn't mean to snap at you. This has been a hard day."

"All around," I murmured. I took a long drink of the coffee, felt my scalp begin to tingle, and decided I'd had enough caffeine for the day. Setting down the cup, I went on. "I take it you're looking into whether or not Carlos bought one of those knives."

"Yes, but it's not as easy as you think. If you pay cash, stores don't keep records of who bought what."

"Then you may not be able to prove he bought one," I said, thinking aloud.

"You may not be able to prove he didn't either," Frank countered, again with that same edge to his voice.

I felt as if I were being talked to like a member of opposing counsel. I found it odd but let it go. "Let's go back to this nine-one-one call."

"I know what you're thinking," he replied. "But it could have been genuine. Between us, I don't think so. As you say, it's awfully convenient."

"You don't think Carlos did this, do you, Frank?"

"Of course not," he huffed. "I've known that boy almost as long as I've known you and Richard. I can see him killing another man in a duel over the honor of a woman or for God and country, something like that. But a knife in the back? That doesn't sound like Carlos."

"I would have thought that too," I muttered, thinking of the recent accounts of Carlos's strange behavior. I decided to keep my doubts to myself.

"Not that it matters what I think. I can be a character witness later on, but first, I've got to keep him behind bars. It doesn't look good, Lee. It doesn't look good at all," Frank said more to himself than to me.

"Is he still here? Can I see him?" I asked, knowing the answer.

"Not unless you're his legal representation. You get a law degree in the past couple of days I don't know about?"

"Just testing the waters." I grinned. "You know, for old times' sake."

"I'll test your waters," he bantered easily, his dark eyes flashing. "You know, for old times' sake." We both smiled for a moment and felt the tension ease a little. Frank sighed and looked away. "You'll have to wait and see him down in San Jose, probably Monday after the arraignment. They're moving him down there as we speak, for his own protection. This is considered a high-profile case, him being a rich Stanford boy and all." He drained the last of his coffee. "I wish he could stay here so I could keep an eye on him, but that's the way it goes." He shrugged and studied the inside of his empty cup. "By the way, Carlos says he doesn't have a lawyer yet." He looked up at me. "You want to take care of that?"

"Sure," I said. "I'll call Jim Talbot, the world's oldest practicing attorney." I was only half kidding. Mr. Talbot was in his early eighties, a little hard of hearing but with a mind as sharp as the heel on one of Mom's Ferragamo pumps. "He may not be available, but I'm sure he can recommend someone. By the way, this has been gnawing at me. How did you get a warrant so fast?" I asked. "The cops were at the apartment with a search warrant in less than two hours."

"The detective on duty got hold of Judge Frye on the golf course with a list of probable causes. I was there playing golf with Frye today, just like I do every Saturday. The phone call came in at the thirteenth hole. Really threw off my game."

"The judge was carrying his phone during a golf game? I thought golf links were sacrosanct."

"Had to. Frye's the emergency-call judge this weekend. Something bad always happens on that thirteenth hole, I swear. Last week one of the caddies got bit by a squirrel."

"I thought you weren't superstitious," I teased.

"If this keeps up, I will be. Even though I don't work weekends, I came in today because of who was involved. See what was going on, you know."

"You're a good guy, Frank." I watched him shrug in embarrassment. I knew under that tough exterior of Frank Thompson was an even tougher interior, but he was an honorable man and loyal to his friends. Carlos was lucky to be able to call him friend.

"Yeah, well, I found out what was going on, all right," he said.

"So let me see if I've got this straight. Probable cause was Carlos's fingerprints on the murder weapon, a nine-one-one caller reporting him at the scene of the crime, and other witnesses hearing him threaten to kill the victim the night before. It's quite a list."

"It doesn't get much better." Frank nodded. "Frye was on the phone for less than five minutes, and it was done. We went on with our golf—you don't walk off in the middle of a game with Josh Frye and live to tell about it—and then I came straight here. I wanted to be here before they took Carlos away. This is the kind of case the prosecution dreams of, Lee." Frank stared me dead in the eye, saying, "What are you going to do?"

"Well, after I get hold of Mr. Talbot," I said, thinking out loud, "I'll talk to Carlos about bail. It's going to be pretty high, and he may have to pull some funds out of Mexico. Fortunately, money is something…"

Frank interrupted with a dry, empty laugh. "You need to back up and face reality. He's not going to get any judge in the world to give him bail. Carlos Garcia is not getting out any time soon."

I stared at Frank. "You mean there isn't even a hope of bail? Even if it's a sum that could buy a tropical island?" He answered me by staring back. I thought for a moment. "Flight risk."

"Serious flight risk," Frank agreed and continued to stare at me in a way I found unnerving. "On Monday, at the arraignment, the judge will hold him for a prelim, and I'll bet my pension the charges will be murder one."

"Murder one! That's premeditation," I said, jumping up. "That means they believe he went there with the intent to kill. That's punishable by death."

"Bingo. So I repeat" — he glared at me — "what are you going to do about it?"

"Well," I started lamely, "aren't we all — I mean you and me — going to try to prove him innocent?"

Frank slowly shook his head, and I began to see what all the stares were about. I am nothing if not slow on the uptake. "Lee, until someone brings me some other facts I can work with, I have to stick with the ones I've got," he said, pointing his finger at his chest. "My job is to see that Carlos stays in jail. My job is to help the prosecution come up with enough evidence for a conviction." He leaned as far forward over his desk as he could and pressed the same finger on the tip of my nose. "And your job is to see that I don't. Get it?"

"Got it."

"Good."

I rose, walked across his office, and opened the door. I could feel his black eyes boring into my back as I closed it behind me. For the first time since I'd known Frank, we were on opposite sides of the law. Or maybe it was the opposing sides of the intent of the law. Frank's job was to prove Carlos's guilt. Mine was to prove his innocence.

For as long as I can remember, Frank has been haranguing me to become something other than a PI, and he wasn't fussy about what it was. He didn't much care if I became a dancer, real estate agent, cruise director, butcher, baker, or candlestick maker. Even though my own father started the family PI business, Frank has always felt that his goddaughter — me — was above such gritty work. His preference would have been for me to go to med school like his daughter, Faith, and become a doctor.

Recently, Frank and I had come to an uneasy truce about my lot in life, but I had never found him to be what I would call accepting. Now it looked like he not only accepted I was a PI but was counting on it. At least for as long as Carlos was in jail for murder.

Even though it was the weekend, I was determined to reach Jim Talbot, legal counsel for Discretionary Inquiries and family retainer since Mom was in diapers. In all that time, I don't think anyone has dared to bother him over holidays or the weekends. *There's a first time for everything*, I thought as I punched in one of the myriad of numbers I had in my iPhone for him.

The phone rang on the other end of the line while I reflected on the man who started out as my grandfather's junior law partner until Grandfather Hamilton's death decades ago. After that, he carried on the firm of Hamilton and Talbot, Esquires, alone. In his eighties, Mr. Talbot had the same skills as when he was clerking for Presiding Judge Walter B. Beals during the Nuremberg Trials in the 1940s.

I knew the octogenarian had been promising his wife he would retire since the first Bush took office. I was sure hoping he wouldn't be keeping his promise to Mrs. Talbot anytime soon. His service answered, and I left a message for him to call me.

Then I phoned Mom to see how Mira was doing. Tío had fed her homemade chicken soup, and she had fallen asleep wrapped in a blanket in my old room while watching one of my favorite movies, *Dark Victory*. If you think you have problems, wait until you get a load of Bette Davis in this tearjerker. It's enough to make you count your blessings.

Chapter Four

Saturday Night Fervor

Before I went home Saturday night, I dropped by the fourth floor of the university garage, just to eyeball the murder scene. There wasn't much to see initially—cars silently waiting, half enclosed by cement walls, little else. The crime-scene area was taped off and looked like it had been scoured within an inch of its life. Not even a cigarette butt remained. Undaunted, I got out my trusty flashlight, the one you can self-wind to recharge the battery and, winding it up, went under the tape and dropped down on all fours. When I found the area to be clean, I widened my scope and began to search beneath nearby cars. My theory is, you never know. An hour went by, and I wished I had some kneepads.

Then three spaces away, something sparkled when the beam of light hit near the inside back right tire of a gray SUV. It could have been a candy wrapper or a piece of cellophane, but I crawled under the car anyway. Once I grabbed it, I could tell it had been a stud earring at one time, sufficiently crushed by the weight of a car or two to be almost unrecognizable as anything other than a shiny glob. On turning it over, I saw that the five-prong setting still held a large, sparkling stone. The stone itself was virtually undamaged, which led me to believe it just might be a genuine diamond. Otherwise, judging by the condition of the setting, it should have been reduced to little more than powder. If I showed it to Lila later, she would know in an instant whether it was real and, probably, where the stone was mined.

Valuable or not, it couldn't have been there long. I knew these garages were swept of debris nightly by a street-cleaning machine. My stomach did the flip-flop that it does when I'm onto something. But what? Did it mean an unfortunate woman lost one of her earrings, or could this mean the murderer was a woman? A knife wasn't the usual female weapon, but it has been known to happen.

Maybe there was no way to tell if this had anything to do with the murder, but if it did, I'd tainted the evidence by picking it up. Maybe I should turn it over to Frank. Flipping the earring up in the air as if it were a coin, I caught it just like George Raft does in his movies. No, I decided. I found it outside the taped-off crime scene. This bauble was mine.

I put the remains in my pocket and thought about going home, suddenly tired and depressed. My mind came back to the last of my conversation with Mira. A silver-haired appraiser at the Mesoamerican gallery told her the stolen statue was worthless. Yet it was worth enough for somebody to steal it, practically in the middle of the day. Why?

The Mesoamerican gallery was only about a block away, but what could I learn by going there? I could call Richard and ask him to do a run on it, but that would only glean facts and figures. Right now, I wasn't interested in how much they grossed. I wanted a rundown on the place by someone knowledgeable in the field, with a little gossip and innuendos thrown in. That meant Race Holbrook.

Race is a six-foot-three Australian art dealer with a year-round tan and a gold chain collection rivaling most jewelry stores. Shirts open to the navel in order to display this abundance of gold. He tops the look off with his Akubra military slouch hat and drives around Palo Alto in a green-and-black monster truck with a dual-exhaust system. Not someone to be overlooked in a crowd.

He's had a huge crush on Lila since I can remember. With four wives under his belt, he wants nothing more than to make Lila wife number five. Shortly after Dad died, Race moved in fast on Mom, inviting her to go away with him on a two-week spearfishing trip to the Great Barrier Reef. Putting aside that, Mom does not do sports, boats smaller than the QE2, nor would she spear anything other than a Cartier bracelet at a charity raffle. Furthermore, she was appalled the man had asked her less than two months after she'd become a widow.

Bless his heart; he's not even deterred by the fact she insists on addressing him as Horace, his given name, something no one else has the nerve to do, not even his mother. If ever there was a man who acted less like a Horace, it's Race.

But back to my interest in him. He was big into the Palo Alto art world, not to mention president of the chamber of commerce. Even though his specialty was medieval art, I believed he could give me an insider's take on Mesoamerican Galleries. I gave him a fast call at his small gallery off Ramona, and he answered on the second ring.

"G'day! Holbrook Galleries. You have the honor to be speaking with Race Holbrook, himself." Not only did he drop his "h's" and clip his vowels, but the greeting climbed the scale in volume and pitch. The longer he lived in the States, the heavier his Australian accent got.

"Hello, Race. It's Lee. Lee Alvarez."

"Lila's little girl! How is your mother, luv? Still thriving?"

"Oh yes," I said.

"Well, you tell my lovely lady I've got some amber fluid in my fridge with her name on it, anytime she wants to drop by."

"I'll do that, Race." Right. Like my mother would drink beer. "Meanwhile, I'm hoping you can help me."

"Anything, my luv. You name it. Good old Race at your service."

"What can you tell me about Mesoamerican Galleries?"

He took a deep breath and held it for a moment. "They're fairly new, you know. Only been open a little over a year but keeping in the black, unlike a lot of them. Two owners, Spanish, Mexican, something like that. You know, south of the border. One of them a Nancy boy."

Slightly taken aback, I asked, "You mean gay?"

"That's right, a banana bender. He brought his new boyfriend to our monthly commerce meeting last week. If that didn't start tongues a-wagging. Wait half a mo. You know the one I mean, Douglas somebody or other. You went to school with him."

"Douglas Albright?" I couldn't believe my ears. Douglas and I had been friends since college.

"That's it. Douglas Albright. He's the manager of that restaurant where I sometimes take a meal. The Creamery, isn't it? I've seen him around town. Born to be a Sheila. Remembered he was a friend of yours too."

I let his comments about Douglas pass. "What can you tell me about the gallery owner?"

"There are two of them. The one I've seen is a gray-haired bloke, a little younger than me, but I can't remember his name, luv. Even if I could, I can't pronounce it. It isn't American."

"Said the Aussie," I replied without thinking.

He laughed. "I may be a true blue, but I'm one hundred percent American." I could feel his mood shifting over the phone. "I'll tell you, though, those Mexicalis, they've got a good thing going. I wish I could sell half the volume the pre-Columbian stuff does. Not that I'm hurting." His voice carried a false brilliance, so I let it lay.

"Race, what's your overall impression of the place?"

"You want me to bag on them?"

48

"If that means I want you to give me an honest assessment, then yes."

"Well, they've been going great bangers since they opened their doors. As far as I can tell, they haven't had the year or two slump that usually happens before a business gets established, especially in this financial crisis. 'Course, they're working all hours. When I drive by there, ten thirty, eleven o'clock at night, sometimes they're still open. They pay their membership dues on time, contribute to the widows and orphans fund, keep the sidewalks swept, so I can't place it."

"Place what?"

"The feeling that I have they're too good to be true."

We hung up after I promised to give Mom his love, which I had no intention of doing. Not unless I wanted to hear a sixty-minute diatribe of her dislike of him.

On the off chance Mesoamerican Galleries was suffering financially more than they let on, I made a quick call to Richard's department, asking for a copy of Meso's tax returns. Richard was out of town at a conference, but I knew someone would get back to me if I left a message and instructions.

That done, I drove home and put sliced cucumbers on my eyes just as Mom suggested. I'd fished them out of a Greek salad one of the bridesmaids had brought for the occasion. The salad had hardly been touched, since next to Tío's culinary offerings, it didn't stand much of a chance. Finishing off the rest of the wilted mess as an early dinner, I fell asleep on the couch with the Tugs nestled in my arms. True, I should have been cleaning up the apartment after the afternoon's festivities instead of napping, but fat chance. Should this ever get back to my mother, I'll say it was totally Tugger's idea.

The old duffer—Mr. Talbot's expression, not mine—woke me around 6:30 p.m. my time or 9:30 p.m. Boston time, which is where he was. Through a sleepy haze, I could hear the background sounds of music, clinking china, and happy, chattering people. That made me even more depressed. Saturday night and a man in his eighties is out on the town, and I'm at home with my cat. The thought sent me straight for a Milky Way bar I'd found under the sofa the day before.

I gnawed on it while I briefed Talbot on Carlos's situation. He, in turn, either muttered, "What a shame, just a shame," or made tsk-tsking noises.

When I'd finished, he shouted through the phone, "I remember that nice young man and his mother from some of your holiday office parties. Just a moment, my dear," he added.

He covered the mouthpiece and said to someone, probably a waiter, "Yes, that's my lobster, not the crab, and my baked potato as well." *Lobster and baked potato*, I thought. My oh my.

"I have to go soon, Liana," he said, piercing the airwaves. I held the phone as far away from me as I could. "My dinner has arrived, and I do have guests. I just wanted to get back to you as soon as the phone service reached me with your messages. I'll make the necessary calls and see what I can set

50

up for late afternoon upon my return tomorrow. If he wants to retain my services..."

"Oh, he does, he does," I interrupted, feeling I could speak for Carlos.

"Well, I'll call him from here in the morning to confirm things. He's being held down in San Jose until his arraignment, correct?"

"Yes," I replied. "Do you need the number?"

"No, I have it," he said, clearing his throat. Shouting at the top of your voice can be a strain.

"Could I see him tomorrow as well?" I asked. "I'd like to ask him a few questions."

"I think it would be better, Lee, dear, if you met with him after the arraignment on Monday. I would prefer that no one meet with him until he and I have a chance to go over things. I'll tell him as much in the morning."

It was easy to see why James Talbot the Third was such a success. Here was a man who dotted all his i's and crossed all his t's. Sort of like a good PI. Add to it that he was one of the few people in the world who could intimidate Lila Hamilton-Alvarez, considered a Komodo dragon by many. It was a winning combination.

"Would you care to join us Monday evening around six?" he asked.

"That would be great," I replied.

"In that case, I'll call you tomorrow after I speak with Carlos. Good night, Lee, from Boston Harbor," he added, hanging up.

I put the phone down and sprinted to the kitchen, putting together my own fish feast, a tuna sandwich with mayo, liberally sprinkled with peanuts and just a hint of wasabi mustard. Not quite the same as lobster, but one must be flexible.

* * * *

Sunday morning I slept in even though I had taken a long nap the night before. I woke up thinking about my longtime friend, Douglas, whom I hadn't seen in a while. I stroked the cat curled up on my chest. Tugger was getting a little heavy for that sort of thing, weighing in at seven pounds now, but he was so cute I didn't want to move him. Lying there caressing his glistening fur and watching his whiskers twitch, it occurred to me I hadn't spent much time with him recently, quality or otherwise.

Realizing I hadn't done so with my man, either, I sat bolt upright and dialed his number, tossing Tugger onto the bed. John's voice mail picked up. While soothing a miffed cat, I left a message saying I had the entire morning free and would love to see him. Then I phoned Douglas's number and his vm picked up too. I left a chatty message about the two of us getting together sooner rather than later, hung up, and tried not to think about my Benedict Arnold tendencies.

Instead, I played Bite the Toes Under the Blanket with Tugger for the better part of an hour. Criminy, not having to do anything was fabulous. The phone rang twice close to noon, just as I was having coffee.

The first call came from Mr. Talbot confirming the fact he was now officially handling Carlos's defense and telling me to meet them at the San Jose jailhouse at six on Monday. The second call was from Tío.

"Morning, Tío. *Qué pasa?*"

"*Nada, mi sobrina,*" he uttered in his soft Spanish. Tío Mateo is my dad's only sibling. The fifteen-year difference in their ages and the loss of their parents in a landslide in Vera Cruz made Tío more of a father figure than a brother. He was barely twenty when he walked across Mexico and up to the Central Valley of California, bringing along his five-year-old brother, Roberto. Night after night as a child, Tío would tell me in Spanish how he worked his way up to become a distinguished chef at a prestigious restaurant in San Jose. He always ended with his proudest story — and I was proud too — that of Dad carrying a 3.9 average in high school and being offered a track scholarship to Stanford. Tío keeps my Mexican heritage alive and kicking. I will always love him for that.

"How's Mira doing?" I asked, guilty about not having rushed over there and comforting my friend in the a.m.

"*Mucho major.*"

Then Tío called her "Our Sweet Mira" in Spanish, throwing in "angel from heaven" for good measure. Sometimes I get jealous about how much my family adores Mira. To my credit, it's not often and it never lasts for long.

"She sleeps soundly after eating my huevos rancheros," he said, switching to English. Tío still tries to perfect his English, which isn't bad, though his accent is heavy.

"Tío, can I speak to Mom for a minute?"

"Liana," she said, coming on the line. "What do you have for me?"

"Well, I've got good news and bad news. The good news is Mr. Talbot just phoned and said he's going to take the case. He flies back from Boston this afternoon and will see Carlos then. The bad news is I can't see Carlos until tomorrow evening at six. Nobody can."

"Hmmm," she answered. "I thought you would have had things more under control by now."

"More under control? It's the weekend and Carlos is in jail!"

"I understand," she interrupted, "but you *must* be persistent."

"I'm doing my best," I said, feeling angry and guilty at the same time, "but I'm not sure —"

"Nonsense, Liana," she said, her voice overriding mine. "Surety is in the mind. I realize the fatigue you must be experiencing in your long hours of dealing with the Fogel case in addition to the wedding, but one must remain focused."

The Fogel case was my current assignment, and it was true; it had me draggin' my wagon. One of our ex-employees, Leonard Fogel, had asked us to save his duff before his start-up internet search engine and online advertising company, Bingo Bango, went down the tubes. Leonard left DI about eight months ago, forming this start-up, which had just received its first venture-capital round of funding. It was very similar to Google, MSN,

Yahoo, Silo Junction, and so forth but giving pretty fierce competition to one and all due to Leonard's particular algorithms.

An algorithm links something to something and enables the user to zip through all the junk on the internet and get to the junk they really want to see, plus other junk suggested by the program itself. I hope that's not too technical.

These algorithms were touted to be innovative and advanced even for Silicon Valley. I really didn't get the significance of it myself, but Richard, my thirty-one-year-old brother and the computer genius "from whom all things flow," got it and thought Leonard was a wizard. High praise coming from someone who has written several articles and managed to be on the cover of *Wired* magazine for his own technical skills.

The long and the short of it was, Leonard Fogel, a skinny, clean-shaven geek of about twenty-four, suspected someone was copying and selling his in-house web encodings shortly after he created them. They kept showing up a day or two later on Silo Junction's website, a start-up with a reputation for a no-holds-barred attitude.

No matter what security measures Leonard put in place, it still came down to the fact these encodings were accessible only to him and five or six loyal workers, who helped put him where he was. Before he accused anybody, he'd better be damn straight he knew for sure.

This made for an odd assignment for DI because we specialize in the post-mortem version of what, when, where, how, and why. We gather after-the-fact evidence, so when the case comes to trial, the prosecution can go right for the jugular. The DA likes nothing better than knowing the only thing the defense can do is to throw itself on the mercy of the court, hoping, in the end, their clients might be allowed to keep their pants.

Normally, I'm what is called a ferret, although I'm sure there's a more official term. Dressed in my finery and wielding a lot of power, I'm sent in while distraught personnel are mopping up the mess left behind. I find out exactly what happened when no one was paying attention, and I am quite good at what I do.

However, this time I was in beforehand and undercover. Bingo Bango only hired computer techies, software engineers, and programmers on the sunny side of twenty-five. Even I couldn't fake that. They had no need for any level of administration at all, like most start-ups. The officers with initials after their names like CEO, CFO, and COO were used to doing all the secretarial work themselves in between learning how to shave. Any small amount of administrative work left was done by the office manager, a nasty kid called Robby Weinblatt, or by Leonard himself.

They did, however, have an opening for an absolutely horrible job labeled Office Clerical Assistant and paying bupkis. Leonard "hired me personally" without going through normal office procedures. Thus was born an underpaid, struggling Hispanic, single mother of three from East Palo Alto trying to make ends meet. It was a far cry from the glamour-puss jobs I held during our normal investigations and required doing everything but cleaning toilets.

No Versace dresses, Bruno Magli heels, fancy offices, or power lunches. And I was feeling slightly put out about it, although I would never have admitted it to Lila. I like to pretend I'm above that sort of thing. You know, that I can take or leave my Prada.

On the bright side, every morning I climbed into a pair of baggy, black polyester slacks, one of three K-Mart blouses, and my thrift-store tennis shoes. I would slick my short, wavy hair back with gel and hit the road. No makeup, jewelry, stockings, or heels, none of the trappings of the modern-day executive businesswoman. The total time of office preparation was four minutes, if you counted my three-minute shower.

Then I would drive my car to a parking lot in East Palo Alto, only to take public transportation to Mountain View, a township south of Palo Alto. The woman I was supposed to be lived in EPA and couldn't afford a heap, much less my own classic '57 Chevy, an expensive gift from my father before he died.

In my current guise, I waited for buses or walked wherever I went. By the time I arrived at work at 8:00 a.m., I was already pooped. I reversed the process at the end of the day, getting home at around 7:30 p.m. when I became the wedding planner. All this cloak-and-dagger stuff, combined with taking on a soup-to-nuts wedding, takes its toll, let me tell you. I hadn't even had time to watch any black-and-white movies on AMC in weeks. I was having Barbara Stanwyck withdrawals.

"Tell me about the problems you are encountering at Bingo Bango," Mom said.

"There's this jerky office manager, Robby Weinblatt, a kid who gives the word 'dork' new meaning. He's been hovering around me for the last few days."

"Why is Mr. Weinblatt hovering around you?"

"Let's not call him 'mister' even though he wears the label of office manager. He's barely nineteen years old."

"Do you think he suspects?"

I sat thinking about Robby Weinblatt for a moment. "I'm not sure. He is on my case, and I catch him looking at me all the time, but I can't think of anything I've done. You know how careful I've been about taking public transportation. I devote three -and-a-half hours a day to just commuting. I don't know how people from Los Baños commute to the Bay Area every day. I just don't."

"You're getting *sidetracked*, Liana. We don't *care* about the people in Los Baños."

"That's a little heartless, I must say."

"Liana," Mom threatened quietly.

"Sorry. Anyway, my Latino accent is good. I don't think I could get tripped up except by getting into a deep conversation with a native speaker. My demeanor is very subservient. I do a good job, and there have been no complaints I know of. I don't talk on the cell phone unless I'm by myself in what is laughingly called the ladies' room. I haven't used the mini-scanner or flash recorder because I haven't found anything yet."

"Do you think Leonard is wrong? That no one is *actually* stealing his encoding?"

"You mean, is it just a coincidence?" I mulled that over for a moment. "Mom, Richard says there's no way two people in two separate companies could be coming up with the same strings of coding simultaneously. He says they're too intricate and involved. I'm going with Richard's gut on this. He should know."

Lila sighed. "Very well. This has *already* cost Leonard quite a bit of money for our services even with us giving him a discount." Mom always has her eye on the dollar.

"One thing I have noticed, Lila, is these computer guys are very careful about what they put online or on their computers, but when it comes to what they throw in the trash can, it's another matter," I said, using her given name. When it came to business, calling each other by our first names was less confusing for clients and had become habit after all these years, even privately. "You'd blush at some of the things I've found going through their piles of waste every night. If I see one more picture of a pair of gigantaboobs — "

"Young men are *known* for their raging hormones," Lila interrupted. "But we'll talk about it later, Liana, when we meet."

Richard was back from his conference in Las Vegas, so the plan was to meet a little after five, when my karate lesson was over. I had been sloughing off lately, and I needed to keep up my level or turn in my black belt.

"Oh and Mateo wants to speak with you again." She handed the phone over without saying goodbye.

"I have made something special for you, *mija*." Tío's voice came as a welcomed contrast to my mother's. "I will bring it now while it's warm. Then I will show you one of Tugger's new tricks. We have practiced throughout the week."

"Tugger knows a new trick?" I asked with excitement.

"*Si*. You will be pleasantly surprised, I think. Now is good?"

"Now is perfect, and I'm starving," I said, laughing. "And by the way, I will probably be amazed, not surprised. I can't get the cat to do squat, Tío."

I had just finished setting the dining room table when he arrived. I opened the door to the smells of a tray full of *machaca con huevos* and jalapeño corn cakes. After giving Tío some coffee, I sat down and stuffed my face while he watched.

When I came up for air, I looked at Tío, noticing that despite his youthful smile, his hair and eyebrows were flecked with white. Tío was getting older, and the thought of it made my throat tighten.

With my Aunt Tia's recent passing and my dad's death two years before, he and Mom decided to try living together under the same roof, at least for a while. That roof being atop a two-story, five bedroom, six-bath structure, complete with carved columns at the front door and a hot tub and pool in the back. Mom roams the second floor with the study, and Tío's taken the ground level with the kitchen, where he cooks for her and some of the dietary cases from the local SPCA. He's a big animal person.

"Tío," I said, putting my fork down, "how are things going with you and Mom? Everything all right? Are you happy?"

"*Si, si.* I am happy. She is happy. We are happy." He reached out and squeezed my hand.

"I'm glad it's working out, Tío."

"We are family. What is not to work out? So do not have the worry lines in your face. And now," Tío said, rising, "I go to find my star pupil." Returning with a yawning cat, Tío placed him on the dining room floor. After a good stretch on Tugger's part and a couple of scratches behind Tugger's ear by Tío, my uncle went into the kitchen and called out clearly, "Tugger, come."

I watched as my cat's ears went erect, following the sound of Tío's voice. He paused for a split second and then ran into the kitchen. I trailed behind. With an alert look, Tugger went to Tío's feet and sat expectantly, staring up at him. Tío had placed one of the kitchen chairs in front of the counter and to the left of the refrigerator.

Using his forefinger, he tapped on the seat of the chair twice saying, "Tugger, come." The cat jumped onto the seat of the chair, sat, and looked at him again.

Tío tapped twice on the countertop with the finger, this time saying nothing, and Tugger jumped to the exact spot Tío's finger had touched.

I must have uttered a sound of surprise because Tugger lost focus and looked in my direction. Snapping his fingers to gain the cat's attention back again, my uncle held his forefinger near the feline's face, subtly demanding total concentration. Tío tapped the top of the refrigerator, once again without saying a word. Tugger jumped to the top of the fridge and sat down.

Tío turned his back to the cat while tapping on his own right shoulder. Tugger leapt onto his shoulder, balanced himself, and went down again on his haunches. At this point, Tío put his hand up to his shoulder and stroked Tugger's head as he lavished praise upon him. Then he gave him a small treat and turned to me.

"What do you think, *mi sobrina*? Is he not a smart boy?"

I babbled my usual about Tugger being the smartest and most beautiful cat in the world, as he sat on Tío's shoulder. Then Tugger jumped back to the top of the refrigerator, where he sat serenely taking it all in, front legs together, tail wrapped around his feet, looking more beautiful than any Egyptian sculpture I've seen.

"People forget that animals, like most humans, want to feel needed and useful. He knows he pleases me when he does as I ask," Tío said. "The most important thing, *mi sobrina*," he continued as he waggled his finger in my face much as he had done with Tugger, "is to make it clear to the animal exactly what you want and to be kind but firm. You must, above all, be consistent. That is the word, is it not? Consistent?"

"Yes, it is, Tío," I said as I quickly hugged him. I had a thought. "Will he do that for me?"

"*Como no.* Turn around and tap your shoulder twice with your fingers."

I did and nothing happened. I waited with my back to the refrigerator feeling pretty foolish. Tío snapped his fingers over my head, I think to get Tugger's attention, and then tapped on my right shoulder twice. The cat's sudden weight as he lithely jumped on my shoulder startled me. I moved a little, and I felt his nails go into my flesh as he tried to steady himself. "Ow! I have to trim his nails, Tío. That hurts."

"Stop moving, Liana. You have to remain very still so he may get his balance. He is not a tightrope walker," Tío added and then burst into laughter.

Chapter Five

Sunday's Child Is Full of Grace

Later that afternoon, I was pummeled by my karate instructor for two hours and told to practice more. Yeah, right. Like at three o'clock in the morning, maybe. Then I showered and turned my cell phone back on. In the two hours I was lying on the mat screaming in pain, there were six calls. The first was from Mom, the second from Richard, and the next three from Mira, who I thought was supposed to be resting.

The theme of the first five calls was pretty much the same. Apparently, I'd changed my name to Wonder Woman and didn't know it. Mom said I "owed it to the family to be ever vigilant and handle this problem." Richard, back from the convention, said he "knew he could count on me to solve this," and Mira repeated three times in her messages that "if I didn't find out who really killed the thief, their lives would be ruined forever." No pressure there.

Thoughts of our obligations to Bingo Bango flitted through my mind as I drove home. Maybe I'd have to bail if I was going to try to free Carlos. DI didn't usually abandon a client in the middle of a job, and I felt bad just thinking about it, but there were only so many hours in a day. I was already burning the candle at both ends. I decided to table this line of thought until the family meeting.

The last message had been from my old friend, Douglas, returning my call and telling me he was dying to see me. I was dying to see him, too, though mainly, I wanted to pump him for all he was worth on his new boyfriend. Mata Hari, move over.

Before getting out of the car, I tried John's number once more. I got his voice mail again and left another, terser message. As an immigration officer, he usually listened to and returned his messages within an hour, so I didn't know whether to be worried or mad. When the phone rang seconds later, I scrambled to fish it out of my handbag, but it wasn't John. It was Douglas.

"Lee, darling! I finally get to talk to you in the flesh. Where have you been?" he demanded with that dramatic edge he does so well. "And what's this I read in the papers about Carlos being arrested? And for murder? I nearly had a stroke." While running up the stairs to my apartment, I brought Douglas up to date.

Douglas took it all in and then said, "You know, even though I find Carlos just as yummy as all the other women in the world do and am devastated at not being able to have a shot at him—"

"I don't think he's ever going to turn gay, Douglas," I interrupted, laughing. I opened the door and heaved myself onto the sofa. Every moving part of me ached.

"I know, darling, but if he ever does, I'm first in line."

"I'll tell him you said that."

"Don't you dare, you vixen. This is our little secret," Douglas said. His tone changed, and he became serious. "Lee, what can I do to help? You know I wish him and Mira only the best. Speaking of Mira, how is she taking it, being sick and all? Does she need anything? I can send her meals from the restaurant. Three times a day, if necessary. You have only to ask, sweetie."

That's my Douglas, one of the most generous people on the face of the earth. As the manager of one of the oldest restaurants in Palo Alto, the Creamery, this was not an idle offer of sending Mira food. And he'd pay for it out of his own pocket too.

"Douglas, that's so sweet, but we've got it covered. Mira's staying with Mom, and Tío is healing her with his cooking."

"Well, no one can compete with Mateo's masterpieces. He is the Shakespeare of culinary artistry. So, pray tell, my tantalizing Bartlett pear, my connubial crimson rose, my winsome Welsh terrier, when shall we two meet again?"

"Hey, did you just call me a bitch?" I asked, laughing.

"If I did, it's in iambic pentameter, darling, so it doesn't count. I've got some very exciting news, sweetie," he taunted.

"Oh, you do, do you?" I asked, feigning ignorance. "Like what?"

"Oh no, darling, only in person. I must drag this out," he said. "How about tonight?" I let out a deep sigh, and he picked up on it immediately. "What is it, Lee? Tell Papa."

"Well, I'd hoped to see John this evening, but he's not returning my calls."

"Uh-oh. Trouble in paradise?"

"I think so," I answered.

"Darling girl, come over to dinner but leave your phone on. If the man calls, even in the middle of my soufflé, and you feel the need to tear out, leaving me to eat it all by myself, I will completely understand. What do you say?"

"I say thanks, Douglas. I'd love to. Around seven?"

"Is six thirty too early? After dinner, I need to put the sunshine back in my hair." That was a euphemism for dying his hair.

"I'll see you then, Douglas." We hung up laughing about something or other, and for a split second, I felt guilty as hell. Then the phone rang. Seeing the number, I remembered my meeting with Lila and tensed up again.

To the phone's ringing demand, I threw open the door and ran down the stairs, heading for the main house. Once inside, I followed the sound of voices coming from the family room.

Done in soft beige tones and dark oak, the family room has a floor-to-ceiling stone fireplace against one wall. In warmer weather, such as now, the hearth is filled with candles. The soothing scents of vanilla and lavender lightly perfumed the air.

Mira lay on one of the sofas, wrapped in blankets despite the temperature. Mom sat at Mira's feet reading her day planner, Richard diddled on a laptop, and Tío was pouring lemonade into glasses. When they heard my footsteps, all four looked in my direction. The first to speak was Mira.

"How's Carlos doing?" she asked, attempting to sit up. "Is he all right?"

"I can't see him until tomorrow evening," I told her. "I thought you knew that." I looked around at everyone for confirmation.

Richard came over to me, giving me a quick hug. "Mom told us, but we thought you might have something new to add. I just found out about this nightmare a little while ago. I'm still trying to wrap my mind around it."

"That's what you *get* for being incommunicado, Richard," said Mom. She rose, picked up a thermometer, shook it, and without warning shoved it into Mira's mouth. She'd have made one feisty nurse.

"I told you I forgot my phone, Mom," Richard explained. "With Vicki in New York on this buying expedition, she wasn't there to pack for me. I didn't even remember to bring shirts. I had to buy a bunch of T-shirts in the hotel gift shop." You would never know that he and Vicki had only been married a short time. He settled into being an old married man within seconds of saying "I do."

I sat down, gratefully taking a glass of lemonade from Tío, and gave them a verbatim of the conversation I had with Mr. Talbot, down to the lobster. Then I asked, "Does Tex know yet?"

They shook their heads, but Mira spoke up, saying, "When Carlos phoned last night, he said he wanted to be the one to tell her. I won't hear from him again until visiting hours tonight, so I don't know if he called her or not. I do know he doesn't want her dropping everything and coming here, if he can help it."

"And you know Virginia," Mom added. "She'll do just that even though she feels she shouldn't leave the ranch." Her foreman had retired three years before, and the replacement couple wasn't working out. Carlos planned on hiring someone new when he took over. Mom went on, "Before she learns about this, we need to have a plan in place. We should make the freeing of Carlos our number one priority. We'll put all of our resources into it."

"What about Bingo Bango?" Richard and I said in unison.

"I've been *thinking* about that," Lila said, pulling the thermometer out of Mira's mouth and reading it. "Still *over* one hundred, Mira Louise. You're to stay *inside* and *in* bed. No leaving this house until it comes down."

"But I have to—" Mira protested.

"No you *don't*," Mom contradicted with a smile. "Now, about Bingo Bango, Liana, stay with it for the next couple of days, and see what you can find. Toward the *middle* of the week, if there's *still* nothing, we can either abandon the project or put someone else in."

"I know Leonard's counting on us," Richard said, looking at me, "but I agree with Mom… ah… Lila." Sometimes it's hard for one of us to slip into the work-mode names. He continued, "Getting these charges dropped against Carlos has to be our number one priority."

"Agreed." I looked at my watch and then around the room to each face. "If that's it, I'm having dinner with Douglas at six thirty, so I need to get going. Douglas sends his best, Mira, and wants you to know he's there for you and Carlos, should you need anything."

"Please thank him for me," she said and then had a coughing fit. It wasn't as bad the day before, so I knew she was getting better. I headed for the door.

Mom followed me and whispered, "*Still* no word from John, Liana?" I looked at her in wonder. How did she know my relationship with John had taken a nosedive? I hadn't spoken about it with anyone except Douglas. Sometimes her skills at detection, especially regarding me, are scary.

"I don't know what's going on with it." She reached out and touched my arm. I turned my back on the others while retrieving the crushed stud earring from my bag. Changing the subject, I said, "Mom, I want you to look at something, and tell me if you think it's genuine." She took the earring and went over to a nearby window in the hallway. I followed her.

After studying it for a moment, she turned back to me. "This is a *high*-quality diamond, judging by the clarity and cut. This appears to have *been* a Tiffany setting. What happened to it? How did you come by it?"

"I found it near the murder scene. I think it was run over a couple of times by cars. How much do you think the stone is worth?"

"A one-karat diamond of such a quality is usually worth about ten or twelve thousand dollars."

"That's a lot of money to leave on the floor of a garage."

She thought for a moment. "Whoever lost it *should* have filed a report with the police or, at the very *least*, put an ad in the lost and found of the newspaper. Should I put someone on that?"

I nodded. "But I don't want Mira to know yet. It might mean something; it might mean nothing." I took the earring from her hand and dropped it into the pocket of my slacks. We stepped back into the family room as Mira struggled to her feet.

She said, "I wanted to thank you all for what you're doing for Carlos and me. I don't know what we'd do without you."

"Don't you worry, Mira," Richard said from across the room. "Lee's on top of this, and she always gets her man."

I looked at Mom, and she looked at me. Yeah, right, unless I'm romantically involved with him.

****

I was ascending the elevator to Douglas's apartment on the top floor of the chic ten-story condominium, when I suddenly got teary eyed. By the time I stood at his door, I was sobbing full out. Delayed reaction, I guess, to John's apparent rejection, combined with knowing I was about to take advantage of the most sympathetic person in the world. When Douglas opened the door and saw me, he folded me in his arms, crooning, and had me laughing in less than a minute.

For a man who wears as many pastel and ice cream colors as Douglas does, his apartment is completely the opposite, decorated in an ultra-modern design and accented with glass, black marble, and bright red globs of modern art. Not for the faint of heart. I sat on a black leather stool in his up-to-the-minute kitchen, watching him prepare our food with panache. The smell of a cheese soufflé, filled with sautéed onions, wafted from the oven. It was almost more than I could bear.

"So this ass has the unmitigated gall to ignore your phone calls? What a loser." He whisked the green goddess salad dressing. Another smell filled the air: garlic. Yummy.

"Maybe he's tied up, although it's been almost a week and no word."

"True," Douglas reflected. "Maybe he is tied up, lying in a ditch somewhere, unable to free himself to get to the phone."

This is what I love about Douglas, always looking on the bright side. "The last time we got together, it wasn't so good," I said. "Forced, you know?"

He stopped whisking and looked at me. "Well, it's his loss. I'm sorry, Lee. You deserve better than that. You really do. You'll find the right man someday... unless I find him first," he added wickedly with a wink. We both laughed.

"Speaking of that," he said, pouring the mixture over the salad, "I've met someone. We've been seeing each other for two months."

"No!" What an actress.

"Yes! In fact, he's moving in this weekend."

I kept my smile going, but inside me, I could feel my heart thudding. "Douglas! This sounds serious."

"Could be. Could be."

"But you never said a word." I was torn. Should I tell him about Mira and Carlos's experience at Mesoamerican Galleries or not? Douglas rattled on, so I let it go.

"I didn't want to jinx it, darling. Something like this doesn't come along all that often." He opened the oven door and hauled out the soufflé. It no longer smelled so great to me.

"I'm happy for you," I managed to get out. "What's his name? Who is he? Tell me everything."

"Hand me the plates," he said, laughing. I took them out of the warming tray and passed them over. With a large spoon, Douglas scooped out the steaming soufflé. "His name is Stefano Ramírez de Arroyo, and he's from Barcelona," he added with a fake lisp, reflective of the Spanish spoken in Catalonia, Spain. "That's his picture over there."

73

Douglas gestured to a spot on the gleaming black marble countertop separating the kitchen from the living room, dining room area. I walked over and picked up an eight-by-ten photo. Within an ornate silver frame rested a picture of a handsome, silver-haired European-looking man wearing a diamond stud earring. The photo was nestled in between two other photos, one I had given him of the two of us at Christmas and the other of his late and adored mother. My heart sank.

I remembered that my friend had purchased the silver frame at Sotheby's in Geneva several years ago. It had set him back a new winter coat plus gloves and had sat empty all these years. Douglas was waiting for just the right person's photo to fill it.

"Come on." He carried the two plates to the dining room table. "Let's eat this while it's hot." I crossed to the round glass-top table, elegantly set with black place mats, napkins, sparkling crystal, and sterling silver. Flickering candles and fresh flowers finished off the decoration. I felt both honored and guilty that he had gone to so much trouble.

"Get the salad, will you?" he asked. I went back to the kitchen and grabbed the bowl and tongs as he continued. "Isn't Stefano gorgeous? And such a nice man, Lee. I don't mean to say all of this with you having a broken heart—"

"Don't be silly, Douglas," I interrupted. "My heart isn't really broken. I mean, maybe I'm overreacting." Douglas gave me a look. I stuck my tongue out at him.

"Besides, one thing doesn't have anything to do with the other. If this is the man for you, I'm happy for you, truly."

"Are you, sweetie? I knew you would be."

I doled out the salad, and we began to eat. "Tell me about your friend. What does he do for a living?" I asked with a mouthful of fluffy cheese, egg, and onions. Between his and Tío's cooking, I was having a day worthy of James Beard.

"He's an art dealer here in Palo Alto, Miss Please-Eat-With-your-Mouth-Closed," Douglas answered with a wide grin.

"Sorry." I wiped my chin with my napkin. "It's so good."

"Thanks." Douglas smiled. "Stefano's been in town for about a year. He and his cousin own the gallery on University and Emerson. You must have seen it, 'Mesoamerican Galleries, purveyors of genuine and model art throughout the ages,'" he parroted from memory.

"What's 'model art'?"

"That means it's a reproduction. He carries a lot of those. If they're not marked, sometimes you can't tell the difference between the real and the imitation unless you have a professional tell you."

My mind flitted to Carlos's stolen statue.

"Look here," Douglas said, putting down his napkin, getting up and walking to the other side of the room. Thrown over the finial of a lamp, a small carved stone dangled from a slender strip of leather. He unhooked it, saying, "This is a model right here. Stefano gave it to me last night." He held it out to me as he came back across the room.

"Why, it's a cat!" I took it with delight. "It reminds me of Tugger." I moved it around in my hand and examined it from all angles. "And you're right. It looks old, very old."

"I know. It's actually a copy of an Aztec leopard done from a mold. Stefano says he gets about fifty dollars apiece for them. He's got them for sale at his gallery. Why don't you take it, Lee?" Douglas offered impulsively. "It's so you... and Tugger."

"Oh no," I started to protest, pushing it back at him.

"Oh yes," Douglas said. "No arguments. For the nonce—that's an Olde English phrase that means for the moment. Tugger is your main squeeze, so I want you to have it." He put the leather cord around my neck and kissed me on the cheek.

"Thank you, Douglas," I said, touched by his generosity and his friendship.

"Let's finish our dinner, shall we?" he said and we did, chatting about this and that, like the old friends we were.

I didn't know it at the time, but hanging around my neck was not an Aztec leopard but a sleeping tiger. And it had me by the tail.

Chapter Six

Bingo Bango

Monday morning I arrived at Bingo Bango twenty-five minutes late because I missed the bus. The timetable said it wasn't supposed to have arrived for another five minutes, but apparently the bus hadn't read the schedule.

I was greeted at the door by Robby Weinblatt, who glared at me as if I had eaten his firstborn. "You're late, Maria Theresa," he growled, addressing me by my masquerade name. I noticed he still had his knapsack slung over his arm. That probably meant he had only arrived moments ago himself. Do as I say, not as I do, presumably.

"I'm sorry, *Señor* Robby," I said, rolling my r's and using a halting Spanish accent. "The bus no come. I am mucho sorry, *Señor* Robby."

"Well, see that it doesn't happen again, Maria Theresa," he said, emphasizing my two names. He was his usual nasty self, but his eyes blinked nervously. "We wouldn't want to have to replace you, would we?"

My inclination was to smack him with my own knapsack, but I thought better of it. I lowered my head and said, "No, *Señor* Robby. It will no happen again."

I moved past him and on to my desk, the smallest of the lot, shoved in a corner and already piled high with everything needing to be copied, stapled, sorted, or delivered.

Bingo Bango was located in a huge loft in one of those buildings off the Central Expressway in Mountain View, where the real estate per square foot doesn't cost nearly what it does five miles north in Palo Alto. The loft was sectioned off into several dozen cubicles in the center of the space. Software engineers and computer techies sat and worked fifteen to eighteen hours a day, six or seven days a week, surviving on coffee, donuts, and youth.

Along the far wall of this enormous room sat the copy machine, as well as areas for the lunchroom and playroom, where the guys could work off some steam by playing pinball machines. I say "guys" because 99 percent of the thirty-eight people working here were male. The remaining 1 percent was a loner who went by the name of Pat. Possessed of a low voice and crew cut, Pat dressed like a dockworker, but had just a hint of hips and possible bosoms. I chose not to investigate further, so the gender was still an enigma to me.

The only places with any sort of privacy were the restrooms. The men's room was in the hall near the staircase, and the ladies' room was down one floor, sharing amenities with janitorial supplies. I never saw Pat use either facility. Bladder like a camel, I guess.

The ladies' room being on another floor made it difficult for me to do my sleuthing. Whenever I found anything that might be useful, I would have to cram it into one of my pockets and run downstairs to the bathroom, sharing my findings with a damp mop.

Just when I thought it was going to be just another horrible day, I hit pay dirt. One of the things I'd noticed when I first started the job was that Weinblatt always carried a black knapsack and tended to drop it in various places around the office, depending on where he was using it. I went out and bought a similar one. Mine was a cheap knockoff from Walgreens, but they looked pretty much the same. I'd been waiting for any opportunity to get inside his sack, so to speak, and that day I kept my sights on him while pretending to sort the mail.

Right after bawling me out, the nasty little twerp went to the copy machine. He looked around, unzipped the front pocket of his knapsack, took out a single eight-by-eleven-and-a-half piece of paper, copied it, folded the original plus the copy in quarters, and put both inside the sack. He then dropped the sack on the floor by the copier, and whistling, headed for the coffee machine on the other side of the room.

I was up like a shot. Grabbing my own knapsack, I rushed to the copier. After a quick glance around, I switched my bag for his and headed to the janitor's/ladies' room. I locked the door and rooted around the innards of the sack until I found the paper he'd just copied. It was a memo, and boy, was it worth the chance I was taking.

Apparently, Silo Junction, already on NASDAQ, had agreed to give Robby Weinblatt 2 percent of their shares if he continued to hand over the coding that had made Bingo Bango a front-runner. And if he could bring down Bingo Bango in less than six months, he would receive a cool three-quarters of a million dollars on top of everything else. Other smaller things were outlined in what read, essentially, like a contract. It was all right there in that stupid memo *Señor* Snot Face had left in his knapsack.

I danced around with the mop for a minute or two, us having become friends over the past few weeks, and then called Lila on her private line with the glorious update. She answered on the first ring.

"This is Lila."

"Lila," I singsonged into the phone, "the Leonard Fogel mystery is solved. I've got something in my hand that you're going to love."

"Oh?"

"And I'm about to take some pictures and send them on their way. If this doesn't burn up in the airwaves on the way over to you because it's so hot, it should be at DI within minutes."

"From what little I know about airwaves, I would say that's physically impossible," she countered, almost spoiling my fun.

"Well, wait until you read it," I insisted, keeping my voice down. "The office manager, Robby

Weinblatt, is the culprit, and I'm so glad 'cause he's such a mangy little twerp."

"Interesting. Why do you think he has mange?"

"I don't, Mom. It's just an expression. I could leave this disgusting job right now, but it might look too suspicious, so I'll wait until tomorrow morning. Then I'll call in sick for the rest of my life. Yippee," I whispered.

"If you're that sure, Liana, contact Leonard, and have him come to the offices at nine this evening. You're meeting with Carlos at six, aren't you?"

"Yes."

"Well, that should give you enough time. Hopefully, you won't run into traffic. We'll go over everything with Leonard at that time and finish off the assignment."

"Will do," I said and waited a moment, for what I don't know. "Okay, Mom. Gotta go."

"Liana?"

"Yes?"

"Good job."

"Thanks, Boss." I grinned into the phone.

I checked again to make sure the door was locked and looked at my phone. Odd, I thought, why is this off? I didn't turn it off. Then I realized I forgot to charge the phone the night before. I must have used what remaining juice I had on the call to Mom. I panicked. Then I remembered the scanner I carry in my pocket "just in case."

It's about the size of a business card holder, only slightly fatter, so it's easy to tote. Once I scan the doc, it does its magic and then I send DI the completed WYSIWYG — What You See Is What You

Get or an exact image of the document. Bada bing, bada boom.

Uh-huh. When I turned the scanner on, nothing happened. No little ping-ping sounds to indicate it had been turned on. No sharp red lines shot out on the page beneath it, delineating what area was going to be scanned. Nothing. Nada. I turned it on and off several times. I shook it. I cursed at it. Stifling the urge to throw it across the room, my eyes crossed studying all sides of it as if I could possibly understand why it wasn't working. After about five minutes of this insanity, I gave up.

"I'll just have to make a hard copy and bring it to the office tonight," I said to the mop.

The mop didn't answer.

"This is all Richard's fault. You know that, don't you?"

The mop still said not a word. There's nothing more annoying than a disinterested mop.

I refolded the memo and copy Weinblatt had made, and put them both in my pocket. Heading upstairs, I tried to come up with a plan for making an extra copy for myself, returning the original two sheets to Weinblatt's knapsack and switching back his sack for mine, all without being noticed. Good luck to me.

I could see Weinblatt having a conversation across the room with one of the techies and stuffing his face with a donut. Everyone else was occupied with a major project that had come in the night before. The time was now. I screwed my courage to the sticking post, wherever that is, and hurried to my desk.

The first thing I did was to plug in my phone. I thought about waiting until it charged enough to take the images, but couldn't chance it. He might miss his knapsack at any moment.

Grabbing my dirty coffee cup from Friday, a stack of papers that needed to be copied, and still clutching Weinblatt's knapsack, I made a beeline for the copier. I figured no one would pay attention to the copy "girl" as she went about her job, not even Weinblatt.

I placed Weinblatt's knapsack in front of my own on the floor, put the coffee cup on the edge of the machine, the stack of papers beside it, and withdrew the original memo from my pocket. Unfolding it, I made a quick copy, retrieved said copy from the bin, and placed it under the stack of papers on the machine. I then took the original memo out of the copier, while deliberately knocking over the cup with the other hand. Remnants of cold coffee dotted the floor. Bending over to ostensibly pick up the mess, I unzipped Weinblatt's knapsack, refolded and replaced the original and copy he'd made, rezipped the sack, and without straightening up, reached up and set the cup back on the copier, one-two-three.

Still hunkered down, I took out a Kleenex from my pocket, swiped at the coffee on the floor, grabbed my knapsack, swung it onto my back, stood up, and picked up the stack of papers, preparing to copy them. Another one-two-three. No sooner had I accomplished that than Weinblatt came over and stood behind me, his mouth covered in powdered sugar.

"What are you doing?" he snarled.

I let out the breath trapped inside my body and answered sweetly, "I am to make two copies of these papers and then bring them back to Jerry and Zack. Do you want to see them?" I asked, taking the chance he didn't. He didn't.

He glared at me and opened the lid to the copy machine, which revealed nothing. Somewhat satisfied, he closed it again. He looked at me with a scowl on his face, but it didn't completely mask a case of good, old-fashioned bad nerves. Interesting.

I smiled. "Can I help you with something else, *Señor* Robby?"

"No, I just came back for this," he said, snatching his knapsack from the floor. "Did you touch this?" He held up his sack.

"Oh no, *señor*. I did not know it was there," I said in mock surprise.

Suddenly he returned my smile, asking, "Why are you carrying yours? Going somewhere, Maria Theresa?"

"No, *Señor* Robby. I was just to take some medicine, which is inside my *bolsa*, I mean, my knapsack." I continued to smile. "I must learn to use the English words."

I opened my sack, took out a small bottle of aspirin, and went to the nearby water fountain, while he watched. Sucking down a pill, I hurried back to the copier, smiled at him again until I thought my face would break, and put the stack of papers into the automatic feeder. He studied me for a second and left.

After copying all the papers but the one I'd concealed at the bottom of the pile, I returned to my desk, stashing my hard-won treasure inside my slacks. I sat down, allowed my heart rate to return to normal, and mentally patted myself on the back.

A few hours later, I grabbed my knapsack again but this time to go outside and have lunch under the trees. It was a gorgeous day as it usually is this time of year, and I wanted to enjoy it and revel in my victory. Charged phone in hand, I took a chance and called John again once I was far from the madding crowd.

This time he answered. "Hi." I could tell he had read my number and knew it was me, yet his voice was expressionless.

"John, at last! Didn't you get my other messages?"

There was a moment of silence, and then he said, "Ah, yes, I did, Lee. I, uh, didn't get a chance to call you back yet. Ah, how are you?"

All these "ahs" confused me, but I said, "I'm fine. How are you?"

"Okay. Okay. Ah, we need to talk, Lee. Ah." More silence.

"Well, apparently we do. So talk, John."

"Ah, Lee, I think you're wonderful. Really, I, ah, do. You're beautiful and smart and, ah… ah…" His voice trailed off.

Oh no, here it comes, the "you're beautiful and smart'" speech. The kiss of death. Prepare yourself, sailor. Bad news coming on board.

"Go on," I urged.

"But Angela and, ah, Angela and, ah —"

"Angela Ann?" I interrupted. "Who's Angela Ann?"

"Not Angela Ann. Just Angela," he answered and a little testily, I might add.

"Okay," I said, matching his testiness. "Who the hell is Just Angela?"

"Listen, you know when I met you I had, ah, just ended a six-year relationship with someone."

"I do remember you mentioning that to me. Once. You said it was over."

Finding a spot under a shady tree in the parking lot, I plopped myself down. I had a feeling I should be sitting down for the rest of this conversation.

"Ah, look, there's no easy way to say this, Lee," he began. "When I met you, I thought Angela and I were through, but I was, ah, wrong."

"Ah, wrong?"

"Three weeks ago, we ran into each other again. We've… we've talked things out, and we're getting, ah, married."

"Ah, married?"

Wow, I thought, *there must be something in the water; everybody's getting married. Wait a minute. He's getting married to someone else, and all the while I thought he was my boyfriend? And he's telling me this over the phone? Now, that's being dumped, deluxe style.* In retrospect, there are a thousand things I wished I'd said, but all I could think of to say was, "I see."

He took a shallow, anguished breath, and I could tell he was upset. I guess being the dumper isn't all it's cracked up to be. "I'm sorry, Lee," he said. "I never meant to hurt you."

"I'm sure you didn't," I said, trying to rise above it all.

Then he uttered the most damnable phrase in the English language: "I hope we can still be friends."

"Up yours, John," I said, hanging up. I guess I don't rise well.

Sitting on the ground, I thought about having a good cry but couldn't decide if it was because I was angry or heartbroken, so I elected to eat. Leaning back against the tree, I unzipped my knapsack, opened the small cooler, and ate the *gorditas* Tío had made for my lunch. I particularly liked Tío's small seafood sandwiches with the chunks of crab, flavored with a lime cilantro sauce. Food brings me through every time.

After lunch was over, I went back to the office to continue my job but couldn't help counting the minutes. I phoned Leonard at his cubicle even though he was only about six steps away from my desk, to plan a meeting with him. It wouldn't do for me to be seen talking to him in person. I was way too lowly for that. I looked around to make sure no one was listening or watching me.

Leonard finally picked up on the fifteenth ring. If I hadn't been able to see him from where I was, I would have thought he wasn't there.

"Yeah. What?" he answered.

Great telephone manners, I thought, looking around me. It's a good thing he's a computer guru. "Leonard. It's Lee," I whispered. "Can you hear me?"

"Who is this?" he bellowed into the phone. Obviously, he couldn't.

"It's me. Lee," I repeated a little louder.

"Oh, yeah. So? What do you want? Do you have something for me?"

"Yes I do," I answered, looking around me again. Robby Weinblatt appeared out of nowhere and was heading in my direction. I spoke fast. "Listen, show up at DI tonight around nine p.m. Okay?"

"Yeah."

I hung up, just as *Señor* Robby descended on me.

"Who were you talking to?"

"Rosita, my *niña*. She is home from school sick today," I said, smiling in what I hoped was a sincere and humble manner when all I really wanted to do was kick his spine up through the top of his head. The boy had really taken the Simon Legree character from *Uncle Tom's Cabin* to heart.

"We don't take personal calls here, Maria Theresa," he said even though he and I both knew that everyone did just that.

"Oh, *si, señor*. It will no happen again."

"See that it doesn't," he said, leaning down into my face, putting on more of his tough-guy act. I was pretty sick of him by now, this pimply-faced kid, and as it didn't really matter anymore, I stood up quickly, forcing him to back up. Also, instead of slouching down, as I had been doing, I stood erect. My five-foot-eight-inch frame towered over him by about four inches, the little nerd.

"I will go now and add the paper to the copy machine. Then I make a delivery to Office Max on the bicycle," I said, using my best Spanish accent. "Did you want anything else, *Señor* Robby?" I asked, striding toward the copy machine that was directly behind him.

"No. Go ahead," he said, stepping aside just in time. I would have knocked him over, but he was too fast for me. He was baffled by my aggressive body language but didn't say anything. As for me, I didn't give a damn whether he was baffled or not, fed up as I was with him and men in general.

At the end of the day, throwing caution to the wind, I called for a taxi to pick me up and take me to my car. If I was ever going to get to San Jose on time, there was no other way. Getting into my car, I glanced over my shoulder to see if I could spot anyone watching me. I didn't but that doesn't mean much.

I drove to a nearby gas station, gassed up, and then hauled out an overnight suitcase from the trunk. The suitcase contained a change of D.R.O. or Designer Rags Only. Not without some merit, there is a persistent DI rumor that anyone who shows up to work dressed in less than what you'd see in a 1960s sitcom will be flogged by the CEO, personally. A slight exaggeration but just. I happen to know that Lila H. Alvarez has not renewed contracts based on PIs having worn polo shirts and jeans into the office even on a Saturday or Sunday.

As an impressionable eleven-year-old, I once saw my mother clean fish in a beaded Halston original. When asked, she retorted that she *was* wearing an apron, after all, and went on scraping the scales off the halibut. I won't go into what she wore as den mother to Richard's Cub Scout group. Let's just say he has yet to recover.

This mandate does not include the IT Department, which has little if any interaction with the clients, so Richard is off the hook these days. As a result, he wears faded T-shirts and ripped jeans exclusively.

I pulled out a black, three-piece suit made out of a non-wrinkle fabric that in a pinch could probably be used by NASA as a space suit. The bias-cut skirt, with a slight flared hemline, had a matching long-sleeved jacket, both reminiscent of the '30s. The sleeveless blouse was patterned with wide, diagonal, turquoise-and-black stripes. The suit was not only stunning, but it wore like iron and was machine washable. It was a shame it spent its life in the trunk of my car, but it packs so well and looks so great after months of being crushed, that's where it has to live. I added chunky Mexican silver-and-turquoise earrings, sheer stockings, and Ferrigamo's basic black pumps, that also wear like iron. I ran quick fingers through my hair, trying to coax a do — succeeded minimally — and put on some lipstick and mascara.

I must have looked okay when I emerged five minutes later from the station's ladies' room because one of the attendants tripped over an oil can while staring at me. Back in the car, I reached under the passenger seat for my black snakeskin Judith Lieber handbag, containing all my identification. I kissed the all-revealing memo and thrust it inside my bag.

After starting the car, I headed south with the rest of the traffic toward the Santa Clara Hall of Justice, based in San Jose, some twenty miles away. Out of nowhere came the memory of the crushed stud earring I had shown to Lila on Sunday. Actually, I had forgotten about it with all the noise about Bingo Bango.

I had a small panic attack wondering where it was or if I'd lost it, when I remembered I had transferred it from my pants pocket to my change purse late Sunday night. Keeping an eye on the road, I grabbed at my handbag, found the small leather coin purse, and dug at the contents with my free hand, all while driving with the other one. I am nothing if not the consummate California driver.

Fortunately, I located the earring among all my change when the bent post pricked at my finger. I snatched it out and, holding it over the steering wheel, studied the mass of contorted gold holding what Lila said was a genuine, one-karat diamond. Even with the gathering rain clouds, the stone sparkled in what sunlight managed to sneak through. Balling it in my fist, I pressed that hand against my mouth, deep in thought. I could feel the crushed-metal-and-stone concoction locked inside my tightly closed hand and knew, just knew, it had something to do with the murder.

Large drops of rain pinged at the windshield, bringing me out of my trance. I returned the jewelry to my bag, turned on the wipers, and concentrated on the road ahead.

Government buildings are contained within several blocks on a multilane street called West

Hedding, most notably among them Santa Clara County's Hall of Justice and main jail. These two imposing buildings are on the same side of the street, numbered 190 and 150, respectively, separated only by a small common green. Plunked in the middle of the common is a three-story elevator with an overhead walkway crossing West Hedding's many traffic lanes and connecting to the five-story parking garage on the other side. I pulled in, parked the car, trotted across the enclosed walkway, and joined several other people taking the elevator down to the ground-level common.

Ordinarily, I would have turned left and headed for the Hall of Justice, which contains dozens of courtrooms trying criminal cases continuously during the forty-hour workweek. I've been to the hall many times to testify for our clients in the past but never to its neighboring jail.

Opening my umbrella and now turning right, I headed for the modern glass-and-cement complex holding hundreds of people against their will, albeit for the protection of society. It was a sobering thought that Carlos was one of them.

I entered a lobby that looked like it could belong to a condo or apartment building if it weren't for the metal detector, scan belt, and uniformed officers scattered here and there.

"May I help you?" said a smiling, blonde female officer from behind a black metal counter. I noticed that despite her youthful smile, she was wearing a revolver at her side.

Before I could answer, from across the lobby, the doors of a chrome elevator opened, and Mr.

Talbot stepped out. He saw me, came out the exit side of the detector, and shook my hand. He looked a little frazzled, so I could only imagine the condition Carlos was in.

"Carlos is waiting for you," he said, taking me by the arm and pulling me out of blondie's earshot. "Before you go in, let's chat a little." He drew me over to a corner of the lobby.

"How's he doing, Mr. Talbot?"

"He's a bit down, Liana, but that's only to be expected."

"What happened at the arraignment?" I asked. "I called your office on the way over here, but your secretary said you wanted to talk to me yourself."

"It's not good," he answered. "No bail. He's been remanded over for trial."

"Damn." I wasn't surprised but was still disappointed in the outcome.

"Most of Carlos's assets are in Mexico," he explained, "and even with his mother offering all the cash she could raise, a million five, the prosecution protested. They could have saved their time and energy. I knew the judge would never consider such a flight risk. And if the prosecution decides to go for murder one, the judge knows Mexico would never let the US extradite him back to the States under those circumstances."

"So he has to stay locked up until the trial," I said, chewing on my lower lip. Mr. Talbot nodded. I went on, "When will that be?"

"There won't be a preliminary hearing until at least six weeks from now. Carlos might not come to trial for months," he said. He started to say more but hesitated.

"What is it, Mr. Talbot? Tell me," I insisted.

"Frankly, Liana, we're going to need all the time we can get to prepare his defense," he replied. I studied his aged face, not liking the doubt I saw behind the pale-blue eyes.

"There's more to this, my dear," he said, leaning in. "There's something going on inside of Carlos, here." His two hands clapped dramatically at his chest. "I haven't seen this behavior myself, but there were a couple of erratic flare-ups witnessed by others. What I've been reading in the police reports describe him, more or less, as a..." He stopped speaking for a moment, reluctant to go on.

"What?" I prodded.

"A hothead, a man who might lose control and kill someone. Indeed, he has threatened to."

"Carlos? A hothead?"

"As I say, I have not been witness to this, but that's why I wanted to see you before you went up," he continued. My mind flashed back to Mira and Frank's comments about Carlos's recent behavior. "Something's going on with him that he's not telling me about. I have an instinct for these things. Whatever it is, it has already done him serious harm, and I need to know what it is."

"I see," I said, feeling an invisible fist punching away at my solar plexus like nobody's business.

Mr. Talbot studied my face as he said, "Talk to him. Perhaps you can get him to open up. I don't have to tell you the prosecution has a very good case of circumstantial evidence, and unless..."

"Unless what?"

"Unless the real murderer is found out, this trial may not go the way we want it to go."

My thoughts flitted to a wedding supposedly taking place in a short time and the carpall tunnel syndrome I got from writing out two hundred wedding invitations. Was it all for naught?

"Then I guess what I'm going to have to do is catch me the real killer," I said. "And I've got to do it before the wedding. That gives me three weeks."

He nodded. "It's a tall order."

"I'll have the help of my family."

"And through the years I've seen you and your family do some pretty remarkable things," he replied, putting his hands on both my shoulders and looking directly at me. "But it's still a tall order."

"I know, and I'm scared to death."

"Don't worry." He smiled. "I won't let it get around the neighborhood."

Chapter Seven

Life Is Not a Dress Rehearsal

Mr. Talbot left, and I signed in with smiling, pistol-packing blondie. Fortunately, Carlos had left my name as a visitor, and it was already logged into the computer. Otherwise, it would have been an hour's wait to be processed. Clipping on an identification card, I was handed a yellow piece of paper with a three-digit number written on it and given instructions to hand it over to the guard at the visitors' door.

I took the elevator to the fifth floor, along with several others holding yellow slips, and waited my turn. After snatching the slip from my hand, the guard took me into a large room. A line of plexiglass-enclosed cubicles ran dead center, separating inmates from visitors. Red plastic chairs, in various stages of decay, strained under the weight of live bodies, many of whom looked to be in various stages of decay themselves. Black phones hung to the right on either side of the plexiglass dividing the fifteen or so cubicles from each other.

It looked like every TV movie-of-the-week prison I'd seen. Only it was real.

I went to where Carlos sat in his orange jumpsuit on the other side of the plexiglass, nervously clasping and unclasping his hands. Even his golden tan couldn't hide the pallor beneath. Bloodshot eyes looked up at me, and he tried to stand. A hefty guard came over and pushed him back down in the chair. Carlos looked stunned but compliant. As I took my place in the empty chair, we picked up our phones simultaneously. Carlos spoke first.

"How's Mira?" he asked, his normal melodic baritone sounding stressed. "I wasn't able to call her today. I'm only allowed so many minutes on the phone, and I talked longer with Mom than I should have."

"Well, I'm sure your mother needed you," I consoled him. If I could have, I would have reached over and hugged him. Damn and blast, he looked worse than I thought he would. "Mira is doing better, Carlos," I said. "Try not to worry about that. Her temperature's down, and the cough has subsided."

"Good. Good," he said and gave me a slight smile. His words rushed on. "Give her my love. Tell her I love her very much, and when I can, I'll... I'll...." He stopped speaking and blinked several times, not knowing what else to say.

"Sure, Carlos. Sure." Searching his face for a moment, I decided a full frontal attack was best. "Carlos, before we get into anything else, we have to talk about your recent odd behavior. You need to be honest with me."

"What are you talking about?" His whole body froze. He stared at me through the glass. "What odd behavior?"

"Oh, come on, don't give me that. What's with all the redneck, tough-guy stuff? Who is this macho idiot I've been hearing about, yelling, banging on walls, making threats, and scaring everyone, especially Mira?"

Gaping at me, he nearly dropped the phone. "What? I've been scaring Mira? Did she say — ?"

"Yes, she said," I interrupted. "And so has Frank and anybody else who's been witness to your Neanderthal routine. Even your own lawyer has mentioned it. What's going on?" I demanded.

Dropping his head to his chest, he shook it imperceptibly. "It's nothing, nothing," he murmured.

"Really? Well, I don't believe that. Your erratic behavior has Mira worried more about you than she is about getting better. She says it's like she doesn't know who you are anymore. She doesn't need this added stress, my friend." When I want to, I can slather on the guilt like nobody's business. After all, I am my mother's daughter.

"Oh God, Lee," he said, raising his head. "I'm sorry. I'm so sorry."

"Well, being sorry might be a step in the right direction," I whispered into the phone, "but it's not going to cut it with a judge and jury. You're not doing yourself any good by keeping silent. If something's going on, you'd better tell me."

Carlos stared at me with such a look of sadness, my heart did a flip-flop. He almost replied but instead tapped at his chin with the end of the receiver, his eyes a thousand light-years away. Setting the phone down, he covered his face with his hands. I could see he was grappling with a monumental decision, so I let him have at it. We sat for a minute or two, Carlos with his head in his hands and me holding on to a dead phone watching one of the guards by the door clean his nails.

Just when I was wondering how much longer this would go on, Carlos lowered his hands and began to speak. I gestured that I couldn't hear him, pointing to the phone. He picked it up, and his strained voice replaced the silence in my ear. "Lee, I'm going to tell you something nobody else knows, not even Mira."

Carlos took a choppy breath and went on. "Before I was adopted by Mom and Dad, I spent the first four years of my life watching my birth mother being knocked around by my real father. You know about him, don't you?"

I nodded, saying, "Columbian would-be drug lord, right? Spent part of his time in Mexico City."

His head jerked up and down in agreement. "That's where he met Rosa, my… my birth mother. She was sixteen. His name was José Louis." His voice, so filled with emotion moments before, now took on a monotone. "Rosa worked in a brothel but was involved with him on and off. He got her hooked on drugs, which she used even when she was pregnant with me. I was born with a clubfoot.

The doctors say it wasn't the drugs, but it kept her family from wanting anything to do with me. One day he... José Louis... went berserk and beat her to death right in front of me."

"Jesus," was all I could say.

"He took off right after that," Carlos said. "I don't think they ever caught him. I went into an orphanage. That's where Mom... Tex... found me a few months later. They say I didn't speak for weeks after it happened. Just sat and stared. Mom paid for the operations to fix my foot before she knew she could adopt me. She's that kind of lady."

"I-I had no idea, Carlos," I stuttered. Through the years, I'd noticed the scars on Carlos's foot, but Tex had said it was an old childhood injury.

"I know the sisters at the orphanage told Mom about how I got there, but we've never talked about it. Ever since, I can't stand to see a man beat up on a woman or animals. I once took a dog away from a jerk who was beating it. You remember Rocky, don't you?" I nodded mutely. "The sweetest dog God ever made." I reached out for his face but touched my side of the plexiglass, forgetting it was there.

Carlos went on haltingly. "The night of the robbery, when I thought that brute hit Mira, it was just like it was happening again to Rosa. I didn't think about how it looked to everyone. In fact, I wasn't thinking at all, just... being." He reached up and touched his side of the barrier where my hand rested. "I'm sorry, Lee."

I shook my head numbly, not daring to speak for the tightness in my throat. Carlos went on. "Will you tell Mira what I've told you? Tell her I'm sorry I frightened her. And tell her I love her. Keep telling her that."

"I will," I managed to get out. I took a few quick breaths to steady myself. "I'm glad you told me this, Carlos. It explains a lot. I'll tell Mira tonight verbatim. I can repeat conversations from weeks back word for word. It works great with used-car salesmen and old boyfriends," I said, trying to lighten the mood.

Carlos forced a smile, and we both dropped our hands from the glass. When he looked away for a moment, I took the opportunity to brush at wet cheeks with my free hand.

"Once I was in here, I had a lot of time to think." He went on. "I realized what was going on inside me. But I didn't want anyone else to know because, well, I was afraid it might help build an even stronger case against me. People might think it gives me more of a reason for wanting the man dead."

I nodded in agreement.

"But I don't want to frighten Mira, and I don't want her to think I'm crazy. Or any crazier than I am." He let out a raspy laugh and cleared his throat.

"You're not crazy," I reassured him. "But things like that aren't good bottled up. They tend to come out when least expected. Carlos, Mr. Talbot has to know about this too. I'm not sure if anyone else does, especially if it could hurt your defense. That's for you and him to decide. Tell him tomorrow just as you've told me."

He looked at me and nodded in agreement.

"Let's go on," I said, shaking off the past. "Tell me what happened Saturday when you got the phone call from the robber."

Carlos sat up straighter, relieved to be free of what went before and to talk about the present. "I got the call around noon, the day after the statue was stolen. The man on the phone said he would sell it back to me for fifty thousand dollars. I couldn't believe it."

"What couldn't you believe?" I leapt in. "That he called you? What?"

"Lee, Mira and I had that statue appraised just days before and were told it was worth nothing. *Nada*. So why would a man steal a worthless statue in the first place and then call me the next day offering to sell it back for that amount of money? None of it made sense. That's one of the reasons I went there. I was curious."

"Well, curiosity killed the cat. No offense, Tugger," I muttered under my breath. Louder, I said, "Why else did you go there?" He shrugged but said nothing. "Don't close up on me now. Did you want to hurt him or pay him back for what he did to Mira?" Carlos and I looked at each other for a moment. Carlos shook his head, but I stared hard at him, doubt filling my mind.

"No, not hurt him. I just wanted to confront him, Lee. I swear," he said, running slim fingers through jet-black hair. "Face him, let him know he couldn't do what he did to Mira again and not answer to me for it. It sounds stupid when I say it."

"And? What else?"

"I've already told you," he said, not bothering to hide the irritation in his voice. "I've never been blackmailed or had anything held for ransom before, let alone a statue I was told was worth next to nothing. I was curious, I tell you! So I went to the bank and took out the money —"

"You were walking around with fifty thousand dollars on you?"

"Yes."

"Carlos," I said, reeling in my chair. "Do you know how that looks? It looks like blackmail that went wrong."

"I know. It looks bad."

"It looks bad? You are a master of understatement," I said dryly. "Where is the money now?"

"I don't know. They took it with the rest of my things. I guess the police have it."

We were running out of time. "Did you kill him, Carlos? Tell me the truth now. No bull. I can't help you if I don't know the truth."

Carlos looked me directly in the eyes and said, "Lee, I am innocent. He was already stabbed and dying when I got there. I swear to God. I swear on everything and everyone I hold dear. I swear on my love for Mira. I did not kill that man."

"Okay, okay," I said, letting out the breath I'd been holding since all of this began. "I believe you."

"Thank you," Carlos whispered.

We instinctively knew we had crossed a hurdle. A basis of faith had been reestablished between two lifelong friends.

"Now that we've got that out of the way, tell me more about this statue," I said. "Where did you get it?"

"I found it on one of the dirt roads on the rancho a week or so ago. It was lying near the side, under a clump of bushes. I dropped my canteen and when I went for it, I saw the statue. I thought it was interesting, so I brought it back for Mira. She likes things like that. Mira thought it might be real, so we took it to be appraised."

"Didn't you wonder where it came from?"

"Yes, I did, but frankly, it's just one of several strange things going on there lately."

"Like what?"

"When I go home, sometimes I see weird lights out by the abandoned mine. Mom keeps blowing it off, saying it's nothing but a *vaquero* driving one of our trucks or a car cutting through our property. At first, I thought so, too, but it keeps happening more and more. That's really why I've been taking those early morning rides. I've been trying to see if something is going on at the mine. You know the one."

I did indeed. When we were kids, and my folks visited the rancho, Carlos, Richard, and I would ride out to the abandoned mine, them on ponies and me on a rickety mountain bike, and try to get inside. We never could though.

"But each time I rode out there, nothing." Carlos continued, "The place is sealed up like it's been for the past thirty years. I've been thinking about this a lot. Ever since our old foreman retired three years ago and his nephew took over, it's been different around there. I know it doesn't sound like much, but, Lee, you're good at this."

"Good at what?"

"Finding out about things, you know, after they're over."

"Well, thank you, I think."

"Lee, go to Los Pocitos Minerales," Carlos said, nearly jumping out of his seat and then stealing a look at the guard before sitting down again. He lowered his voice, saying, "I think all of this is tied together. It has to be. I mean, finding the statue on the rancho, having it stolen here, and then a man from Mexico getting murdered. It's too much of a coincidence."

"I was going to start here in the Bay Area. How can I—?"

"Please!" he begged. "Help me. Besides, Mom's there by herself, and you know what she's like when she has a jumping competition coming up. She doesn't see or think about anything else. She could be in danger."

"Why do you think Tex may be in danger?" I could feel my eyebrows rise up to my hairline.

"I'm not sure. Maybe it's all in my mind," he admitted in a dejected tone, once again running fingers through his hair, adding to his disheveled look, so out of character for the well-groomed young man I knew. "No, it's not," he contradicted himself. "The rancho is different now."

"In what way?" I asked.

He thought for a moment before speaking. "Well, the lights, for one thing. But also, sometimes I see a few of the hands whispering to each other and then looking at us. Like there are secrets or something."

"Has your mother noticed it? Has she said anything?"

"Other than saying they're behaving squirrelly? No, but I know Mom. With me being so far away, she wouldn't want to worry me. Besides, she's got a competition coming up in July, and there's no way she'll leave her Aztecas. She works with them several hours every day."

Aztecas are by way of being the national horse of Mexico, a cross between the Andalusian stallions and Criollo mares but highly refined. Tex Garcia was a real rootin' tootin' cowgirl, tortilla style, in that when she took off her handmade Stetson, it was only to don her charro hat for a jumping competition. She was well known for sleeping on bales of hay in the stables whenever her horses sneezed or something like that, just to be near them. You could say she was devoted.

"I don't like her being there alone without us knowing what's going on. She's been training one of the *vaqueros*, Paco, to take over for her when she comes for the wedding. She trusts him but says he isn't ready yet to run the ranch by himself. I don't think she'll leave no matter what I say." Carlos looked at me. "Please use that ferreting skill you've honed so well. Go to Los Posos. Will you?"

"You really think the answer is there?"

"Yes I do. And if isn't, I'm screwed."

"All right," I said after a moment. "I don't know if I can find out anything at the rancho, but I'll give it my best shot."

"That's all I can ask of you," he said simply.

I replaced the phone, got up to leave, and glanced back over my shoulder. There, burned in my brain, was the image of Carlos sitting in the red plastic chair, looking hopeful and bereft. And about a hundred years old.

On the drive back to Palo Alto, my mind ran through a dozen scenarios, not the least of which was leaving the rest of the family to do the investigation in Palo Alto while I went to Los Pocos by myself as I promised Carlos I would. It all seemed such a mess. With murder charges against Carlos here in the States, what was the purpose of going to his rancho? Yet Carlos seemed so certain that the rancho, the dog statue, and the murder were somehow tied together.

Noshing again on my lower lip while driving down University Avenue, I noticed a parking space on a side street near one of our entrances and couldn't believe my good fortune. Usually I have to park several blocks away, no matter what time of day. I was in the space in less than fifteen seconds.

Getting out of the car, I thought more about my conversation with Carlos than I did about Leonard Foley. It was eight fourteen. I had to get back in sync for my nine o'clock meeting on the Bingo Bango project before Leonard showed up.

DI is located on the third floor of one of the few remaining designated historical buildings in Palo Alto. The northeast corner bears a bronze plaque with an official California historical building seal. This designation is due in some part to an early twentieth-century bank still living on the first floor, having once occupied the entire building. Mostly, though, it's due to Lila's efforts in the mid-'90s.

The building still has the original everything, including the ornate, glass-enclosed elevator that makes more noise than an aerobics class filled with out-of-shape oldsters. This lift dangles from a cord no thicker than a jump rope I used in the eighth grade. Yet the yearly inspector has the effrontery to state it can support the weight of all that brass and glass plus two full-grown people. Maybe it can, but I will never be one of those people.

I raced up the stairs and across the burgundy plush carpet toward the black polished double doors bearing a rectangular gold plate on which were written the words:

Discretionary Inquiries Inc.
Data, Information, and Intelligence
Room 300

As I turned the polished brass handle, the door opened on silent hinges and into my family's and my world.

Even though it was after 8:00 p.m., Stanley, who keeps the front office hopping, was speaking to what sounded like a potential client over the phone. He hadn't seen me in several weeks, so his face showed happy surprise as I trotted by even though he didn't miss a beat of the conversation.

I looked forward to being in an office I hadn't visited for a while and closed the door happily behind me. Unlike the opulent but impersonal décor of the rest of DI, my office is done in pale apricot tones with modern Mexican touches. Sergio Bustamante sculptures, whimsical and colorful, are everywhere. They fill me with delight every time I look at them. The office interior is in direct defiance to one of Lila's edicts that all offices be in line with the rest of DI's furnishings. That would be gag-me-with-a-spoon maroon and gray.

On this matter, I dug my heels in and threatened to go to the board if I didn't get my way. Lila was scandalized and backed down, but to this day, refuses to set foot in my office, an unexpected bonus. No worries about a surprise visit from the boss.

Once settled in, I opened my bag and took out the copy of the memo, still riled that the scanner hadn't worked. Making several copies on my desktop copier, I popped them inside the file. When Leonard showed up for our nine o'clock meeting, we would give him several copies with our blessings and tell him to do with them what he will. Then I would tell Richard what to do with his scanner.

Before Leonard arrived, I had scheduled ten minutes for a debriefing meeting with Lila to fill her in. For the next five, I entered the day's information into the database with fingers flying over the keyboard. Fortunately, I had been going into my email and voice mail after work each day from home, so there wasn't much of a buildup. Most of my other assignments had been passed on to Pete or Manny, so after I wrapped this up tonight, maybe I could get some sleep and play with my cat before going to Mexico, finding the blue dog statue, and, oh yeah, getting the murder charges against Carlos dropped. My stomach clenched as I thought, *how am I going to do it all?*

I glanced at my watch again and got up. Grabbing a quick cup of coffee, I headed for the South Conference Room, one of my favorites. Another untouched by Lila's decorating mandates, this was originally created as a smoking room for the bank manager and other gentlemen back in the 1920s. It remains pretty much the same now as it did then.

Sometimes, when the windows have been closed a long time, you can still smell the faint lingerings of pipe tobacco. When the windows are open, you can hear the water spraying into the three-tiered fountain outside on the patio and the chirping of bathing birds. The furniture and wall paneling is done in cherrywood, with accents of forest-green leather. Several brass hanging lamps sporting real abalone shades from the 1920s throw a soft glow on the walls and the burnished wood of the long conference table. Abalone shell shades are very Old World, very beautiful, and very politically incorrect. According to California law, today the only thing the average person is allowed to do with abalone in the ocean is to pat it lovingly on the rump if it happens to swim by.

I walked into the room and found Richard seated at one end of the table, tapping on the keyboard of his laptop. I don't think he goes to the bathroom without dragging that thing along. Speaking of Richard, it was unusual for him to be included at these meetings. Not only is he the technical side of things, with a heavy leaning on computer research, Richard is what we refer to as our "loose cannon." Yes, he has a brilliant mind and computer know-how up the wazoo. His genius at statistical compilation has given DI the bleeding edge in detective work, not just in California but also throughout the country. I use the phrase "bleeding edge" because it's what the techies say when something surpasses the industry's idea of the leading edge on things. It is the highest form of praise. I find the metaphor squeamish myself, but I try to stay up on these phrases, so when the family has dinner together, I know what the hey Richard is talking about.

Getting back to him being a loose cannon, the last time we let him meet with clients, he was twenty minutes late and arrived carrying mounds of paperwork in a plastic laundry basket tucked under one arm. In his free hand, he was gnawing on a liverwurst and onion sandwich, which stank up the whole room for days afterward.

That was three years ago, and this is the first time he has seen the inside of a conference room since that time. However, as he used to be Leonard's boss and wanted to give good ol' Len the information we'd gathered, face-to-face, Lila thought we'd take a chance and let him sit in with us. She gave me a smile as I entered the room.

Richard looked up, saying, "Before we do anything else, here's the tax report you asked for on Mesoamerican Galleries." He tapped several papers by the side of the computer. "You know, we're not supposed to be able to get other people's

111

tax returns unless we have their permission, so it would be better if you did that kind of thing only through me, okay?"

"Sorry. It might help Carlos's case though," I said. I updated them briefly before snatching at Meso's papers, leaving out my conversation with Race.

"Having glanced over it myself," Lila said while I read, "their first year's income is commendable. It's not a great deal of money, but justifiable for keeping a business open and promises a bright future."

Richard grunted, still pecking away. He looked up again. "Unlike many of the other galleries around. Victoria told me she heard a rumor at the gym the other day from the interior decorator of Race Holbrook's gallery. She said if Holbrook doesn't get a cash infusion soon, he's probably going to go under."

"And that's with four ex-wives to feed," I said. Mom sniffed, while I wondered just how desperate Race might be to keep his gallery open.

"That's *enough* gossip," Lila said. "We should be concentrating on the matter at hand: Leonard Fogel's dilemma."

Mom, Richard, and I went over the process, hours spent, and outcome, in preparation for Leonard. He was ten minutes late and showed up wearing the same ratty Home Depot T-shirt, baggy jeans, and worn-down rubber thongs that covered him nearly every day. You'd never know this was a kid worth over four million bucks.

"Good evening, Mrs. Alvarez," he said deferentially. "Hey, Richard, my man," he said gregariously, and they did that masculine hand-slapping thing that looks pretty silly to me, but men like doing it, so there you are. He turned to me and became serious, saying, "Whatcha got for me, Lee?"

"Why don't you sit down, Leonard?" Lila said, taking command and gesturing to one of the fourteen high-back chairs surrounding the long, oval table. He chose a chair opposite me and looked at all three of us expectantly.

Richard threw a clipped stack of papers down and said, "Len, we always thought it had to be one of just five people. Two we eliminated early on, as they just don't have the steady access to your encodings like the others do. The next two not only have access, they have had telephone communications with Silo Junction's main office."

"You're kidding," Leonard said with a surprised look on his face.

Richard continued. "We weren't sure if they were just looking for a job or something else pretty benign. Come to find out, they each had a friend working there and were trying to do some headhunting for you. You pay five thousand dollars to whomever brings in a hiree, don't you, no matter where you get them from?"

Leonard shrugged but said nothing. Proving once again we are right to keep Richard under lock and key. He went on hotly. "Well, you know you do, and I'd appreciate it if you'd stop trying to take my staff away from me, Len. I had to give a ten thousand dollar bonus to Phil Makiato to keep him from leaving me for you."

Leonard opened his mouth for a rebuttal, but Lila quickly took charge of the conversation with the command of a four-star general, thank God. "*Gentlemen*, I think we should *continue* with the reason we are here," she said, glaring at Richard, who folded his arms and glared back at her, loose-cannon style. She turned to Leonard, smiling. "Those two were *never* our leading contenders, anyway. The one that stood out to us from the beginning was Robby Weinblatt. He had means—"

"No! No way," Leonard exclaimed, shaking his head. "He would never do anything like that. You're wrong."

"*And* opportunity," Lila continued as if she hadn't been interrupted. "Liana has brought all the *proof* you'll need. Richard has the rest of the research done on your employees. I'd like to draw your *attention* to Mr. Weinblatt's phone calls," she said, gesturing to a printout of names, dates, times, and phone numbers. "You can see he's made about three in the last month to a Jeffrey White at his private number."

"Jeff White owns Silo Junction," Leonard said, barely audible.

"We know," I said. "That combined with this memo should be all you need." I slid the memo across the desk to him without saying another word.

He read it quietly several times as he pulled at the neck of his T-shirt with trembling fingers. "Why that miserable son of a bitch," he spat out.

Lila blanched but did not call him on his language. I guess that's reserved just for me. She said, "I know this is a shock, Leonard, but let us try to remain calm."

"He and I grew up together," he said, not hearing her. "He owes me everything. I gave him his first job out of high school with no college degree. That miserable mother fu — "

"Leonard!" Lila stood up, interrupting him, "*Control* yourself. Try to concentrate on what you should do about this. There's no *point* in name calling."

He ignored her and turned to Richard and me, saying, "You know that a-hole is downstairs right now waiting for me in my car?"

"What?" all three of us exploded in unison.

Our voices crossed over one another's, saying, "What did you bring him here for? Does he know about us? You said nobody knew."

"He needed a ride home," said Leonard. "I told him I had to make a stop on the way. I didn't tell him why I was stopping here, but I didn't think it was him. I didn't think it was him," he repeated.

"Well, what's done is *done*," Lila said, sitting down and leaning back in her chair. "Let's try to remain calm."

"You are such a dork, Len," Richard stated, obviously still annoyed about the headhunting thing.

Leonard ignored him, saying, "Jeff White's tried to buy me out twice, but I wouldn't sell, so I guess he went through Robby. Robby, who I trusted." He pulled at the neck of his T-shirt again, stretching an already out-of-shape garment even more so. "What do I do now?" he wailed.

"Well…" began Lila, becoming more controlled and businesslike the more emotional Leonard became. "There are *several* options open to you, and we can discuss them, but first, why don't we take a brief break? This will give you a few moments to *compose* yourself and *calmly reflect* on what you want to do next." Wow! Three emphasized words in one sentence. A lot, even for Mom.

"What I want to do next is kill the son of a —" Leonard shouted, writhing in his chair. Apparently, I'm the only one who pays attention to Lila's emphases.

"You're the one who's going to be killed if you don't start watching your language," I interrupted, noticing Lila's red complexion and pinched mouth. "Just a friendly warning," I added, patting him on the arm.

"Len, my man," Richard interjected, with a forgive-and-let-live attitude, "go have a cup of coffee and pull yourself together. When you come back, we'll go over some of the legal options you have. You'll straighten this out, buddy." And with that, Richard clipped him on the shoulder with his fist. I love it the way techies get macho.

"Listen," I said, rising, "I accidentally left my cell phone in the car. While you guys take a break, I'll run down and get it. Where did you park, Leonard? I want to make sure I don't run into Weinblatt."

"In the parking lot off Emerson," he replied. "I couldn't get anything closer than a block away."

"That should be all right, then. I'm downstairs at the side door." Lowering my voice, I said to Lila, "We need to talk about that other matter. There have been some updates." Lila raised one eyebrow but said nothing. I felt Richard's eyes on me and turned to him. "And you. I've got a bone to pick with you," I whispered to him.

"Can't wait," Richard whispered back and rolled his eyes.

I turned my attention back to Leonard, who sat hunched over, looking deflated and unbelievably young. "Leonard," I said, "a piece of advice. Listen to Richard and keep it legal. Don't do something that's going to come back and bite you on your backside."

He leapt up, suddenly very much the gentleman. He took my hand and shook it earnestly. "Thank you so very much, Lee, for all you've done. I know it can't have been easy doing the job you did."

"It pretty much sucked, Leonard, but don't worry, it will be reflected in the bill," I said, laughing. "I'll be right back."

I clomped down the stairs and was pushing the side door open when who should I see darting by along the sidewalk but good old *Señor* Robby. Backing up, I closed the glass door between us and stood in the shadows, watching him cut across the street in front of oncoming traffic. I don't think he saw me, but I knew he saw something that terrified him. It was written all over his face. He kept looking back over his shoulder, like he was being chased by the hound from hell. How he managed to do that without falling down or running into something, I will never know.

I surmised he must have gotten tired of waiting and started tracking Leonard by walking in the same direction. Once on our block, he saw our inconspicuous but readable sign over the doorway. Knowing Leonard had once worked at DI, and combined with the recent troubles, Weinblatt must have put two and two together, freaked out and took off.

Watching him disappear into the dusk, I opened the car door while humming a snatch of one of Blondie's songs, "One way or another, we're gonna find ya. We're gonna gitcha, gitcha, gitcha, gitcha..."

I reached in for my cell phone and saw what I thought was a flyer on the windshield. *Another stupid advertisement from a car wash,* I thought. Annoyed, I seized the offending paper, crumpling it into a ball. About to toss it, I noticed childlike scribbling on one side. I smoothed it open on the hood of the car and read, *If you don't want to wind up like the Mexican in the garage, you'd better mind your own business.*

With a pounding heart, I spun around in every direction, seeing nothing but people and cars going about their business. I got into the Chevy, slammed the door closed, and locked it. Shivering, my eyes were glued to the wrinkled note I clutched in my hand. It occurred to me my fingerprints were all over it, and the way I'd initially handled it, I'd probably smeared anyone else's.

118

Nonetheless, I dropped it on the passenger seat. I did what I should have done when I'd found the diamond. Opening the glove compartment, I took out a clear plastic bag and a pair of thin rubber gloves. With shaking hands, I put the gloves on and folded the note in such a way that when it was placed inside the bag, the contents could be read, which is what I again did. I wanted to make sure I had read it right the first time.

I'd read it right. Someone knew about me, my association with Carlos, and wanted me to know that they knew. They wanted to scare me off. Well, they scared me but not off. But one out of two ain't bad.

Chapter Eight

Just Memo Me

On the way up the stairs to the office, I listened to my voice mail. Mira had called, anxious to know about my meeting with Carlos. She also let it drop that she, Tex, and my mother had been burning the wires most of the day, so I guessed Lila had a few things to tell me.

Clutching the plastic bag, I decided to give the note to Frank, once I'd shown the family. Maybe there was a print or two left on the flyer, besides mine. One could only hope. I hadn't decided about whether or not to give him the diamond. I'd see what Lila had come up with.

When I returned, I found her writing in her journal while Richard leaned over his laptop. I noticed an absence of Leonard.

"Where's Mr. Bingo Bango?" I asked.

Richard pointed with his thumb saying, "He's lying down in the Quiet Room with a headache." That was an area with a cot, pillow, and blanket for ailing staff or those twenty-four-seven days.

"I gave him a cold compress for his *head*," Lila said, "and an Advil. He should *be* there for a while."

"Good," I said, dropping down in one of the leather chairs. "Because there's no need for him to hurry himself on account of his fellow passenger. *Señor* Robby *se fue*."

"He's gone?" Richard stopped typing and looked up at me. "You're sure?"

I nodded. "Just saw him careening down the street like a man with a rocket in his drawers. I think he's onto us."

"Well," Lila said, "we might have *expected* something like this, once we knew he was waiting in Leonard's car."

"At least Len doesn't have to face him when he goes back downstairs. That's something," said Richard. Lila and I stared at him. "I like to look on the positive side of things," he said defensively.

"Try looking on the positive side of what I found on my windshield," I said, with more bravado than I was feeling. "I've got a pen pal." I extended my arm and dangled the plastic bag in front of Lila's face.

"What's that?" Lila said. She looked up and read it, pursing her lips.

Richard pushed his chair back, rose, and stood behind Lila, saying, "I hope that's a parking ticket." He bent over, giving it a closer look. "It's not."

"I don't like this, Liana," Lila said, taking the plastic bag from my hand and studying the message.

"You're going to have to stand in line on that one," I retorted.

"Do you have any idea who it's from?" Richard asked.

"Not a clue. I'll give it to Frank tomorrow," I said, pulling the baggie from my mother's hand. Lila said nothing. Feeling it was best to distract her from obsessing over the threatening missive, I changed the subject. "Did you find anything on the diamond? Police reports or ads in the paper?"

"Nothing, Liana. Of course, it's early *yet,* and maybe whoever dropped it hasn't discovered its loss yet. We should wait a few more days unless you want to give it to Frank along with the note."

"I don't. The note we know for sure is part of this mess. The crushed earring is still a maybe. By the way, I got a voice message from Mira, and she says you, she, and Tex have been conferring much of the day and it involves me."

She looked up at me with her clear blue eyes and said, "Yes, we have and it *does.*"

"I'd like to know more, so if this is a good time," I continued, "let me call Mira, and let's do a conference call." I stashed the flyer in my handbag and pulled out my phone. Richard returned to his laptop, and Lila put the cap back on her fountain pen. I could see all of us changing mindsets, going from one problem to another, as we so often have to do.

"Why don't you use the conference phone?" Mom said, gesturing to the beige phone on the end of the table.

I shrugged. "This is easier. The number is on my speed dial, and I'll put it on speaker."

After speed-dialing the house, I set the phone in the center of the table, crossed over to the side table, and picked up the water carafe. Pouring some into a paper cup, I drank, and wondered how many people still used a fountain pen besides Mom. While our home phone rang, my thoughts flitted from my mom to Carlos's mom. "How is Tex doing, by the way?" I asked in between sips.

A look of assessment crossed Lila's lovely face, and she said, "Virginia was, of course, shocked and *deeply* distressed. She wanted to fly here immediately to be with the children, feeling Mira needed her just as much as Carlos. I *managed* to persuade her to stay once she found out you and I would be there sometime tomorrow."

"Excuse me?" I choked out, spitting water all over myself.

"Hello?" answered Tío before I could go further into Lila's response.

"Tío, it's me, Liana," I said, wiping at my chin with my hand. "Is Mira there?"

"Oh, *si*," he replied. "She is right here."

"Let me talk to her, Tío, please," I said, still thinking about my mother's last remark. "In fact, why don't you use the speakerphone button? I'm using mine."

I heard a jiggling sound and took the opportunity to say, "Mom, what did you just say right before Tío answered the phone? I must have heard you wrong."

"Hi, Lee," Mira said. Her voice filled the room and sounded more energetic than it had in days.

"Mira Louise, it's Lila," Mom said, taking charge. "I was *just* informing Liana that you, Virginia, and I discussed a trip to Mexico because we think there's a connection between where the statue was found and the murdered man."

"Yes, we do," said Mira.

"As I was telling Liana, she and I going to the rancho is how I persuaded Virginia to stay home. I convinced her that in order for us to do any investigation that didn't look too suspicious, she should be there acting as our hostess."

"Yes, but—" I said.

"I'm sure it will take *only* a few days," Lila went on as if I hadn't spoken, "knowing how quickly Liana can get to the heart of a matter."

"Yes, but—" I said again.

"Then, if need be, Virginia can join Carlos and you here in the Bay Area upon our return," she finished.

"Yes, but when you say 'us,'" I managed to get in, nervously squeezing the paper cup into a ball. "Do you mean you and me, Mom?"

"Well, you didn't think you were going there alone," Richard called out, banging away on the keyboard.

"*Como no*, you go together with your mother, *mi sobrina*," said Tío, adding his voice to the mix. "I would go as well, but—"

"Listen here—" I interrupted my uncle.

"It's not necessary, Mateo," Mom said, overriding our two voices. "We're merely going to look around for a couple of days to see what's going on down there, if *anything*. You're of better service here taking care of Mira Louise and Liana's cat until we return. Also, you have your commitments at the SPCA, don't you?"

"*Si, si*," he agreed, letting out a small sigh. "We all must do what we do best."

"Exactly!" I said, taking the opportunity to repeat Tío's words, "'We all must do what we do best.' A man was killed and this could be dangerous. I'm the one that should go—and by myself—as I am the one who is a trained professional."

"Well, la-di-da," Richard sang out. I threw the balled up paper cup at him but missed.

"So am *I*, dear, so am *I*," Mom said, looking me directly in the eye again.

I sat for a moment, filled with reflection. God help me, it was true. Lila does have to go through the same training as everybody else does in California in order to hold a PI license. The state requires you to have six thousand hours or about three years of compensatory investigative experience just to qualify to take the state examination. And if you carry a firearm, the qualification card expires every two years from the date of issuance. An applicant must requalify four times during the life of each two-year permit; so every six months or so, it's back to the classroom for written and range exams, no matter how many times you renewed your license.

Surprisingly, Lila Hamilton-Alvarez is a better shot than most and can hit a popcorn kernel at twenty feet with her Beretta semiautomatic pistol. She's also been taking karate lessons recently from my instructor. I keep forgetting all of that. Or maybe, like Carlos, I'm good at blocking things out. It's hard enough dealing with Lila being the CEO of DI, and being my mother, thank you very much. But she and I as Charlie's Angels Minus One was enough to make my toes curl.

"Besides," Lila said, "the man was killed *here*, Liana, not *there*. Remember, we're ostensibly going to go down to help Virginia get through this."

"That's the story, and we're sticking to it?"

"Yes. That is the official story."

"*Sí*," Tío said into the speaker, his voice reverberating in the room. "I will take care of Mira and *el gatito* until your return."

"Peter will take care of anything that can't wait until my return as he has done from time to time in the past," said Lila.

Pete was an ex-cop from Boston who started working with DI after getting a masters at MIT and moving to the Bay Area. He's one smart cookie.

"And I'll take care of you two from here via satellite," said Richard. "I've already fixed up two satellite phones, and I'm nearly done putting in the AT commands on the WiFi laptop. All three have satellite uplink, so you can communicate from anywhere in Mexico using direct linkage from one of their satellites straight to DI. *El fin*," he said, ending his tapping. "It's done. You should be able to reach me, get information from DI, and vice versa within a matter of seconds. The sat phones are also walkie-talkies, ladies, with a five-mile radius, so you can talk to each other," he added. "Plus, they have photo and video capabilities. This way you won't have to carry a camera or scanner with you. I still don't like you going by yourselves," he threw in.

"It's *settled*, Richard," Lila said, uncapping her pen and writing again in her damned journal. "Liana, I do *believe* we've thought of everything."

"Apparently so," I said, falling into the nearest chair.

"I've booked us two first-class tickets for midnight tomorrow to Leon," she continued, scribbling away. "Of course, we have a thirty-five-minute layover in Houston. There are still no direct flights from here to there. More's the pity. With the time change, we'll arrive first thing in the morning. Virginia will meet us at the airport and drive us back to the rancho. The element of *surprise*." She smiled.

Unlike me, during this entire exchange, Mira hadn't tried to say anything. Now she spoke up. "You don't know what this means to me, all of you. I'll be grateful to you till the day I die. Especially you, Lee," she added. "Carlos and I know you're the only one who can find out what's going on."

"Let's hope your faith in me is justified," I said, clearing my throat. "Mira, about Carlos, I need to tell you something privately. How late can I call you?"

Lila and Richard exchanged looks but said nothing.

"As late as you want," Mira answered. "I do nothing but sleep these days."

"Good." I changed the subject. "Before we hang up, let's talk about the man who appraised the dog statue again. What exactly did you say to him? Did you tell him you might get a second opinion?"

"Yes, I did, and he didn't like it."

"I'll bet. Can you describe him for me?" Now that she was better and codeine free, maybe her description would be different, and he wouldn't sound so much like Douglas's Stefano. I could feel her thinking about it over the line.

"Middle-aged, silver hair, distinguished looking, spoke with a Spanish accent. Oh yes... he had a big diamond stud in one of his ears."

Crap, I said to myself. "Okay, thanks. By the way, Mira, Tío says you hardly eat anything. You have to promise me to try to do better."

"*Si*," said Tío, his voice scolding her gently. "You have had nothing but a piece of fruit all day. Do not try to fool me. I know this is so."

"Well," she said, "I wouldn't mind a little something right now."

I could hear Tío's voice perk up as if he'd just won a door prize. "I have on the stove cooking my *sopa de pollo*, which, if I must say so myself, *es mejor del mundo*." The best in the world. As a recently retired but renowned Bay Area executive chef, Tío might be exaggerating, but not by much.

We hung up on this upbeat note, and I got up, stretching my muscles.

Richard must have noticed because he said, "Mom, Lee, you both look worn out, and you've got a couple of big days ahead of you. Why don't you go home? I'll take care of Len when he wakes up."

"Works for me," I agreed and started gathering my things to leave. "By the way, speaking of scanners..." I said.

"I didn't know we were," Richard replied with a smile.

Removing the nonfunctioning doodad from my handbag, I dropped it on the table, saying, "This one is a dud."

"What are you talking about?" asked Richard, losing the smile. "All of our equipment is checked out at least three times."

"Well, this one's not working," I said, crossing my arms and staring at him. "I tried to use it and nothing."

Richard picked up the device and studied each side of it before saying, "Here's your problem. See? You've got it set on pause."

"P-pause?" I stuttered. "I never set it on pause."

He shrugged. "Well, pause it's on, Sister mine." He depressed a button, and I heard a small sound, reminiscent of a robotic vacuum cleaner. "There you go."

"I didn't know there was a pause button," I babbled. "No one ever told me."

Richard handed it back to me and started typing on his laptop, saying, "Note to self: better training for operatives using equipment, even the most basic of instruments," he added, looking at me. "And I'd better go over the sat phone and the laptop with you several times before you leave."

Lila got up, saying, "I won't go just yet, as I have one or two things I *need* to take care of in my office." She turned to my brother and smiled. "However, I will leave Leonard in your capable hands, Richard."

"Since when do you consider my hands capable?" Richard teased.

"Since Leonard went from being our client to your friend," I answered.

Lila ignored our banter. "Be sure to inform him that Robby Weinblatt has fled the scene and is *possibly* aware of the situation."

"Sure thing," said Richard, swiveling back to his laptop or rather, my soon-to-be laptop.

"And no more contention about headhunting, Richard," she warned, "theirs or ours. It's a business practice none of us is happy with, but the less said about it the better. *Understood?*"

"Got it," Richard said. "Besides, I don't like to kick a man when he's down."

It was nearly ten thirty when I pulled into the hedge-lined driveway and toward my garage apartment. About three-quarters of the way down the drive, I thought I saw movement out of the corner of my eye, and then my headlights bounced off what looked like someone's eyeglasses. It happened too fast to be sure, but I stopped the car and idled for a moment, deciding what to do. For my money, it looked like Robby Weinblatt in that brief flicker of an eye, although how he found out my real name and where I lived, I couldn't imagine.

On further thought, the research Richard did on him previously showed when he was thirteen, he was given a two-week detention at school for enabling the library computers with porno websites. He could probably find out a lot of information on anybody, even someone as carefully screened as me. Never underestimate the power of a hacker and his computer.

I took the flashlight out of my glove compartment, lowered my window enough to stick it through, and searched the brush for any signs of life. Then I decided to get out of the car and do a thorough search. I figured if I found somebody, between my karate and the metal flashlight, I had the edge. I am nothing if not cocky.

There was a soft rustle in the bushes, and it wasn't the wind. Dashing the five feet or so to the hedge, I yanked some aside and aimed the light toward the sound just in time to see an astonished *Señor* Robby fall to the ground on his back. The look of terror on his face would have made me laugh if I wasn't so hopping mad. As he tried to claw at the ground backward to get away, I grabbed the front of his T-shirt with my free right hand, jerking him into a standing position. He was a lot lighter than I thought he would be, and I overcompensated, pulling him to the side of me and almost into the brush behind.

Robby struggled like the proverbial greased pig and somehow managed to stretch the shirt over his head and off his body before I could drop the flashlight to make use of my other hand. He wound up breaking free, his thin, little half-naked body fleeing into the darkness, while I held an oversized T-shirt with "Artificial Life Beats Real Stupidity" written on it.

Flinging the T-shirt onto the back seat of my car, I was furious that he had gotten away. Seconds later, though, I found myself chortling over the fact that the temperature had dropped to around fifty-five degrees, and he was going to be one cold puppy by the time he got to wherever he was going. I toyed with calling the police and reporting him for trespassing, but I figured he was in enough trouble without me adding to it.

After driving the car inside the garage and climbing the steps to my apartment, I phoned Mira for that one-on-one chat we needed to have. It was brief, and I must say she took it well. Her sympathies were all in the right places. Carlos was one lucky man. I think this slight chink in his armor made Mira love him even more. Knowing they would sort it out in the morning, I said good night and was asleep in less than ten minutes.

Several hours later, I was roused by Tugger growling softly in my ear. I had never heard him make this sound before and was at first confused by it. Even though it was dark, I felt him rise, standing taut, his growling intensifying. Then I heard a noise in the kitchen. Before I could move, Tugger leapt off the bed and ran toward the sound. I didn't turn on the light, feeling it was better to stay in obscurity, but that decision slowed me down.

I felt my way along the wall listening to a growing commotion in the kitchen. Within seconds, there were sounds of shuffling, and Tugger's ever-increasing growling turned into a loud howl. Then came a man's exclamation and cry of pain.

That's when I began to run and fell over the coffee table. I let out a scream and grappled for the five iron I keep behind the sofa for just such an emergency. Rounding the corner to the kitchen, I heard the man shriek, things being knocked over, and a sound of pain from Tugger.

Brandishing the golf club, I lost precious moments trying to find the light switch. When I turned it on, my vision was blurred by curling puffs of flour and the intensity of the light. A form pushed past me and out the open kitchen door before my eyes adjusted. When they did, all thoughts of pursuit were gone. On the kitchen counter, the canister of flour lay on its side, a still Tugger beside it.

I felt another scream escape me and dropped the five iron, rushing to my pet. He was covered with flour but still breathing. He opened his eyes suddenly. Afraid to pick him up, I helped him struggle to wobbly feet, looking for signs of cuts or bruises. So intense was my concentration, I didn't hear footsteps running up the stairs until there was a banging on the front door.

"Liana," cried my mother from the other side of the door. "Liana! Are you all right?"

"Liana, *por favor*, answer us," said Tío.

"Just a minute," I yelled, looking at Tugger. He was steadier on his feet now, and I felt I could leave him for a moment or two. Racing to the front of the apartment, I bellowed that I was all right while unlocking the door. They barged inside.

"I'm all right. I'm all right. It's Tugger," I said, with a catch in my voice. Turning, I ran back to the kitchen. I found my cat sitting where I'd left him, his eyes half closed. He was breathing slowly and deeply. Mom and Tío followed on my heels and stopped right behind me.

"What happened?" demanded Mom, looking at the disarray in the kitchen.

"Someone broke in, and Tugger got in his way. I think he's hurt."

"Let me see," Tío said with quiet authority. He stepped in front of me and began to examine the cat. Tugger leaned into Tío's gentle hands.

"I should bring him to the vet emergency hospital," I said, fighting back sobs. "There's one in San Mateo. He could have internal injuries or something."

"Shhh, Liana!" Tío ordered. Tugger shook himself free of flour, stood, and turned around as Tío continued his inspection. "I think he has had the air pushed out of him, *mi sobrina*. I think he will be all right in a moment," Tío said.

"You mean the wind knocked out of him?" asked Mom, leaning on the counter and stroking Tugger.

As if to emphasize that fact, Tugger freed himself from their hands, jumped down, and shook his body again. He went to the middle of the floor and began cleaning his paws. I grabbed a kitchen towel, followed, and sat cross-legged beside him, gingerly wiping the remains of the flour off his back and legs. "He does seem better, doesn't he, Tío?" I asked, my voice still trembling a little.

"Look at this," Mom said. "I think this is blood on the refrigerator." Glancing up, I scrunched my eyes and noticed several droplets of blood, too small to drip down the white enamel. "And there on the floor," she said, pointing to another spot.

"*Dios mio!*" I exclaimed, carefully taking Tugger in my lap and looking all over his body for a wound.

"I do not think that has come from *el gatito*," Tío remarked. "Look, there is more on the cabinet door." Tío pointed to the cabinet over the fridge. This was a streak of droplets as if splattered from a small paintbrush.

I set Tugger on the floor, and the three of us watched as he cleaned his paws but not his body, which still wore traces of flour. Picking him up again, I took one of his paws in my hand and pressed down to splay open his talons.

"Mom, Tío, look at this!" They came over to where I sat on the floor with the cat in my lap. "There's blood on his claws, and I don't think it's his." Ears back, Tugger freed his foot from my clutches, hopped down again, and strolled out of the room, annoyed by all the attention.

I stood up and went to the refrigerator, examining the top. I noticed the vase of flowers that had been upright when I went to bed was now on its side, water and flowers everywhere. "Tugger must have jumped up here on top of the refrigerator, just like you taught him, Tío, only when he pounced, his claws were extended."

For the first time, I looked at the opened kitchen door that led out to the back deck. The pane nearest the lock had a neat, round hole in it. We crossed to the door, stepping over the few drops of blood on the floor, and I flipped the switch for the deck lights. In the flood of light, we could see that one of the window boxes had several geraniums broken. I ran over to the railing, where I saw a rope ladder dangling by a metal hook.

"The guy wanted to get in here real bad," I said to my uncle, who had followed me outside. "It's almost a twenty-foot drop."

Mom stood at the door, saying, "What I don't understand, Liana, is how he got the door opened. Didn't you have it dead bolted? And what about the alarm? Why didn't the alarm go off? If we hadn't had our windows open, we wouldn't have heard your screams."

Wordlessly, I went back inside, shivering from the night air and my stupidity. Reluctant to admit it, I said in a small voice, "I didn't put the alarm on, Mom. I don't use it unless I'm going away for a while."

"What about the dead *bolt*?" she demanded.

"This dead bolt. What is that?" asked Tío.

"It's a key that locks the door from the inside," I said. "It's often used on doors that have windowpanes in them, like this one. Even if someone breaks the window, like he did, the door still can't be opened unless you have the key to unlock it." They both looked at me expectantly. "The key is in the cookie jar. I haven't used that, either, in months and months."

"Oh, *mija*," Tío commented, shaking his head.

"I see," Mom said. "I'm *disappointed* in you, Liana. I thought you were smarter than that."

Even as a child, that was the ploy my mother used on me when I did something wrong. She never punished me, just expressed her disappointment and made me go to my room to "think about what I'd done." It undid me every time. It still does.

Crossing to the counter, I took the key out of the cookie jar. "Okay, I admit it. I was careless, lazy, and stupid, and if it hadn't been for Tugger, there's no telling what might have happened." I shut the door, locked it, and returned the key, not to the cookie jar but to the nail head near the door, just out of reach of anyone from the outside. Both mother and uncle regarded me silently.

"From now on," I said to both of them, "I promise to use both the dead bolt and the alarm every night. This won't happen again."

Mom touched my face lightly with her fingers, saying, "I'm sure it won't."

"*Si, si, mi sobrina,*" Tío said as he hugged me briefly. "A lesson well learned, *espero.*"

"I hope so too, Tío."

We went back into the living room where Tugger was sprawled out on the sofa, cleaning his fur. "There's my hero," I said. He looked up and blinked, just like a cat. I walked over and sat next to him, caressing him. "Even though he looks all right, I still think I'll bring him into the vet tomorrow."

"We should call the police, Liana," said Mom.

"Not now. I'm too tired. All I need is Frank and his men crawling all over the place. Besides," I added darkly, "I'm pretty sure I know who it was."

"Who?" they asked in unison.

"Robby Weinblatt," I spat out and went on to tell them about my run-in with him just hours before. "Len was right. He's a miserable son of a bi—"

"Liana," Mom interrupted me with a look of warning.

"He could have hurt Tugger," I said through clenched teeth, stroking a now purring cat.

"Ah, but judging by the blood in there," said Tío. "I would say *el hombre* got the worst of it. I believe he has deep scratches on his face, neck, and shoulders. Maybe even puncture wounds. Those can be *grave*."

"Good. Let's hope they're *very* serious," said my mother uncharacteristically, sitting down by my side. "If you don't call tonight, then you should tell Frank about this break-in tomorrow morning, when you give him that note." She put an arm around me. "For now, why don't you come over to the house and sleep there?"

"No way," I said, wiggling free and standing up. "I don't get scared out of my home so easily. When you go, I promise I'll put the alarm on." I raised my right hand as if being sworn in. "I've got my trusty five iron and, of course, the bravest cat in the world to protect me. I'll be fine."

Mom let out a deep sigh and shook her head. "Very well. Besides, I know you. When you're like this, nothing can persuade you."

"*Exactamente,*" I replied.

Tío insisted on getting a board and nailing it over the broken pane before he would go back to bed. After dead bolting the doors, turning on the alarm, and checking the windows, I fell asleep on the couch, waking only to the sound of birds chirping to the rising sun.

Tugger was sitting on the sill intently watching the customers at the bird feeder. I called his name, and he jumped down, talking as he ran over to me. I picked him up and examined him for any repercussions from the night before even though he appeared completely normal. Satisfied, I set him down. He followed me into the kitchen, chatty and hungry.

The kitchen was still a mess, a sober reminder of what happened the night before. I fed Tugger, made an afternoon appointment with the vet, and then phoned Frank. The morning was spent with police reports, cleanup, and windowpane replacements. The afternoon was spent organizing my thoughts, making lists, packing for Mexico, and checking out My Son the Cat's health, which was just fine. Robby Weinblatt's health, on the other hand, was going to be a lot worse once I came back from Los Posos and got my hands on him.

Throughout the day, though, slivers of doubt would pop into my mind. Stuff like why would Robby Weinblatt break into my apartment? What did I have that he could possibly want? But then, what was he doing in my driveway hours before? And if it wasn't him in my kitchen last night getting ripped to shreds by my cat, who the hell was it? Could it be the person who left the nasty little note on my car? Or was that Robby Weinblatt too?

Unable to stand the random thoughts anymore, I took my mind off everything by going shopping and sprang for a new Kate Spade handbag, topping it off with a mocha frappaccino with double whipped cream from my favorite coffee shop. Stress can be expensive and fattening.

Chapter Nine

Down Mexico Way

The entire time Richard drove us to the airport, I spent being pissed. Lila has this thing that when you fly first class, you have an obligation to dress for it. She always wears her finest. As for me, I feel that when you fly, you should be as comfy as possible. I don't care if you're going first class, tourist, or tied to the wing.

My plan was to wear sweats, but here I was in full makeup, dressed in a red silk blouse, matching wool gabardine slacks, and the red leather slingbacks Mom gave me for Christmas. Completing the ensemble was the stone leopard necklace.

I am a woman who has been known to carry a gun, chase people over rooftops, and occasionally, send them to jail. If necessary, I can be one pretty tough cookie. When it comes to my mother, however, half the time I roll over with all fours in the air. This was one of those times. I'm sure Sam Spade would have been mortified by my behavior, but I'll leave Sam to handle his own mother. I've got enough to deal with.

Seated on the plane and clicking my seat belt together, Mom noticed my necklace. "What's this?" She took the charm in her hand.

"Douglas gave it to me." I answered in a cool tone, since it was her fault I would be uncomfortable all night and look like last week's laundry in the morning. Okay, so maybe it wasn't completely her fault. I am nothing if not fair, so I tried to move past it and smiled. "It's very unusual, isn't it?"

"Why, it looks a little like Tugger."

"I know! It's actually a model of an Aztec leopard," I said, warming up a little. Deciding to show off, I added, "You know, a model is —"

"I *know* what a model is, dear," Mom interrupted with a smile. "While one prefers the genuine article, it is often a question of availability and finances."

Just then, the stewardess leaned over and asked us for drink orders. As it had already been a trying flight, and we hadn't even left the ground yet, the prospect of a gin martini straight up, briskly shaken with three olives set my mouth to drooling. Mom decided to have the same thing but with a twist and without the drool.

While we waited for our drinks, Lila started a running diatribe on Mira's father — or rather, the lack of him. "I don't know *why* that man isn't here for his daughter, Liana. When Mira phoned him about Carlos, all he said was for her to break off the

142

engagement, which, of course, our Mira would *never* do."

"Not ever," I chimed in, secretly glad it wasn't me who was getting dumped on.

"Putting aside that Carlos is *innocent*," Mom continued on a roll, "Mira is not the sort of person who…"

"Cuts and runs," I finished for her.

"I was going to say deserts a friend in need."

"And well said, Mom."

I thought about Mira. She was the first person I called when things went right, when things went wrong, and when things just went. I know I couldn't have gotten through my divorce without her. If the situation were reversed, she would have boarded this plane on my behalf in a heartbeat.

"Never *once* did Warren offer to be by her side." I heard Mom sniff. True, Warren McFadden was the kind of man who gave the word "shallow" new meaning. But he was still her father.

"Not to change the subject, but wait till you see what he did to the bridesmaids' gowns," I gossiped, finding I was enjoying myself. "Holy chamole. If one of us isn't mistaken for a tropical bird on steroids during the trip down the aisle and captured by *Jungle Jim*, I will be surprised."

"And who is this *Jungle Jim*?" Mom asked with a frozen smile on her face.

"That's the movie series that Johnny Weissmuller did in the late forties after he was too old to play *Tarzan*. *Jungle Jim* was this great white hunter in Africa who—"

"This *obsession* you have with old black-and-white movies eludes me," my mother interrupted with a sigh. "We should have thrown the television set out the day you were born."

"Dad liked them, too, you know. That's how I got hooked." Silence.

The stewardess brought our drinks and small bowls of mixed nuts. I was happily sipping and munching, mentally recalling my favorite episodes of *Jungle Jim*, when out of the blue, my mother leaned over and kissed me on the forehead.

"What's that for?"

"That's for being a good friend. You're doing the right thing, going down and trying to help Mira Louise and Carlos. I'm very proud of you."

"Well, you too. You're a good friend. You're going down because of Tex."

"Like mother, like daughter," Mom replied.

Mulling that one over, I took a healthy swig of my eighty-six-proof alcohol before chomping down on an olive.

"So here's to the next few days," she continued, clinking my glass with hers. Finding my drink nearly finished, I was about to ring for another, when the ever vigilant and smiling stewardess delivered one.

"This is from the gentleman four rows back," she said, white teeth sparkling. "He had me make it with the private stock he sends on board every time he flies."

Both Mom and I craned our necks to look around and down four rows. There, holding a frosty martini glass, sat a gorgeous, tanned specimen of a man, with blond-streaked hair, green-gray eyes, and a lopsided grin.

"Now aren't you glad you're dressed for the occasion?" Mom whispered.

When he saw me staring at him, he jerked his glass up in a toast, causing some of the martini to slop over the sides and spill onto one leg of his gray tweed slacks. His grin was replaced by a look of surprise and then embarrassment. His free hand mopped at his pants with one of those small, useless square paper napkins they give you on planes. Meanwhile, the forgotten drink began to list to the side. The remaining liquid flowed out of the tipped glass, drenching his lap. Suddenly all arms and legs, he undid his seat belt and stood up, banging his head on the overhead bin.

I turned my head back around. "Oh yeah. I am soooo glad, Mother."

Looking up at the stewardess, who was not even bothering to control her laughter, I said, "Please thank the gentleman for me, and give him the name of a good dry cleaner."

"Don't worry, Liana," said my mother while sighing, who seems to do a lot of that when I'm around. "I'm *sure* Mr. Right is out there somewhere."

"But with a little luck he won't find me."

"And you look so pretty too. Red suits you. Not many women can own the color red the way you can," Mom offered graciously. Thanks to a good snort, she was now in a very mellow mood.

I threw a quick eye back to my gorgeous gin guy, but he had disappeared. I tasted the gin concoction he'd sent up and had to admit it was delicious. I don't know much about booze, but I know a good juniper berry when I taste one, and this was first rate.

Turning my attention back to Lila, I'd hoped she hadn't said anything important while I was zoned out. "I found out something interesting today, Liana. Leonard has no idea where Robby Weinblatt is. He seems to have disappeared."

"Check our backyard," I said half jokingly.

"In a way, it makes little difference." She sipped her cocktail. "Leonard has decided not to press charges."

"He's not? I thought Leonard was going to have the culprit drawn and quartered, once we found out who it was."

Mom shrugged. I shrugged. "Well, we did our job," we said in unison and laughed. We finished our drinks in companionable silence, falling asleep shortly after.

I woke up five hours later, about fifteen minutes before the plane was due to land in Houston. I took two aspirin for my hangover and was dying to brush my teeth that tasted like I had been eating dirty socks. Mom was still sleeping, as was the gorgeous gin guy four rows back in the now-dry gray slacks. I grabbed my toothbrush, undid the seat belt, and ran to the restroom, only exiting when the captain told us to prepare for landing. GG Guy was still asleep.

We arrived late and had to scurry through the airport for our connecting flight to Leon. My head was pounding by the time we got seated. I looked around and found myself, once again, four rows in front of Mr. GGG. What the hell was that all about? Was he also heading to San Miguel? Just as I was debating about getting up and chatting with him, he waved at me and put on an eyeshade, settling in for a snooze.

It was a smooth landing in Leon, and my head was grateful. After picking up Mom's two suitcases, and a brief stint at customs, I looked for Mr. GGG again but never saw him. Covering my disappointment, we headed outside to meet Tex.

I knew Tex would have her bright yellow Hummer, and as we exited the glass doors, there she was, pacing back and forth in front of it. I think you can see that hulking car from space. While Tex greeted us with her usual warmth and enthusiasm, her face looked pale and drawn. There were lines around her eyes and mouth, something I'd never seen before on the eternally youthful and bubbly Tex Garcia. But then it's not every day your only son is arrested for murder.

"How's my boy doing? Is he all right?"

Mom embraced her. "Liana saw him yesterday — well, the day before — and he's fine. Didn't you speak with him last night?"

"Yes, yes, of course I did." She leaned into Lila, more crushed than I've seen her. "I can't believe it, Lila. I just can't. I should go to him right now."

"Let's talk about it over some breakfast," Mom said. "Isn't there a restaurant close by? I seem to remember —"

"Oh, forgive me, hon," Tex drawled, hustling the luggage and us into the car. "You two must be

147

starving. I don't think about food anymore, since this whole thing happened."

"We're going to remedy that right now, Virginia. It doesn't do *anyone* any good if you become ill from all of this. You'll have a nice bowl of oatmeal," Mom added, her cure-all for anything and everything.

Tex smiled, and I felt her spirits momentarily lighten. She pulled out from the curb, and I compared her profile to my mother's. Both women were knockouts: Mom in that understated Grace Kelly sort of way, straight out of *High Society,* and Tex in that Rita Hayworth *Lady from Shanghai* way, only with a Stetson.

Tex was born Virginia Mae Madden in Carrabassett Valley, Maine, population 450, if you count the dogs. She ran away from home at fifteen, when, after her father died, her mother remarried, and the man started sexually abusing her. Tex's mother didn't believe her, an all-too-common story, and she wound up in Las Vegas. Being tall, good looking, and well developed for her age, she went to the Flamingo Hotel and applied for a job as a showgirl. In them thar days, all you needed was a doctored-up driver's license to prove you were of drinking age. Today it wouldn't even fool a nine-year-old.

Three months later, she met and married Bart Garcia, a Mexican-American who'd struck it rich by inventing a little thingy-hooky that sits at the base of an oil rig and pulls up an additional 5 percent oil. When Bart was alive, they lived six months in Texas and six months in Mexico, with the occasional stint in Palo Alto.

She dabbed at her eyes with Kleenex as she drove. "I should be with my son," Tex said again. "What am I doing here?"

"We need you here, Tex, to help us," I said. "Besides, Carlos said there was a jumping competition—"

"Screw the competition," came Tex's sharp reply. "Paco can take care of the horses for me while I'm gone. I won't stay here in Mexico if my son needs me just because of a jumping competition!"

Mom shot me a look. "Of course not," she said soothingly. "But Carlos is"—she hesitated a moment—"in *confinement* right now, and Mateo is looking after Mira. Before you decide to go to the Bay Area, we could use your help here. Let's see what the next few days bring." Tex nodded, but I could see her lips quiver.

"Right," I mumbled. "I didn't mean anything when I said that about the competition, Tex. I..."

"No, you didn't, little darling," she said, reaching over the back of her seat and grabbing my hand. She squeezed hard. "Forgive me, hon, for jumping all over you. I'm not myself right now. You're just a doll to be here, a doll." She turned to Mom. "My sweet Carlos would never hurt a living thing. You know that, Lila."

"Of *course* we do, Virginia," Mom answered. "That's why we're here. We'll talk about it more over breakfast. And you're going to eat all your oatmeal," Mom ordered.

Forty-five minutes later, all three of us fortified with the aforementioned oatmeal, we were heading toward Los Posos, about an hour-and-a- half drive. Mom sat next to Tex again, and I stretched out in the back. Just as I was wondering if Carlos had let his mom know he'd told me his big secret, Tex brought it up.

"Lee, Carlos told me he's spilled the beans about how his birth mother died," she said, looking at me in the rearview mirror. "Have you told your mother yet?"

"No, I haven't." It wasn't just that I thought either Carlos or Tex should be the ones, I hadn't had the time. True, I could have told Mom on the plane, but two martinis took care of that.

"I knew there was something after Liana returned from seeing Carlos," said Mom.

"Lila, Carlos and I have never talked about this, not once, until last night. We probably should have, but we didn't. It's like the elephant in the room, you know?"

While Tex let 'er rip, I looked out the window to a sky that was endlessly blue, dotted with an occasional cloud drifting above flowering trees and lush, vibrant foliage. A flock of chattering, wild green parrots flew overhead and settled in a nearby jacaranda tree.

I love this area of Mexico, high in the mountains but still very tropical. The same plant and animal life flourish here as do seven thousand feet below, but the air is dryer and cooler, especially in the summer. With only a twenty-degree temperature variance year-round, this part of Mexico is known for having one of the best climates in the world.

Up ahead on the side of the road, I spotted a middle-aged, sinewy man and his burro tilling a field with an ancient-looking plow. Small and wooden, the plow had a curved blade that scooped out the dirt and threw it to the side, creating a narrow ditch. Bronzed by the sun, the man pushed as much as the burro pulled, but neither seemed overly burdened by the process or in any great hurry. A colorfully dressed woman with long salt-and-pepper braids trailed them. Rhythmically, she reached into a burlap bag tied around her waist and threw seeds into the newly created trench. All three, seemingly content with their lot in life, cast a serene and distinctly Mexican glow on the moment. As I watched them, I forgot why I was in Mexico.

About to drift off to sleep, I regarded Tex's white-and-silver Stetson scraping the inside roof of the car, and wondered how many dozens she owned before I mentally pinched myself on the butt and decided to get on with why we were there. I leaned forward and stuck my face between the two of them.

"Tex, Carlos says there have been some odd things going on at the rancho. What exactly?"

"Well, hon, aside from a few of the ranch hands acting peculiar, now and then at night, we see lights coming over the ridge out by the old mine. Each time we ride out the next morning, we never find anything out of place. Everything looks the same."

"No tire tracks or anything like that?" I asked.

"Well, the road we're talking about is used to bring feed to the cattle out in the lower valley. And the foreman and his wife live off it to the south about three miles down. There's somebody riding or driving on that dusty old road almost every day. It's hard to tell if somebody's using it who shouldn't ought to. I never thought about it until now."

"How often do you see these lights?" asked Lila.

"Sometimes months will go by with nothing, and then we'll see them three, four days in a row."

"Where exactly did Carlos find the dog statue?" I asked.

"Close to the mine, near the spot with the crick going by it. You know it, dontcha?" Tex's western accent always made me smile.

"I think I should go to the mine as soon as we get there," I said, looking out the window again. It was around ten in the morning, allowing for the time change, and we were almost at the rancho. I knew I had nearly the whole day before me.

"You don't let any grass grow under your feet, do you, hon?"

"Carlos found that statue nearly ten days ago," I said. "Too much time has gone by as it is."

"We could ride out there, too, Lila," Tex said, reaching for her cell phone. "Let me call Paco and tell him to get three of the horses ready."

"Just me," I said quietly. "I'll take the bike and go by myself."

"Liana," Mom protested. "I think —"

"No, Mom. I work better alone. You should start looking around the ranch while I'm gone. See if you

152

can find anything. I'll take the sat phone with me and put it on 'track.' This way you'll know where I am every moment. The mine is only about two-and-a-half miles from the house, right?"

Mom looked at Tex, and Tex looked at Mom. "You're the boss, hon," Tex said. It was settled. "But about your bike, *se mureo*. Rusted clean through. I had to take it behind the barn and put a bullet through it last summer. How about I tell Paco to saddle up Lupita for you? I know you don't mind her." Tex dialed the number. "Unless you want to take the Hummer. That's fine by me."

"I don't want to attract attention to myself, so I'll just take the horse. By the way, have either of you noticed the car following us?" Both women whipped their heads around. In the distance, what looked like a black Jeep shadowed us on the dusty road.

"Hey, hey. Watch where you're going, Tex," I said as the car started to swerve.

Mom put on her distance glasses, studying the Jeep. "It looks like the same car I saw in the parking lot of the restaurant. The one covered in mud." She shuddered.

"Right now I'm more concerned about the fact it's been behind us for the last fifty miles or so rather than it needs a wash."

"It'd be hard to lose someone on this dirt road," Tex muttered. "Too much dust and ruts. But you want me to try?"

"Oh, don't sweat it," I answered. "Our front is that we are here visiting the overwrought mother."

"I'll try to sob in the appropriate places and at the appropriate times." Tex grinned. I was glad to see her sense of humor hadn't totally abandoned her.

"When we get through the gate, Tex, slow down. I'll hop out and see if I can get the license plate number."

Fifteen minutes later, we arrived at the gated entrance to the cattle ranch that Bart purchased back in the early '70s. Tex removed a remote from her sun visor, punched in some numbers, and the white, heavy wrought-iron gate, emblazoned with the skull of a steer the size of a tyrannosaurus rex, swung open. Twenty feet overhead, a matching wrought-iron arch held the words *Los Pocitos de Oros* — "the veins of gold" — in large, sweeping letters.

We passed through, and Tex screeched to a bumpy stop while the automatic gate closed behind us. I got out, hiding behind one of the oak trees lining each side of the drive and watched her pull away. Amid the backdrop of settling dust, I glanced around the trunk of the tree, catching sight of a grimy, black Jeep zipping by on the larger road. The last three numbers were obscured by caked-on mud, but I pressed the ones I could make out to memory and fired up the sat phone. Richard answered on the first ring.

"Hey, Lee, you got there." He could have been across the street, his voice was that clear.

"Baby Brother, I need a favor."

"Name it."

"I've got the partial numbers of a Mexican license plate. I think it's from Guanajuato, but I can't swear to it. I'd like you to check it out."

"How soon do you need the info?"

"Yesterday. The first number or letter is a 'one' or an L. I couldn't tell which with all the gunk on the plate. That's followed by U, V, and 'seven.' Those I'm certain of. I couldn't get the last three numbers."

"That's too bad. Mexico's a large country, so there could be a lot of possibilities. Just a heads-up. I'll get back to you."

"Counting on it."

We disconnected, and I started the two-mile hike to the ranch house only to realize I was wearing four-inch stilettos already hurting my feet. Just as I was about to take them off and walk barefoot, I rounded a corner and saw Tex and Mom waiting for me in an idling Hummer, nicely polluting the environment. Swallowing any reprimands I might have had, I yipped and tottered toward them, glad for the ride.

The ranch and bunkhouses sit about two miles in on this single-lane road, filled with enough spine-jostling ruts and gullies to send you to your local chiropractor. The main house dates back about one hundred years, with additions made more recently by the Garcias. It is now a sprawling, single-story, eight-bedroom, five-bath, wooden structure, with lots of windows and a wraparound porch decorated with cattle horns.

Directly across the road is the bunkhouse, where wranglers sleep and eat, complete with a hitching post to tie up the horses. As there are about eight hundred head of cattle grazing somewhere on the fenced-in property at any given moment, there are usually six or seven *vaqueros* or cowhands riding herd and living at the bunkhouse. Right off its kitchen door hangs the loudest triangle I've ever heard in my life, used by Olaf, the deaf transgender cook, to call the ranch hands in for meals. He makes one mean tostada.

At the end of the dirt road looms an enormous three-story, red barn. Four horses, hitched up in pairs, can pull a train of hay wagons through one set of double doors, unload the bales of hay for storage on the second and third floors, then pull the empty wagons out the matching doors on the other side. Meanwhile, milking cows and calves stay undisturbed in their stalls. Any hay not consumed by the Garcia herd or the Aztecas, is sold to nearby ranchers. As a kid, I loved coming to what I considered the Wild West, Mexican style.

Once we came to a stop, I jumped out and ran inside to the small but sunny room in the back of the house I call mine when I'm here. I reached into the closet for my jeans and Gortex all-weather boots. After a quick trip to the kitchen where I made a couple of peanut-butter-and-jelly sandwiches, I headed out to the barn.

I remembered to bring carrot sticks, a treat for old Lupita, the sweetest and most docile horse I've ever ridden. She was tied to a post and ready to go. I called her name and proffered the vegetables in my open palm. A mottled gray-and-white mare, small in size but large in heart, she whinnied softly as I approached and took the treat in a very ladylike manner.

Stowing the sandwiches in one of the saddlebags, I mounted hesitantly, talking myself down from the experiences I've had with horses of yesteryear. I concentrated on the fact that Lupita was a sweetie-pie. Besides, she was my only mode of transportation to the mine from here unless I wanted to walk it. I didn't.

I attached the sat phone to my belt, and we trotted off toward the abandoned mine. About thirty-five minutes later, we arrived at the sealed entrance. I dismounted with a creepy-crawly feeling that someone's unseen eyes were boring into my back. I looked around. No one.

With Lupita grazing by my side, I tried to shake off the feeling and turned my attention to the concrete blocks cemented into the sides of the entrance and the locked, chain-link fence at the center. I went closer and noted there was another stack of blocks behind the fence, too, piled up and filled in here and there with rocks of varying sizes. The ground inside and around the fence was undisturbed and looked like it had been so for decades. Even small nesting animals were at peace in their makeshift condos. I was sure that whatever was going on around here had nothing to do with the mineshaft entrance. I walked back into the brush, surveyed the mine from a distance, and decided to give Richard another call.

He answered on the third ring, booming, "Yo, Lee. What now? You can't think I've gotten those license plates for you yet."

"Richard, I'm out here at the mine, and, I swear to you, it looks like it's been sealed up for the past fifty years."

"Thirty, actually."

"Well, why? I never knew for sure."

"Carlos told me the government had his dad seal it off for safety reasons. Besides, the mine was played out."

"You're sure about that?"

"Lee," he chided me, "don't you remember? Five or six years ago Carlos hired a piloted helicopter with aerial X-ray equipment. This was after the geological survey the year before. I fed the combined data of both findings into a supercomputer that analyzed the physical properties and the probability of any gold being left in that mountain."

"What did you find?"

"Zero probability."

"You're sure?"

"Don't you think Carlos would like to own a working gold mine? It got played out before nineteen fifty. That mountain has so many unsupported tunnels in it, the whole thing is going to collapse in on itself during the next sizable temblor."

I chewed on my lower lip the way Lupita was chewing on the grass. "So whatever's going on around here has nothing to do with gold."

"Nothing to do with gold," he echoed.

"Whoa. I think I see somebody." I strained my eyes. "There's a glint of something on a hilltop."

"Aim the sat phone at them and take a picture. Send it on to me; I'll enlarge it and see what you've got. It shouldn't take more than a few seconds."

I pressed down the "capture" button and heard nothing. "It didn't go 'click,' Richard, so that better mean that all the functions are silent. I'd hate for this thing to be broken."

"Of course they're silent. Even the phone doesn't ring. It vibrates. Do you know how to send the picture to me? I knew we should have gone over this before you left."

I ignored him. "After I take the picture, I punch the thingy underneath the send' button. When I see your phone number in the external display, then I hit the send button. That automatically sends the digital picture to you. Correct?"

"Except for the word 'thingy,' it is correct."

"Where's the flash? Just in case I need it later on."

"The lens is supersensitive and automatically adjusts. It has a form of night vision, similar to what the Navy Seals use underwater. Now, back to the 'thingy' button," he said. "It sets the coordinates. At this time, only DI's number is programmed in, but you could ostensibly send information to anyone in the world."

"Okay, here goes." I pressed the button.

In less than five seconds, I heard Richard say, "I've got it. Now I'll transfer it to the computer and enhance it. Yes, yes," he said more to himself than me. "Not so good."

"What's not so good?"

"It's a person wearing a large hat, sitting on a dark horse. That's all I can make out. That's enough to tell me you're being watched."

"Maybe not. Maybe it's one of the *vaqueros* on the property riding by."

"Take another picture in the same place and send it to me," Richard said in a worried voice. "Let's see if he's still there."

"You sure like to play with this thing, don't you?"

"Take another picture, doofus," he demanded. I obeyed and this time the man and horse were gone.

"See?" I said, "Nobody's there. It was just someone riding by." I was uneasy but didn't want Richard to know. After Dad's death, he'd become such a worrywart that I didn't want to alarm him.

I made a mental note, though, to check the saddlebags for the usual emergency kit Tex kept in each one of them. Aside from water and a flashlight, there should be an extra round of shells for the rifle, tied to the saddle, in case of a recalcitrant rattlesnake. They come in all sizes and shapes.

"I should go, Richard," I said impatiently. "I have work to do."

"Call me if you need me. Mom too. I've got this phone and my laptop with me at all times. I'm right here, Sis."

"Well, take a break. Or get me those license plate numbers. We're fine." I hung up and sat down on the cool grass under a tree about fifty feet away from the mine's entrance, thinking. About twenty minutes later, I had a plan.

"Come on, Lupita," I said. "Let's take a little walk around this mountain. It shouldn't take us more than five or six hours." I grabbed her reins, and she plodded along behind me while I scrutinized the terrain looking for something, anything, out of the ordinary.

Into the fourth hour, I was hot, sweaty, tired of brushing flies away from my face and developing a whopper of a blister on one of my big toes. My repeated check-ins with Mom were becoming annoying, and I would have killed for a cold shower. In short, I was cranky.

I neared the far side of the mountain and found a section of dead or dying flora. I stopped. I had to think about what it meant because I was not the sharpest tack in the pack at that moment. Eventually, I got it.

Being the tail end of spring, there were still frequent showers. We hadn't reached the parched stages of summer yet, where many of the plants wilt or die under the unrelenting sun. Vegetation was green and healthy everywhere else except for here.

I dropped Lupita's reins and watched her amble over to a nearby patch of grass to do more munching while I stepped off the trail and into the brush, some fifteen yards away. Close-up, I could see the foliage had been cut or broken off and then stacked one on top of the other to create pseudo shrubbery. Newer limbs were still greenish, but all were in various stages of death. Behind this first row, small trees and larger limbs were propped up with stones to give a more normal look to unsuspecting eyes that traveled this trail. But there was nothing normal about what was going on here.

While stepping in between some of the larger branches trying to get closer to the mountain itself, instinct told me to move as quietly as possible. From behind the tallest level of camouflage, shrubs and trees, came the faint sounds of a radio playing popular Mexican tunes. I followed the music and found another narrower trail snaking to a four- or five-foot-high opening inside the mountain. Standing at the cave's entrance for a moment, I strained my ears and heard the rhythmic sound of snoring accompanying the music. I ducked down and cautiously went inside, waiting for my eyes to adjust to the lack of light.

The source of the snores was a neatly dressed, lone youth slumped over in a folding chair. A rifle leaned against the wall and a half-empty bottle of tequila lay on the ground by his side. In front of him was a rickety-looking card table holding an unlit kerosene lamp, a half-played deck of cards, and the radio I'd been hearing. The neat, preppy, pink shirt and khaki trousers he wore was in contrast to his drunken stupor.

Fairly sure he would sleep for a while, I relaxed a little, ever listening for a variance in his breathing. I began to look around and was flabbergasted by what I saw.

The cave was massive inside, perfectly spherical, and clearly not nature's work. Directly across from the entrance was a rough-hewn slab of rock resting on two chiseled boulders. It looked to me like an ancient altar. To either side stood sturdy-looking, rectangular, wooden tables each more than twenty feet in length.

Atop them, dozens of burnished statues, bowls, urns, masks, whistles, musical instruments, and idols shimmered in the dimness. Dressed in the richest of colors of terracotta, red, brown, sandstone, gray and blue, some stood only inches tall, while others scaled a height of two to three feet. A riot of exotic patterns and scenic pictures seemed to mock the stillness of the gloomy setting.

Off to one side, smaller jadeite statuettes, masks and incense burners glimmered in shades of dark to pale green. Resting on the dirt floor, and lined against the cave's walls, were ceremonial plates, many nearly four feet in diameter. Mythical creatures, gods, goddesses, and warriors jumped out at me from every direction. My eyes locked on one sand-colored clay urn, nearly two feet tall, on which was painted a realistic-looking black panther. The larger animal looked almost identical to the small ornament hanging around my neck. My fingers flew to the charm, and I enclosed it in a shaking hand.

I crept closer, keeping an eye on my sleeping friend, and noted the relics had been categorized, with a numbered piece of paper before each. Kneeling, sitting, and praying warriors of all sizes banded together. Pots in the form of playing and barking dogs were herded next to ceramic lizards, iguanas, turkeys, and tortoises. If memory of college art history served me, one section contained funereal objects, devoted to ushering the fallen into the next world. I felt as if I were in the working innards of a museum.

Overhead and surrounding me were beautiful red, black, and white wall paintings looking hundreds, if not thousands, of years old. Deities, animals of prey and worship, feathered people in positions of humility and power looking vaguely Aztec, breathed life into the coarse, chiseled walls wherever I looked.

I pivoted slowly in the half light trying to see everything, fretting about how I could retain and report it all, when I thought of the sat phone. I removed it from my belt and, pivoting again, began taking silent pictures. I started with a pair of three-foot-high, black ceramic panthers, so true in detail they appeared to be breathing. I shot them from two or three angles and then moved on to the rest of the cache.

I probably took thirty pictures before I figured I was pushing my luck with Rip Van Winkle over in the corner. I tiptoed back to the mouth of the cave, grateful for the music covering any small noise I might have made. Right before I left, and as a final gesture of contempt, I took a shot of the sleeping sentinel.

I left as quietly as I came but was so excited I could hardly contain myself. I stepped over the brush, careful to leave the flora as I found it and made my way back to where Lupita was patiently waiting. Remembering that a picture is worth a thousand words, I hit Richard's quick-dial number and sent the pictures with a quaking hand, warning him he might not believe what he was going to see.

I led Lupita a little deeper into a clump of trees, just in case my sleeping friend woke up and decided to take a stretch or do something a little more personal.

I sat down behind a tree, filled with the wonder of it all. Accepting my father's old adage, "When you don't know what to do, do nothing," I munched on a peanut-butter-and-jelly sandwich and finished the bottle of water, reluctant to move. A few minutes later, I felt vibrations coming from the phone and knew it was probably Richard calling me back. I answered the phone while looking overhead. The sun was starting to set. I had been gone nearly seven hours.

"Richard, what do you think?" I demanded.

"Lee, it's just possible you've found the largest collection of Toltec artifacts known to man, if they're real. And the wall paintings! Magnificent! I've got at least three people working on the pictures to see what it all means. Who's the guy with the rifle? I don't like that. What if he'd wakened while you' were there?"

"But he didn't," I said and heard a double beep in my ear. The only other person it could be was Lila.

"Richard, Mom's calling. Can I answer and still keep you on the line with me?"

"See the green button below the one marked send?"

"Yes."

"That's for a conference call. Hit it twice and start talking. You know, I tried to go over this with you before you left."

"Yeah, yeah," I muttered before tapping the green button twice. I said hello and heard my mother's voice along with Richard's.

"Liana, we didn't hear from you. Virginia and I were becoming concerned."

"Mom, I've got Richard on the line too. You need to call the police. Something's come up."

"Tell me," she ordered, and I did, with input here and there from Richard.

"Liana," Mom said, "Virginia is phoning the police on the landline right now, but you know it's going to take at least an hour and a half for them to get here from San Miguel."

"I'll wait."

"You should ride back right now. It's not *safe* for you to be there," Lila said, sounding just like a mother.

"No, no, I'm fine. No one knows I'm here. I'm hidden behind a tree. Secondly, I'm not leaving my newfound treasure until the police come, and I know exactly what's going on. Thirdly, I have a rifle, and I'm perfectly safe—"

"You said that, Lee," Richard interrupted. "My vote is for you to leave, as well. Stop being so stubborn. You never know what could happen. Your locator signal had better be on. Is her signal on, Mom?"

"It was, but isn't now. That's why I called."

"Whoops, I must have accidentally turned it off when I called Richard. Sorry. I'll put the locator back on and sit tight until everybody comes. This way I can watch the place. This thing has more gizmos on it," I complained about the phone as I pressed the button. The soft red light began to pulse again.

"If you are determined to stay there, Liana, at least now we can find you," Lila said.

"Great! So I'll talk to you later, Richard, and Mom, I'll see you in about an hour and a half when the police arrive."

I hung up and that was the last I knew. I felt a *thwack* at the base of my skull, a sharp pain, and then *adios amigos*.

Chapter Ten

The Mexican Hat Dance

I woke up to a wet tongue slobbering all over my face and the smell of ingested grass. Thank you, Lupita. Sitting up, I suspected my moaning was what brought her to my side. She's sweet that way, slobber and all.

Wiping my cheeks and forehead with the sleeve of my blouse, I looked up to the sky. It was almost dark. Faithful Lupita still there, I reached for a stirrup and managed to hoist myself to my feet. I heard hoofbeats coming toward me along the main trail. Thinking it was someone coming to finish the job, I grabbed the rifle and cocked it. I've never fired at anything other than a target on a practice range, but I was damned if I was going to go down without a fight. Relief flooded through me when I heard my mother shouting my name as she and Tex galloped by waving flashlights.

Braced against the mare's side, I staggered out to the path and called to the women. The effort added to the crashing cymbals in the back of my head, and I could hear the hoofbeats fading into the distance. Just as I was about to fire the rifle into the air, Lupita gave out with something that sounded more like the trumpet of an elephant than a whinny. She followed it with a loud snort. That got their attention. My God, if I'm ever at the bottom of a well, this horse is better than Lassie.

When Mom and Tex heard us, I could sense their relief, even in my sorry state. They turned the horses around and, flashlights aimed at me, came to my side. It was only a quarter moon, so everything was pale, and it was hard for me to focus. I returned the rifle to the holder, reached inside the saddlebag, and finding the flashlight, flicked it on.

"Anybody got water?" I asked as they dismounted. I was still leaning on Lupita.

"Sure, hon," said Tex, getting a bottle of water and handing it to me. My mother ran to my side.

"Liana, what *happened*?" Mom asked. "Why did your signal go off? We couldn't find you."

"How long ago was that, Mom?" I asked, taking a long drink. I poured the rest on the nape of my neck. A light, spring rain had begun to fall, and that, too, felt delicious on my head.

"Right after we hung up, about an hour ago. We decided not to wait for the police when your signal stopped," Mom said, feeling the back of my head. "What is *this*, Liana? You're *hurt*! What happened?"

"You say the signal went off? Oh, jeesh, where's my sat phone?" I let go of the saddle, searching the ground with my flashlight. I returned to where I'd been hit. "Oh no," I said as I saw it smashed to smithereens, lying by a large rock. "Richard's going to kill me."

"Liana, stand still and tell me what happened."

"Someone conked me on the head right after I hung up from you." I heard her intake of breath. "I'm fine, but I only came to minutes before you found me. The cave!" I said, wheeling around. I aimed the beam toward the fake shrubbery.

"Mom, Tex, shine your lights over there," I said, gesturing with my light. They obeyed, and we saw that the camouflage had been tossed about, revealing the hidden path running along the mountainside. Dropping the bottle of water, I ran over to the mouth of the cave that was now completely exposed. The ground directly outside had been beaten down by footprints and thick tire tracks.

"Oh, crap, crap, crap, crap, crap." I ducked down and stepped inside the cave. Mom followed, not saying a word about my language. She knew how serious this was.

"They're gone," I said. A spent force, I leaned against the side of the cave. My voice echoed in the empty cavern. "It's all gone."

The tables were now bare and several were on their sides. As Tex and Mom's lights shot around the cave, I could see the hasty retreat that had taken place. The card table was upside down and cards were everywhere. The bottle of tequila was smashed against one wall, the still-wet contents sparkling off shards of broken glass.

Tex whistled in wonder, focusing her beam on the walls, "Oh, doggy, would you look at this! This has been on our property all this time, and I never knew?"

Mom went back outside and I followed her. Studying the ground, she asked, "How many men do you suppose there were?"

"I can't really tell, but it looks like quite a few. Maybe Tex…" I began, just as she joined us.

"I'm not staying in there by myself in the dark, ladies. It's too spooky."

"Virginia, you're good at tracking. Can you tell how many men were here?" Lila asked.

"Hmmm," she said, squatting down and playing the light around her. "At least six different sets, maybe as many as eight. Plus the double wheels of a truck. Tires worn pretty thin. That's about all I can tell in this dark. We'll have to wait until morning. Of course, if it rains any harder…" She didn't finish the sentence. She didn't have to.

"Here," I said, rooting around inside my saddlebag for a wool sweater kept there. I tossed it to Tex. "Lie this on top of a section of the tire tracks. Maybe this will keep the rain from washing it away, enough to get a plaster cast for a match."

I stumbled a little, and Mom reached out a supporting arm. "Liana, you're *hurt* more than I thought. We'd better head back, Virginia."

"Sure thing. It's starting to really come down now, anyway," Tex muttered as she stretched the sweater over the ground and looked up at the sky.

"Is there a doctor—" Mom started.

"I don't need a doctor, Mom," I interrupted. "I'm fine." I didn't add I was so mad at myself that

I felt I didn't merit medical help. If I had a headache for the rest of my life, it was only what I deserved.

"The closest doctor is in San Miguel," Tex said, ignoring me. "And they rarely make house calls. In any event, even if we could get someone to come, it might take a couple of hours for them to get out here."

The two of them herded me to Lupita's waiting side. "I don't need…" I began to say again.

"We'll have to drive her to town when we get back," Mom said.

"You're not going to drive me to town. I won't go." My voice was small but mighty.

"I could call my vet, Dr. Gonzales," Tex said.

"I don't want—"

"She's only about five minutes away. She comes over at all hours to take care of my Aztecas."

"Excellent thinking, Virginia."

"Hey! Would somebody listen to me? I'm not going to let a vet check me over!" I put my foot in the stirrup in an attempt to haul myself into the saddle.

"Dr. Gonzales has delivered babies from time to time, when the women couldn't get to the hospital in time. She once set a *vaquero's* broken leg when he fell off his horse." Tex mounted her pinto and looked at me.

"Large animal vets often know a great deal about the human body," Mom said as she gave my rump a push into the saddle. She turned her attention back to Tex. "Could you call her now, Virginia?"

"Sure thing. I even have her number on speed dial," replied Tex.

I gave up. "Well, what the hell. I've been pretty much of a horse's ass, so it's only fitting. Maybe I could ask her what to do about Tugger's hairballs while she's at it."

"*Hush*, Liana. This is no time for levity," Mom said.

Grabbing Lupita's reins, I leaned over, hugging her warm, damp neck. Mom mounted her horse while Tex made the call for the vet to meet us at the house.

We started off at a slow trot, my head pounding and my spirits so low you'd have to take an elevator down to the basement to find them. I had let everyone down with my stupidity. If I hadn't been trying to put on a brave front for Lupita, I would have cried into her soggy mane all the way home.

It was a veritable party waiting for us on the lighted porch—a chubby woman about my age who turned out to be Dr. Gonzales, four or five policemen, and Paco, the horse handler. The doctor had a bag with her that looked a lot like a regular doctor's bag, and she greeted us with a warm smile, blasé about the uniformed and armed company she'd been waiting with.

Paco took the horses from us to unsaddle them and wipe them down. Ordinarily, that's the rider's job and always has been, but these were extenuating circumstances. We climbed the steps, and Dr. Gonzales came over to me. Lila and Tex took the police over to a seating area on the porch

173

while the doctor and I went inside. I would have preferred to talk to the police, but I was outvoted.

Ushered to the leather sofa, I was ordered to lie down. After examining me carefully, Dr. Gonzales proclaimed I was going to live. I could have told her that. It was a "glancing" blow and could have been a lot more serious — I could have told her that too — and some ice and a day's rest should take care of it. She further suggested that I see a regular doctor the following day for a checkup. Fat chance. Glancing blows go with the territory.

Mom and Tex came inside and informed me that three of the *policia* had left. They would question me in the morning. Two officers remained, standing guard on the porch until daylight. When the others returned, they would begin their search. I knew by then the truck and its contents would be halfway to God knows where and the tracks probably obliterated by the rain.

Dr. Gonzalez said her goodbyes to the three of us, and other than to thank her, I didn't talk much. Tex got an ice pack, and Mom fussed with my covers. I lay back on the ice, feeling the headache subside but not my idiocy. I'd been crept up on from behind like a second-grade shamus in a B movie. Man, was I depressed.

Exactly who clobbered me on the noggin? And where did all those men, who made the footprints outside the cave, come from? More importantly, where did they go? Whoever they were, they were able to strip the cave of hundreds of pieces of art in under an hour. They even had a large truck at their disposal that once loaded, departed for a safer, designated place. Whatever was going on, it was big, well organized, and nearby. The nearby part and Tex being here by herself began to bother me. Maybe Carlos was right; maybe she was in danger.

Mom made some soup and green tea for me and brought it out in a tray. Without saying a word, she put the tray down, turned on cable TV, handed me the remote, and left the room. She knows better than anybody that sometimes you just want to be miserable by yourself. I had been ordered to stay awake for a couple of hours, so I propped myself up and sipped the tea while catching snatches of her conversation with Richard in the next room on the sat phone. I didn't have the strength to ask what it was about or to interrupt.

Minutes later, flipping through channels, I found an old Barbara Stanwyck movie, *The Lady Eve*. Even dubbed in Spanish, it was terrific, and I tried to lose myself in it. Sour thoughts flitted into my mind occasionally, but I tried to keep them at bay.

After the film was over, I decided to call my cell and home phones to check my messages even though I'd been gone less than twenty-four hours. Not many people have those numbers, so I wasn't expecting much. I reached for the phone on the end table. The first message was from Tío, who decided to bring Tugger over to the big house. Mira would have some feline companionship, and Tugs wouldn't be lonely in my absence. This sounded good to me on the off chance the apartment was burglarized again. I didn't want My Son the Cat to be there by himself.

The second was a frantic message from Leonard. He had no idea where Robby Weinblatt was and would I find him? I couldn't get the tone of his voice though. It was all over the map—angry, sad, hostile, and wrapped in guilt. Pretty odd, all told, but it didn't hold a candle to the next message from Douglas. I actually had to listen to that one twice in order to let it sink in.

"Lee, it's me, Douglas. Listen, I hate to bother you...actually, I hate to ask this of you... I don't know how to begin... Lee, I'm going to have to ask for that cat charm I gave you, back." Nervous laughter here. "I-it seems that I... shouldn't have given that away. It's not really a copy but the prototype... ah, whatever that is... and it seems Stefano says it's kind of valuable and irreplaceable... well, actually, he says his cousin says it is... and if..." He broke off speaking for a moment. "Lee, I'm so sorry about this, but he really is upset, and he says he will give you another one that looks just like it, okay? I'm so sorry, Lee. I'll make this up to you. If you could just call me back and let me know when I can have it back, so I can give it to him, I'd appreciate it." Long pause. "Call me back, Lee, and as soon as you can, darling girl. Okay?"

I didn't tell Douglas I'd be out of town. Everything happened so fast, I didn't get the chance to tell anyone where I was going. After a moment, I decided to leave it that way, now this Stefano was in the mix. It was 11:30 p.m. That meant it was nine thirty in California. It might not be too late to return Douglas's call, but I wasn't sure I wanted to talk to him even over the phone. I didn't think I was a good enough actor to keep the doubts and worries out of my voice. We knew each other too well.

Tex had gone to bed, but Mom was hovering nearby. She came over when I hung up and sat down on the couch beside me.

"What's troubling you, Liana?" she asked, stroking my hair.

"Mom, do you still have that friend at the Museo de Antropologia in Mexico City, the one who's a curator?"

"Manuel Lopez? Dr. Lopez is not *exactly* my friend. He was more of a friend of your father's."

I removed the leather thong from my neck and handed it to her. "Could you go there tomorrow and have him take a look at this? I don't think there's anyone close by who would either know about this or we could trust. Can you do that for me?"

She looked at me, puzzled. "That actually was my plan, to visit him at the museo, Liana, but for another reason." Now it was my turn to wear a puzzled look. She turned the charm over in her hand again and again absentmindedly. "I have an idea about what might be happening around here."

"Do you? Share with me, Mom. I'm at a loss." I shifted around on the ice pack.

"I think this is much larger than it seems on the surface of it, Liana. The cave was cleaned out very quickly."

"That's what I thought."

"This suggests a finely tuned organization. I suspect there might be a spread-out operation with key people in important and influential places."

"That makes sense."

"In which case, Manuel Lopez is the kind of person who is politically and socially involved in many things, even outside his own areas of expertise. Besides..." She smiled down at me. "He's a man who likes to *gossip*. That could prove useful."

I felt a shot to the solar plexus. She was onto something.

"A little while ago, I gave Manuel a quick call at his home. He's always been a man who stays up late, so I knew he wouldn't mind. We're going to have lunch tomorrow in Mexico City to discuss a few things. I'll ask him about this while I'm at it," Lila added as she held up the necklace, studying it. "Liana, where is the mark? I don't see it."

I snatched the necklace back, turned on a nearby lamp for more light, and scrutinized the small charm in my hand. "I don't see anything either, Mom. What do these marks look like?"

"I have no idea, having never bought a replica, but I would say they should be in a place fairly obvious to the consumer."

Mom looked at me, and I looked at her. I handed her back the panther charm, saying, "Okay, we're going on the assumption that whatever was in the cave is valuable, otherwise, why did they strip it?"

"Exactly, Liana. *Possibly* priceless."

"This doesn't put us any closer to the killer of the thief back in Palo Alto though," I said. "Or does it?"

"What do you mean?" Mom asked, refolding the crocheted afghan I had kicked off in my haste to turn on the light.

I ran fingers through my hair in frustration. "Oh, I can't figure out what I mean. My head is aching too much to think about it. But I know I have to get back home right away. Something's been lurking in the back of my mind, but it won't come forward. Besides, there's no point in sticking around here any longer. Everything's gone, thanks to me."

"Not necessarily thanks to you, but I do agree that at this juncture the *policia* are better equipped to take it from here. Don't chew on your lower lip, dear. It's unladylike."

"Well, this lady can't believe she got snuck up on like that," I said, no longer chewing but rubbing the back of my head.

"Richard feels very badly about that. He said when you tried to convince him you weren't being followed he let it go. He feels he should have tried harder."

"Oh, it's not his fault. I never listen to him, anyway. I've got nobody to blame but myself on this one," I said as I yawned and leaned my head back. It felt like it weighed in at about two hundred pounds.

"Why don't you go to your room and try to sleep now? You've been awake for a couple of hours; your color has returned, and there's nothing more any of us can do until morning." We both listened to the pounding of the rain on the rooftop. "Let's hope it stops raining by then," she added.

I nodded, dragging myself off to bed where I slept like someone who'd been drugged. When I woke up the following morning, every part of my body was stiff, and my head felt like it was in a vise. More to the point, I'd had one of those strange dreams I often have during a case. This one was about a broken cooking pot that couldn't bark that turned into a stone dog that could and then into a knife that spoke Spanish.

Once I was awake, what had been lurking in the back of my mind came forward with a wallop. I knew where I had seen a ceramic knife, in fact, six of them. Douglas's very kitschy kitchen. A set of ceramic knives dangled from an ornate black-and-steel thingamabob screwed into the wall, each knife looking very chic, very expensive, and very deadly. I didn't like to think about one of them being the knife that had broken off in the thief, but I had to know for sure. I didn't want another one winding up in Douglas's back.

Looking out the window, the sun was shining brightly. The ground still looked wet but would soon dry on such a day. I thought about the chances of tire tracks surviving last night's rainstorm and felt a crack in my armor.

The cave and its contents had something to do with Carlos's dilemma but exactly what, I had yet to put together. Now it might be too late. I had managed to lose everything in less than twenty-four hours. That was a record, even for me.

I decided to call Douglas back and headed for the phone in the living room to place the call. I knew Tex's phone number was blocked, an added bonus to this call. I would pretend to be at the Stanford Shopping Center rather than in Mexico. No point in alerting Stefano as to where I was through my trusting friend. Fortunately, Douglas wasn't in, so I left a message for him and phrased it so Stefano wouldn't be suspicious, in case he was monitoring the calls. This time, telephone tag was going to work.

After placing the phone call, I thought about the ceramic knife. The only way to be sure about it was to go to Douglas's apartment and see for myself. Would Stefano have had time to replace it if it was missing? In that case, if all six pieces were there, I'd have to ask Douglas whether or not one had been missing for a time or recently replaced. I checked the calendar on my watch. It was Thursday. He had two standing tickets to the San Francisco Symphony Orchestra every Thursday night from late May through the end of June. Friday nights were given over year-round to the opera. Through the years, I've been dragged at one time or another to these productions, just like his other friends, but when he's involved with someone, the honor goes to that person. I was sure that tonight he and Stefano would be humming along with Rachmaninoff, fifth-row center, while I was playing hard-boiled detective.

While making plans, possible scenarios ran through my head. I should be able to fly back and get into his apartment tonight. I knew where he kept his spare keys. He had told me as one of those "just in case" measures because he didn't have any family in the Bay Area.

I listened to the sound of my bare feet padding through the quiet house. The stillness was eerie. It felt like everyone had disappeared from the face of the earth along with that truck. There were two notes on the coffeemaker for me, plus some fresh brew. One note was from Mom. She'd had the limousine pick her up at the crack of dawn, so she could make the four-hour trip to Mexico City in time for lunch. She told me to call her anytime on the sat phone. I was grateful to be able to reach her so readily. Richard may be an old mother hen about all the equipment he foists upon us, but I have to admit, most of the time it comes in handy. Mom even took her luggage, planning on flying back home from there. She wrote she'd meet me in Palo Alto tonight.

Tex left about an hour before with the *policia*. Her hurriedly scribbled message read she couldn't wait to see what the walls of the cave looked like in the daylight. She planned on being back around 10:00 a.m. *Good*, I thought, *she can drive me to the Leon Airport, so I can catch the first plane back to the Bay Area.*

I poured myself some coffee with thoughts of a shower, when there was a knock at the front door. I slowly moved across the living room, feeling like I had spent the night in a cement mixer. When I opened the door, I saw four very somber-looking Mexican policemen staring at me. One of them proffered my muddy, wet sweater.

"*Senorita* Alvarez? This is yours?"

"*Si. Gracias.*" I took the ruined sweater and tossed it in a trashcan behind one of the wicker chairs on the porch. "Did it help keep the tire tracks from being totally destroyed from the rain?" I asked in Spanish.

In English, the police sergeant and leader replied, "Enough to be able to tell there is a similar imprint of a tire under a large tree that shielded a section of ground from much of the rain." He studied my face, this small angular man with long, straight hair pulled back in a rubber band. "The matching tracks we found at the foreman's house. Do you know where that is?"

"Sure. That's about four or five miles on the other side of the property.

"*Si,*" he nodded slowly. "The truck, it is missing but when we go inside the house we find the bodies of both the foreman, Eduardo Rodriguez, and his wife, Eva. Did you know that?"

While he watched me, I'm sure my reaction gave him an eyeful. I was so startled that I spilled hot coffee all over my robe. "*Dios mio!*" I said.

This was the point that Tex arrived. While I ran for a kitchen towel, he repeated his story to her. Eduardo and Eva had worked for her ever since her previous foreman retired, and she was astounded by the news.

"Both of them? Dead? How?" I heard her say as I was returning.

"They were both shot, *señora*, in the head. Execution style," he said, pulling himself up to his full five-foot-four-inch height. "That is why I must

183

ask all of you to accompany me to the police station in San Miguel. Where is the other lady?" he asked, looking past me and into the living room. I stepped aside, and he entered the house. The three other men remained outside.

"My mother left for Mexico City. I can reach her if you like, but why do you need to see us?" I demanded. "We had nothing to do with the killings."

"That's right," Tex interjected. "Two of your men sat shotgun outside on the porch all night. Why don't you ask them where we were?"

"All three of you may be involved in other ways with the events of last night. Besides, we do not know for sure how long they are dead, although one of the *vaqueros* saw them last night around ten thirty. Then there is the assault on you," he said to me. "I must insist that you hand over your passports and that you come with me." He rested his hand on the revolver at his hip and stared at both of us with an unyielding look.

Frankly, I was impressed by his vocabulary, his dedication to his job and, in all honesty, his cojones. This wasn't the usual behavior of the Mexican police, especially regarding one of the most influential gringo families in the area. We had a Mexican *Serpico* here. I liked this guy.

"Whatever you say, Sergeant." I acquiesced with a smile before Tex could reply. He visibly relaxed, removing his hand from his gun.

"Okay, Toots," Tex said to him, following my lead. She added, "But I don't think the police chief is going to like this one bit." She crossed over to a desk, removed her passport from the top drawer, and handed it over to him.

"Listen, I need to shower and dress," I said, hoping to buy enough time to call Richard and Lila and apprise them of what was going on. "Can you give me twenty minutes? I promise to return with my passport too."

"*Si, si*," he said amiably as he saw he wasn't going to have any trouble with us. "We will wait outside." He turned around and left, shutting the door behind him.

I ran over to the phone in the hallway and began to dial out to the States. "Tex, I've been using this phone, and now I need to call Richard in the States. Hope you don't mind."

"Of course not, hon," she said absentmindedly, pacing the room. "Eduardo and Eva dead! I didn't like the couple. Even after three years, they weren't working out. I wanted to get rid of them, but this! Murdered! I just thought of something. When it rains, it pours. I'm going to have to find a replacement for both of them. She did the housekeeping and gardening, you know. I'll have to let Carlos know too."

"Wait a bit on that part, Tex, can't you?" I said from the hallway as I listened to a ringing phone. "Let's reconnoiter first."

She nodded, shrugged, and went into the kitchen. I heard pots and pans banging around. Obviously, she was taking her frustration out on them.

Fortunately, Richard answered after about a dozen rings. "This is Richard," he said.

"Richard, we've got a situation down here," I said.

"Go."

"Remember the ranch foreman and his wife? They were murdered last night, shot execution style. The police think the truck was at their house last night, too, but now it's gone. No stolen loot anywhere." I heard him give a low whistle. "The police are here waiting outside, and they're insisting on taking us in for questioning about the shootings. I had hoped to get back to Palo Alto today, but that may not be possible."

"Are you finished?"

"Well, I may be finished, but I'm not through. After we hang up, I'm going to call Mom and alert her."

"When you do, use the laptop connection instead of the landline, Lee. I've been uploading tons of information on the pictures you sent me, plus expert analysis. Did you know that Mira is a quasi-expert in Mesoamerican artifacts?"

"No, I didn't," I answered in surprise, although I shouldn't have been. Not only did she minor in archeology at school, she's been on several amateur digs in Central America in the past.

"She's been a big help in directing us to the right sources. We've been working around the clock on this back here, Lee. I've been up all night. You've really opened a Pandora's box. If that cache is real, it's all museum-quality artifacts and could be worth between forty to sixty million dollars on the black market. Just thought you'd like to know."

I felt the room spinning and sat down on the stool next to the phone. Then I looked over to the front door. "Did you say I can get all of this information on the laptop?"

"Sure. Just log on to the uplink, and click on the icon marked DISAT. That'll automatically connect you with the supercomputer. I've created a folder there named Toltec. You can't miss it. By the way, that's an eight-hour battery inside, so you can use it anywhere, anytime, but not on a plane. Safety reasons, you know."

"What about a car traveling from the ranch to San Miguel?"

"Liana," he said as if he were talking to a child who did not believe in air because she could not see it, "I thought I told you we've negotiated with the Mexican government to have access to one of their satellites continually stationed over the country twenty-four hours a day until further notice. Do you have any idea what it's costing us to do this? Never mind, you don't want to know. When Our Lady sees the price tag, she'll have a fit," he said, the last remark referring to our mother and none too kindly. "Help justify the cost. Use it, please."

"And you're saying I can communicate with Mom even though I am using a laptop and she's using a cell phone?"

"Yes. There are two icons on your desktop called Sat1 and Sat2. Each one has an automatic feed to a sat phone. Just think of the laptop as a larger phone. It even has a built-in camera that can send your image to whomever you call, just as it sends your voice. Or you can type on the keyboard and send only text, whichever. When Lila wants to answer you verbally, she'll press a toggle switch called 'conversion.'"

"You and your toggle switches," I interrupted.

"I try to anticipate every need, Sister mine, and when you're around, it's a good thing I do," he said.

"Yeah, yeah. Go on."

"Anyway, while I'm thinking about it, ignore Sat2, as that phone's dead," he said pointedly.

"Right. Sorry about that."

"Don't worry. They only cost about three thousand dollars each. Easy come, easy go," he continued.

"Let's go back to the toggle switch, shall we?" I pleaded. "We can talk about this other stuff later." Which I hoped would be never.

"Okay," he laughed, giving in. "Mom will probably answer you verbally because that's easier. Her answer will either be sent back to you as speech or translated into text, whichever she's decided on her end. All in a matter of seconds," he added proudly. Never challenge a man's computer buttons, I discovered, especially if that man is Richard.

"Richard, how's Carlos doing?" I asked.

"He's hanging in there. Mr. Talbot's thinking of bringing in another lawyer, more for research than anything else. A man named Mike Penn. Do you remember him?"

"Short guy? Looks like a barracuda?"

"That's the one. He's pretty sharp though."

"With a little luck, we won't need him. Richard, there's another angle I'm working on." I told him about the necklace and Douglas's new love, Stefano Ramírez de Arroyo.

"Hmmmm. Maybe I should do some checking on him. Meanwhile, don't destroy any more equipment, if you can help it. Ha ha."

"You know, you could have gone all day without saying that. Ha ha."

Chapter Eleven

Pardon My Enchilada

The trip into San Miguel de Allende was uneventful, if you can call following one police car and being tailed by another uneventful. Tex drove while I contacted Mom using the laptop. While bumping along the back roads of San Miguel, I was "chatting" with my mother who was dealing with commuter traffic on the outskirts of Mexico City. I still can't get used to wireless computers. They don't strike me as feasible; I don't care what Richard says.

When I told Mom about Stefano's request for the return of the necklace, she promised to let me know what *Señor* Lopez's take on it was. I decided, for the moment, to keep my fears about the ceramic knife to myself. I needed to work out a few things first. We left off that we'd touch base in a few hours. I checked the battery. Not bad. I had seven hours and forty-one minutes left.

Once I broke off connection with Mom, I began to search the desktop for an icon named Aztec, when I realized it wasn't the word Richard had given me. After a cursory look, I saw the word Toltec in the upper right hand of the screen, and the summer of my Latin American studies came rushing back to me.

The Toltecs were precursors to the Aztecs by about one thousand years. We don't have much of their art, save their language, because the Aztecs systematically decimated the people and their culture in their quest to take over Mexico back in the 1200s. I knew Mira couldn't get enough of this part of Mexican history. She devoured every book she could get on the subject.

I clicked on the icon and got an eyeful. Richard had been thorough. He'd attached pictures of the scant amount of Toltec artifacts scattered through museums across the world and coupled them with similar artifacts from the cave.

He also included a couple of scientific articles, focusing on two thinly glazed, three-foot-high black panther statues mentioned throughout Toltec literature. The thrust of both articles was whether or not the pieces actually existed. Well, they did, boys and girls, 'cause I seen 'em.

Once it was known about the panthers and the rest of the stash, shock waves would pound the world of anthropology. How would even the hint of these findings strike the curator at the Museo de Antropologia in Mexico City, a place to which Mom was now blithely on her way?

I felt a knot in my stomach and hoped Lila wasn't making a mistake by showing him the necklace. Curators are known to be highly competitive and sometimes unscrupulous when it comes to obtaining works for their museum. The scandal the Getty Museum in Los Angeles had undergone regarding antiquities flashed into my mind. What if the necklace was genuine as we suspected? Would Mom be forced to turn it over to *Señor* Lopez then and there? That wouldn't be right unless true ownership was established first. I reconnected with the sat phone and sent a fast warning to Mom to be careful. She sent back a text message almost immediately.

"Liana, I've already thought of that possibility and have a plan. I am not going to the museum but meeting Manuel across the street at a restaurant. It is more of a social setting. After looking at the necklace, if he determines it's genuine, I intend to use it as a bargaining chip for information about previous activities, rumors, innuendos, etcetera, involving the museum and other museums in Mexico. Possibly, he'll share names of people who have been selling artifacts to them for the past ten to twenty years, people we can contact or follow up on. Through your father, I have known Manuel for a long time. I have always found him to be a kind, principled man. I do not believe he would force me to do anything I didn't want to do. Remember, dear, if the missing pieces are genuine Toltec artifacts, they ultimately should be returned to the Mexican people. Unless there is proper documentation for this necklace, that is exactly what should happen with it too. What better place to start with all of this than with an old and trusted friend? Let me know what happens at the police station." Her answer calmed me down a little but made me think a lot.

I'd just logged off when we made our approach to San Miguel de Allende from the higher mountain road. A thousand feet below, nestled in a valley, San Miguel lay glittering like a dusty jewel in the sun. A timeless, sixteenth-century colonial city, it is a cultural masterpiece, attracting artisans from every corner of the earth and aspect of art.

Starting our descent, I could see the spirals of La Paroquia, built in the early 1800s. The exquisite pale-pink terracotta cathedral is not only a work of genius but has been an elegant shrine to the indigenous people of Mexico for generations.

Commissioned by the Catholic Church, the archbishop chose to use a native architect to construct it, going against the wishes of the pope. The architect, a brilliant local, had never seen a European building but managed to faithfully replicate the front of an ornate church merely by using a hand-drawn postcard given him by the archbishop. Not having any pictures or instructions for the remaining walls, the architect built what he knew best: the simpler, adobe style of Mexico. Everyone was satisfied.

Each time I stand in front of this cathedral, with its intricately carved, resplendent façade and high, Gothic spires, I cannot help but envision the other three sides. For me, it is more than the story of a humble architect who could create a glorious cathedral and the visionary archbishop who would give him the chance to do so. La Paroquia represents the part of the human spirit able to honor and embrace other cultures, while remaining true to one's own.

Entering the *ciudad,* we followed the *policia* through narrow, uneven cobblestone streets, hard on a car but easy on the eye. Single- and two-story stucco buildings, centuries old, swept by in earthen hues and muted shades of ocher, celadon, azure, and mauve. Often decorated with handcrafted wrought iron, fountains or statuary, some were private residences; others were restaurants, mom-and-pop stores, or upscale shops. An occasional discreet sign in a window or overhanging the stone sidewalk announced wares within a particular *tienda.* A few structures wore cracked or peeling façades, yet there was no air of neglect or decay but rather one of character and endless duration.

This wondrous city, unchanged since the 1500s, was declared a Mexican national monument in 1926. Once inside the city limits, no one is allowed to add to, subtract from, or change one iota of its exterior. Chain stores are unwelcome. You'll never find a Burger King, Staples, or Blockbuster here. Unfortunately, not even a Starbucks. But I need to let that one go.

Waiting for us in the doorway of the Estacion de Policia, was the chief, dressed in starched and ironed finery, his arms open wide.

"Ah, *Señora* Garcia, my heartfelt apologies for this disturbance. If I had only known my subordinate was going to inconvenience you like this…" He paused, caressing his lush mustache and bowing slightly. Out of the corner of his eye, he shot Sergeant "Serpico" a conspiratorial look.

Serpico shrugged, handed him our passports, sauntered over to a desk near an open window, and lit a smelly cigar.

"Miguel, no problem. No problem at all," Tex said, brushing it off with a smile.

"And about Carlos, *señora*, you have our heartfelt sympathy. I'm sure," he added, waving his arms around like a conductor of a symphonic orchestra, "it will all be straightened out very soon."

"You bet," Tex replied with false bravado. "It's all a mistake. How are Maria and the children? Fit as a fiddle, I hope?"

"*Si, si.* Although little Louis has the influenza, but he is getting better."

"You be sure to give them my best." She smiled her lady of the manor smile and turned to me. "You remember Liana Alvarez, don't you?"

"How could one forget so beautiful a *señorita* as you?"

He fawned, taking a deep bow. As it was getting a little deep in here, and I didn't have my boots on, I decided to skip to the chase.

"*Gracias.* Now, why don't we get down to business? You have some questions for us, don't you?"

"No, no, no," he said with a flourish and then added, "but now that you are here, why don't we go to my office and discuss a few things?" He gestured for us to follow him, where he dropped our passports on the desk. Then he closed the door and the blinds.

"What is the saying, 'Little pitchers have big ears'?" he said by way of explanation.

"That's the saying, but I've never gotten it, myself," Tex muttered.

"Please sit," he said. I did so, but Tex stood by the door, ignoring his request. "Perhaps some coffee? I have an excellent source from Columbia," he offered. "*Delicioso.*"

"No, *gracias*," Tex said, crossing her arms over her ample chest.

"Listen, Chief," I said, leaning forward, "I've got a plane to catch back to the Bay Area, so if we're not under arrest—"

"*Por supuesto que no!*" he interrupted, again waving his hands in the air. "Of course not," he repeated in English. "But a question or two, *por favor.*"

"Okay," I said and sat back.

"Are you certain?" he asked, gesturing to the coffee. I shook my head, and he poured himself some coffee from a white porcelain mug kept warm on a hotplate. Smiling, he switched to Spanish and asked, "How did you come to find these alleged artifacts that are now missing but of which we have so many digital pictures?"

So they had copies of the pictures already. Richard must have been a busy boy this morning.

"It was just an accident, *señor*. I was out taking a walk. I saw this entrance to a cave, and there they were," I said, returning his smile.

"That is it?" he asked in English. "You didn't come down here with the idea of searching for them? Something has not gone on in Los Estados

Unidos that has brought you here? Not something to do with *Señor* Carlos?"

"Naw. Just an accident," I said, still smiling.

"Who is the *jovan* in the last photograph? Do you know him?"

"The youth? Know him? Naw. I thought maybe you might, as he's probably a local boy. In fact, I have no idea what's going on with any of it. All I know is, I stumbled upon a cave full of pottery, took a bunch of pictures, got hit on the head, and when I came to, everything was gone. I don't even know if it's connected with the death of the foreman and his wife," I added.

He took a sip of his coffee, wiped his mouth with a napkin, and caressed his mustache before he asked, "And that is all you will say?"

"That is all I will say."

"So, if there's nothing else," Tex said, resting her hand on the doorknob.

Miguel ignored Tex and leaned forward, chuckling. "Putting the deaths aside, it is too bad all that treasure is gone."

"Yeah, I bet that won't look too good on your résumé," I murmured. "Well, I've gotta go," I said, rising. I stood looking down at him. He sat looking up at me.

"That is too bad, too bad," he said, picking up the passports and smiling up at me. I watched him rotate and tap them, end over end, on the top of his desk. "I was hoping we could work together on this, you and I. It would be very good for my career to apprehend the culprits and to find the stolen antiquities. There is a promotion in this for me, I

197

know, should I be able to do this." His English was suddenly flawless.

I returned his smile. "No doubt," I said. "But you don't have anything but two murdered people. The stolen artifacts are gone, and I haven't a clue as to where."

"Ah! But you will find out." He looked at me. "And it is possible I could be of immense service in solving this heinous crime and restoring the relics to my country, at least, to Mexico's satisfaction. Especially if you would like to go home anytime soon." His voice hardened. "I think you should sit down, *señorita*. You have much paperwork to fill out. I think you will be here in Mexico a very long time. After all, two people are dead."

"I'll take some of that coffee now," I said, sinking back down in the chair.

He broke out into a smile as he poured me a cup. "Ah! Then possibly we have an agreement? You will continue to search for the stolen booty, as you say in English, and I will, shall we say, deal with the foreman and his wife."

"What do you mean, 'deal with them'?" came Tex's startled reply. "They're dead."

"Oh, *si*. But once the *señorita* finds the antiquities, it will become evident who has murdered the couple, and then I will arrest all who are involved. You see" — he grinned at me — "your reputation precedes you. Carlos and my eldest son are friends since boyhood. Carlos has spoken to him of your exploits *muchos tiempos*, *Señorita* Alvarez. He is very fond of you, the big sister he never had." He smiled and sipped his coffee, an extended pinky waggling in the air. I took a gulp myself and the brew was excellent. It helped to make his blackmail a little more palatable.

He went on. "I want your word that we will work together on this in exchange for me cutting through, shall we say, the red tape and allowing you to go back to this Palo Alto today instead of many weeks from now. Many." He set down his coffee cup, stood up, and put out his hand. "Do we have an understanding?"

I stood up saying, "We get our passports back, and I get to leave today?"

"*Si*. And in exchange, you will keep me informed, shall we say, every step of the way?"

"We shall say it." I took his hand and shook it. "I'll keep you informed every step of the way."

Tex, who said nothing but stood fuming by the door, now came forward. "You know, we shoot rattlesnakes like you on the rancho."

I took her by the shoulders and moved her to the door. "Never mind her, *señor*. She's just kidding. A little American humor. Ha ha. Come on, Tex," I said to my indignant, older friend. "Let's go." I turned back to the chief. "Now when do we get our passports back?"

"In a couple of hours. Take the lovely *señora* for a walk in El Jardin or for something to eat. Come back then. Everything will be ready." He bowed slightly as I ushered an outraged Tex through the door.

"Did you hear that man?" she demanded as we left the station. "Why, he's blackmailing you."

"Yes he is, Tex, but unless you and I want to spend the next few months in a Mexican hoosegow, I'm going along with it."

I dragged her down the narrow, serpentine sidewalk and stopped in front of one of San Miguel's more popular street fountains. Painted a bright blue, the design was the inside of a six- to seven-foot-high clamshell. The shell was set into an ecru-colored cement wall, a wall that typically separates private homes and gardens from the streets of the city. Beneath the shell, a large, silver statue of a fish stood balancing on its tail fin in a bowl. Water spouted from its mouth and down into a small pool. The basin floor was covered with Mexican coins of various denominations. These coins would soon be collected, as they were from fountains throughout the city, and given to local charities.

"Give me some change. I want to throw money in the fountain for good luck." I held out my hand to her.

Tex looked at me for a moment. "Oh, all right, hon. I'll drop it," she said, digging in her pockets. "I hope you know what you're doing, that's all." She handed me a *centavo*.

"I never know what I'm doing, but in the larger scheme of things," I said, turning around, "I need to get back to Palo Alto today." I tossed the coin over my shoulder and heard a wet *kerplop*. "Another life may depend on it."

Tex's face blanched.

"Let's find some food, okay? I'm starting to get a headache," I said.

"Sure, hon," she replied. "Where do you want to go?"

"How about Café Paroquia? They do a great Belgian waffle."

"The best," she said, putting her arm around my shoulder. We began to stroll the six or seven blocks toward the well-known restaurant.

A Bustamonte sculpture caught my eye, and I paused in front of the shop for a moment. Tex continued and began to cross a cobblestone street, chatting and looking back at me. A late-model Volvo station wagon rounded the corner at a high speed. Neither the car nor Tex was aware of the other. A warning cry escaped my lips just as I saw the back of a man run forward and grab her, hauling her back onto the sidewalk. Both barely escaped being hit. The Volvo filled with teenagers drove on, oblivious.

"*Dios mio!* Tex, are you all right?" I ran to her side, looking her up and down.

"I think so. I'm not even sure what happened," she said, shaken. She raised her hands to her head. "My hat! Where's my hat?"

"I've got it right here," said a masculine voice from behind. We turned around to see Mr. Gorgeous Gin Guy staring at us, green-gray eyes and all. He held out a crushed lavender Stetson trimmed with amethyst stones. "I'm afraid it's ruined."

Okay, this was too much of a coincidence for me. First Mr. GGG sits four rows behind me on two planes to Mexico, sends me a fabulous martini, and now he winds up in San Miguel, saving my friend's life? What are the odds? Whatever, I should have them in Vegas.

While I was running through all this in my mind, Tex took the hat and said, "Maybe not. I'll try having it cleaned and reblocked. If you hadn't pulled me back, I might have looked like this. How can I thank you?"

"No need. I'm just glad I was around."

"Hello," I said, half smiling back. "We seem destined to meet again and again."

"Hello, yourself." He smiled back, staring at me with those incredible eyes.

Tex stepped between us, tilting her head at a flirtatious angle. "Well, isn't anybody going to introduce me?" she said. "My champion's name would be?"

"Gurn Hanson, ma'am," he said, extending his hand to Tex. "Are you sure you're all right, ma'am?" he asked.

I focused my attention back on Tex too. "Yes, are you all right?"

She took his hand. "I'm fine, just fine. Tex Garcia. I see you know my friend," she added, gesturing to me.

"No, not really," I said. I felt shy, suspicious, and grateful, all at the same time. Not good.

"We saw each other on the plane, but I never got the pleasure of a formal introduction," he said and waited.

"Liana Alvarez." I put my hand out, and he took it. His was warm, strong, and shot a jolt of electricity through me. *Danger, Will Robinson, Danger*, my brain shouted. I pulled my hand free.

"You can call me Lee. Everyone does. Thank you for saving Tex. I know that sounds trite, but thank you. And thank you for the martini the other night."

"A martini! The other night," Tex interrupted. "Oooooo."

"On the plane," I explained. I grabbed Tex's hand and dragging her behind me, started to walk down the sidewalk. "Well, goodbye, Ger, and thank you again."

"Gurn," he said, matching my stride.

"What?"

"It's not Grrrr, like a dog does over a bone. It's Gurn as in…" He paused for a moment.

"Like Gurn as in gurney?"

I stopped and stared at him. Even though I was attracted as hell, something was not quite right. I decided to go on the offensive.

"If you like." He smiled good-naturedly. "Gurn as in gurney."

Tex stepped in front of me, saying, "Gurn, we were about to go and get something to eat. The least you can let me do is stake you to a good meal after saving my life. How about it?"

"I'd love it, Tex. Where are we going?" he said, and the two marched ahead, linked arm in arm, ignoring me. I trailed behind like a long-lost stepchild.

Café Paroquia is one of San Miguel's institutions. Behind closed doors, as is much of Mexico, it's an indoor-outdoor restaurant in a lush courtyard setting. It serves three meals a day in an arty, yet colonial environment, where each diner has a view of the spires of La Paroquia, while enjoying the tended gardens and tropical clime.

If I haven't mentioned the food, let me do so now. Dishes like chilies en nogada and pollo mole have sent me in search of the chef to throw myself at his feet in supplication.

By the time I caught up with Tex and her new pal, they were already seated at a table next to a climbing vine laden with dozens of fragrant, apricot-colored trumpet flowers. A birdcage hung from one of its tendrils, and a yellow canary was singing its little lungs out. It's hard to be tense in this place, so I relaxed, sat down, and picked up the menu. It was almost twelve thirty. No wonder I was hungry.

"Gurn was telling me that he's a CPA back in San Francisco," Tex said, beaming at me.

"Oh?" I flashed him my best Miss America smile. The one that said As I Walk Down the Runway of Life, Please Know I Am Not Interested in You. "For which firm do you work?"

"Actually, I have my own. Maybe you've heard of it, Gurn Hanson and Company, Certified Public Accountants?" He smiled, and those damned eyes twinkled again in a most distracting way.

"Hmmm," I said. "Maybe I have, but I can't remember." I forced my attention back to the menu. "Now that it's lunchtime, maybe I'll get something a little more filling than waffles. What are you going to have, Tex?"

"May I suggest the camarones in chipotle sauce?" Gurn grinned. "I had that here last night, and it was pretty amazing. You could start with their ceviche as an appetizer. It's a killer."

"Why, that sounds wonderful, Gurn," Tex said, putting down her menu. "That's just what I'll have."

They both looked at me.

"Well, I was thinking of the red snapper," I began but was stopped by the owner of the place, a Swiss ex-patriot, coming to my side with her order pad. I turned and greeted her. "Hi, Ingrid."

"Welcome back, Lee." She smiled at me. "Here for long?"

"Just in and out," I said, returning her smile. Many people are in and out of San Miguel, especially foreigners. She nodded her understanding. "How's your red snapper today?"

Now she shook her head. Arching her brows, she looked back toward the kitchen. "The shrimp is better, Lee," she said, leaning down to me. "The chef is going through a phase. You can't put peanut butter on everything. When it doesn't work, it doesn't work. Move on." She turned to Gurn, "What about you, Gurn?"

"I think it's going to be three shrimp plates, Ingrid," Gurn said. She responded to his dazzling smile by pouring us water and straightening the tablecloth out even though it didn't need it.

"What does Mrs. Hanson do?" Tex asked after Ingrid departed. I tried to kick her under the table but couldn't find her leg.

"My mother is retired and living in North Carolina with my father," he answered. "But before that, she was a teacher. They both were."

"So you're not married," Tex drawled, smirking at me.

"Nope," he replied, smiling in my direction. "Thirty-six and never been married. Imagine that."

"Imagine." I smiled back but deliberately looked at my watch to show him I wasn't interested. Besides, I had to concentrate on other things. It was too early to check with Mom on how she was doing, but if I could find out when the flights for home were, I could make a few plans. I reached for my bag, saying, "I hope it won't be too rude if I search for a flight home today during our lunch. I need to get back to Palo Alto."

"Here," he offered, pulling his iPhone out of his pocket. I had my iPhone with me, too, but didn't want to get into this "how much we have in common" routine. I kept mine in my bag and let him go on.

"I happen to have all the airlines and their schedules on here. I fly back and forth a lot. Let me get to them for you." He pressed buttons on the little machine. "Here you go," he said, handing it to me, "Just scroll down." I did.

"Do you live in San Miguel?" asked Tex.

"I do on and off."

"Funny, but I've never seen you around. Not that I'm here that much, but our rancho is about an hour and a half away. Maybe you've heard of it? Los Pocitos Minerales. I get into San Miguel once or twice a week."

"I discovered San Miguel fairly recently," Gurn replied, "after a buddy of mine told me about it. I came here for the first time about a year ago, and

I've been coming back ever since. In fact, I recently bought a place two blocks off the Jardin."

Even though I had only been half listening to the conversation, while cursoring through the list of flights and times, I raised an eyebrow at his last comment and looked at him.

"You must be doing pretty well in the accounting business. Most houses around the Jardin go for a couple of mil."

He winked at me and said, "I do okay."

The food came. I put the mini-computer down and dug in. I was ravenous, not having had any breakfast.

"I like a girl with a healthy appetite," he commented, grinning at me. He grinned a lot.

Embarrassed, I picked up the iPhone, perusing it again. "You know, Tex," I said with a frown, "I don't know if I'll be able to get back today. The only plane leaving Leon is at three thirty, but I'll never make it. Especially, as we have to return to the police station first."

"The police station? What do you have going on there?" he quizzed.

"Just a parking ticket," I answered, taking a bite of food again.

"Well, I could fly you to Leon, if you like," Gurn said, buttering a piece of warm bread.

"Excuse me?"

"Sure. I've got my jet parked out at the private airport, and I was planning on flying to Leon this afternoon, anyway. I've got to pick up some supplies for the new house. They're being flown in on United. The airport's only about ten minutes from here. Then it's about twenty minutes flying time from here to Leon. I could get you there by two, easy."

"You have your own jet?" Tex glowed and turned to me. "All that and a savior of women as well?"

"Well, I really wouldn't want to impose on you that way," I stammered.

"No imposition at all," he said, popping a piece of bread in his mouth. "Like I said, I'm going there anyway."

"That works out perfectly," effused Tex. She turned to me. "You brought everything with you, didn't you? Not that you have much. Whatever you've left at the house, I can bring to you today or tomorrow when I come to the Bay Area. I've decided to take a chance and put Paco in charge of the rancho. If he loses a few head of cattle, what the hell. I need to be near my son."

"Then that's settled," Gurn said. "Why don't you call the airline and tell them to hold a seat for you?" He leaned over the table, pressed a button on the iPhone, and I could feel his breath on my face. "There! The number should be ringing."

And, indeed, it was. I found out there was space, gave them my credit card number and promised to be there at around two thirty for a three-thirty departure. Modern science.

"That's done," I said, feeling vaguely like I'd been rushed into something. We hurriedly finished our lunch, and around one o'clock, Tex and I toddled back to the police station, having promised Gurn I would meet him in front of La Paroquia at one twenty. The chief was a man of his word, and the passports were waiting by the front desk for us with a handwritten note in Spanish saying he expected to hear from me soon. So far, I'd felt railroaded by two strange men. Not a good day.

Tex and I were heading back to where we were supposed to meet Gurn when I saw a man several yards ahead coming toward me on the narrow sidewalk. It took me a split second to place him, a case of not recognizing someone who's where you don't expect them to be. In the small amount of time I took to connect the dots, he hurried across the street and into a small antiquities shop. Whether or not he saw me, I couldn't say, but when I saw the word "antiquities," I was certain who it was. He looked just like his photograph. But what the hell was Douglas's Stefano doing here in San Miguel?

"Stay put," I said to Tex. "I'll be right back." I raced across the street and into the *tienda*, leaving Tex perplexed and standing on the sidewalk. Once inside, I searched for Stefano but saw no one, save a pudgy, middle-aged man behind the counter, staring at me with disdain.

"Where did that man go?" I demanded, "The man who just came in here?" The shop owner looked at me puzzled and then shrugged. I repeated the question in Spanish but got the same shrug. I walked up to the counter, determined to make him answer me, when I saw the back door to the shop stood wide open. I was about to go through the door when I heard Tex's voice.

"Liana! What are you doing? What's wrong?"

209

"I'll be right back," I called and quickly entered a small alleyway. I looked both ways, but there was nothing except a couple of mourning doves, who flew away when they saw me. I only had a few minutes to get to the meeting place with Gurn. Of course, what was the hurry now? If Stefano was here, I didn't have to worry so much about Douglas there. Or did I? I'd call my friend from the Leon Airport to make sure he was all right once I'd shaken Mr. Gorgeous Gin Guy. I'd call Mom then too. Her lunch with the museum curator should be over about now, although I checked the laptop for a message a short time ago, and there was none. I wasn't worried about her; Lila was famous for her three- and four-hour business lunches, and she had a lot of ground to cover.

I hurried back inside, ignored the pudgy shopkeeper, and pulled a confused Tex out into the street. We just made it to the front of La Paroquia when we heard the sounds of a motorcycle coming our way. A Harley-Davidson roared up and stopped in front of us. Gurn removed his helmet and grinned at me. I was so surprised my jaw dropped low enough for me to have danced upon my tongue.

"Sorry about this," he said. "My car needs a new carburetor and is laid up. This is the only other transportation I have." He reached behind him. "Here's a helmet." He tossed it to me while I remained motionless on the sidewalk. I could tell he was enjoying this. "Well, come on. Do you want to get to Leon in time for your plane or not?"

I found speech. "You know, you didn't strike me as a Hells Angels type of guy. Can I drive?"

"You know how to drive one of these things?" His eyes narrowed, studying me.

"Had a Honda Gold Wing for five years."

"What happened? Did you crash it?"

"Lost it in the divorce settlement. He got the bike, and I got the Christmas tree ornaments."

"Remind me not to hire your lawyer." He pushed down the kickstand and got off, gesturing for me to get on in his place. "You know how to get there?"

I nodded. I'd never flown in or out of the local airport, but I'd passed by it often enough.

"You call me the minute you get there, hon," Tex said, grabbing my hand. I nodded and pulling my hand free, climbed onto the saddle. Gurn straddled the seat behind me and wrapped his arms around my waist, a little too tightly for my liking. I put my left hand on the clutch, the right on the throttle, and my right foot under the gear. Popping it into first, I took off. It felt great. Right from the beginning. It was loud, fun, and fast. Good Golly, Miss Molly, I missed my bike.

The trip to the airport went smoothly. Gurn's jet was already on the runway waiting. After we stowed his bike, I followed him up the three steps into the plane, studying the back of his head.

Everything about him struck me as too convenient and too attractive. As Dad once said, "If something seems too good to be true, then it probably is." That was right after I bought the fake designer handbag on a Manhattan sidewalk for ten bucks. Gurn struck me as one big fake too.

On board, he showed me where to sit. Then, excusing himself, he went into the cockpit and shut the door, separating it from the cabin. It was almost as if once he had me alone, Gurn didn't want to talk to me any more than I wanted to talk to him. Was he really just a nice guy doing a favor and letting me hitch a ride?

I sat down on the creamy leather couch and buckled up. Opening the laptop, I gave a reassuring call to Tex, who answered on the first ring. She wanted to talk about her plans for handing the rancho over to Paco, but the engines revved up, and we began to move. I cut it short and turned the computer off. I was really getting the hang of this laptop thing. I'd even found a headset secured in one of its compartments. This allowed me to speak and listen just as you would do with a telephone.

I settled in, put my head back, and fell asleep, only waking when we bumped to a landing. I looked out the window and saw the words Leon Airport in big blue letters on the top of a building. We taxied for a moment. When we came to a complete stop, I undid my seat belt and waited for Gurn to emerge from the cockpit.

"How are you doing?" he said as he opened the door and smiled at me. "Did you enjoy the flight?"

"Oh, absolutely," I said, glancing at my watch. Five minutes of two. Plenty of time.

Just when I was wondering how to ditch Gurn, he said, "I hope you don't mind if I drop you here. All you have to do is cross the tarmac to enter the main terminal. I'd go with you, but I need to taxi over to where my supplies are."

"That's all right," I said a little too eagerly. "I'm fine. Thanks so much, Gurn."

He opened the door of the plane, dropped the small set of stairs, and stood to the side of the door, allowing me to exit.

"I really appreciate it," I said, standing in the doorway and looking at him. He grabbed my arm, looking like he wanted to say something but changed his mind. "What?" I asked, searching his face.

He shook his head and said, "Nothing. Just take care of yourself, okay?"

"I always do," I answered, smiling. I bounced down the stairs and ran across the tarmac, happy to be free and to be making the plane for home.

Once inside, I checked in at the lone machine for e-tickets. Because I was doing carry-on only, I zipped through the process, including customs, in about fifteen minutes. While sitting at the gate waiting for the plane to load, I went into the laptop for any messages from Lila. Finding none, I called Richard, just in case he'd heard from her.

"Lee!" he bubbled. "You're on the laptop. I knew you could do it. Did you find the headset?"

"I'm using it now," I replied.

"I am so proud."

"Richard, have you heard from Mom yet?"

"Yes, about twenty minutes or so ago."

"Good," I said, relieved. In our business, while we don't like to think about it, you never know what could happen from moment to moment. "So what's going on?"

"Well..." He drew out the word while he thought. "She had a good conversation with this Lopez. After a couple of glasses of wine and her winning charms, he admitted that about a year ago two of his better Aztec pieces—that he knew to be genuine—suddenly showed up as copies during a routine inspection."

"You're kidding."

"He said that someone inside the museo, someone he trusted, managed to switch two fakes for the real. He never found out who, but he's heightened security and goes over all the work logs himself now. It hasn't happened since, but it's been a black mark on his career."

"Did he say how he thought it might have been done?"

"It probably took place during one of their scheduled cleanings, an inside job, although he can't prove it. He says someone high up in customs is probably involved too."

"Wow."

"Yes, it's not easy to smuggle works of art out of the country. Inspectors are trained on what to look for, especially in older-looking pieces. Replicas, by law, are supposed to be marked by the manufacturer, and if a piece isn't marked, it's held for further inspection. Dr. Lopez thinks someone high up in customs is pushing stolen pieces through. He says the authorities haven't found out who it is yet."

"Covered too well? Bought off? What?"

"All of the above, none of the above," he replied. "I think we've only scratched the surface of this."

"So where's Lila now?" I asked.

"She went with Lopez to the museo to run tests on the necklace, and then she's heading for the airport. On the face of it, Lee, Lopez thinks it's real, dating back to about eleven hundred AD."

"What's something like that worth?" I asked, thinking of how I dangled it in front of Tugger and let him bat at it with his paws.

"I don't know, but Lila says Lopez practically did back flips when he saw it."

"She didn't say that, Richard, not our mother."

"No, I did. She made a more reserved comment, but I got the picture. Judging by what pieces, similar to this, have gone for, on the rare occasion they've come to auction, I'd say a minimum of three-quarters of a million dollars."

"And that's a legitimate piece. I'll bet on the black market an unscrupulous collector would pay even more than that."

"There are buyers everywhere. There's no way the Mexican government is staying out of this one, Lee. Not once they saw those pictures, which I had to give them once the homicides were discovered and the matching tire tracks."

"I know, Richard."

"I'd say the cave is swarming with cops looking for clues as to where this stuff has gone. They're sure to find it."

"Not if I find it first."

"You be careful, Sister mine. Remember what happened to the burglar, not to mention the foreman and his wife."

"I'll be careful. I just need to put a few things together in my mind, and I think this will all be over soon."

"And you base this assumption on what, exactly?"

"Don't you feel like we're watching a runaway horse or locomotive?"

"Either way, don't stand in front of it," my brother said.

"I won't. Richard, I'll be back in the Bay Area around eight o'clock tonight, but don't tell anybody, not anyone. Okay?"

"Okay," he answered. "Do you want me to pick you up at the airport? I've got something to do with Vicki, but I can get away for a time."

"No, I'll take a cab. I've got a stop to make before I go home."

"What about Mom?" he asked.

"I'll leave her a voice mail letting her know I'm on the plane. She shouldn't be far behind me if all goes as planned. I have a layover in Houston, but she'll be on a direct flight. We should be landing within hours of each other."

"Okay, Lee, but be careful. Remember the best-laid plans of mice and men," he warned.

"Thank you for that. But as I am neither, I'm not worried."

Chapter Twelve

Back in the US Again

I lied. I was worried. The only thing that could have calmed me down at this point was Valium, fed intravenously. As I boarded the plane, I didn't think the skies were that friendly.

Moving from left to right, there were the missing relics. My goal had been to free Carlos by tracking down the dog statue and its connection with the dead thief. Forget about not finding the statue; I wound up losing a cave full of Toltec artifacts. Then two more people turned up dead on top of the thief. The prosecuting attorney must have loved the job I was doing for him.

Looming overhead was Douglas and his relationship with a man who was becoming more of a major suspect as the minutes ticked by. Once we arrived in Houston, and I'd gone through customs, I decided to bite the bullet and call Douglas at home.

As I dialed the number, I was confident it wouldn't be Stefano answering the phone, having recently seen him vanish inside a store in San Miguel, nearly three thousand miles away. Douglas's phone picked up on the third ring, and his voice message caused me to jump like I'd been kissed by an electric eel.

"Hi! You've reached the home of Douglas and Stefano. We're not here right now, having decided to spend a few days in Napa, drinking great wine and eating good food. We'd like to say we wish you were here, but we don't!" Douglas's voice droned on, dripping with happiness. "So leave a message for either Stefano or me, and one of us will get back to you sometime on Monday. Bye!"

While I sat reeling, the loudspeaker announced the beginning of boarding and called for first class. Fortunately, I don't fly first class unless forced to by Lila, so I sat trying to work this out with what was left of my mind.

Stefano must have left for Mexico after Douglas recorded the message on the home phone, and Douglas simply forgot to change it. A cold blast of fear went through me. Or maybe he didn't forget. Maybe he wasn't able to change it.

Never before had I been so sorry I was so far away from home. Dare I try Douglas on his cell phone and warn him if it wasn't already too late? If I reached him, would he believe me, anyway? No one was blinder than someone in love; I'd stayed in a marriage for eight years where I was the only one who thought it was working. Also, could my phone call alert Stefano I was onto him? I had already lost the "booty" as *El Jefe* called it: I sure didn't need to lose my main suspect as well.

Before I could think this through, they gave the final boarding call. It was like people had been running to get to their seats. Apparently, the only time people hurry to get on a plane is when I have to go to the bathroom or could use some extra time inside the terminal. I put the laptop away and boarded the plane for the last leg of the flight.

The plane ride was tedious but swift. I spent most of the flight gnawing on my fingernails, sighing and being restless, to the point where the woman next to me moved to another seat. We landed forty-five minutes early, and I rushed into a cab.

While waiting for the elevator in the lobby of Douglas's condo, I found I was almost afraid to go upstairs. My initial purpose had been to see if any of the ceramic knives were gone, but knowing what I now knew about Stefano, coupled with more dead bodies, what else was waiting for me upstairs?

The elevator climbed to the top floor and with shaking hands, I searched for the spare keys over the third wall sconce in the hallway, just as Douglas had instructed me. Once at his front door, I rang the bell repeatedly, listening for any inside noise. *Nada*. Glancing around to make sure I wasn't observed, I unlocked the door and went in.

"Douglas!" I called out once I'd closed the door. "Douglas, it's me, Lee. Are you here?" Silence.

Not too sure of what I'd find, I tiptoed to the master bedroom. Nothing, thank God. Same with the two other bedrooms, three bathrooms, and the myriad of closets. The living room/dining room was also clear, even behind the couch. Once that was settled, and I could breathe again, I was drawn to the black marble counter, holding the framed eight by ten of Stefano.

Yup, same guy I saw in San Miguel, I thought as I got closer. I studied it for a moment, focusing on the ear that showed a diamond stud just below his stylish, European haircut. Did I now possess that damaged earring in my change purse?

I looked past the photo into the gleaming, modern kitchen and had to lean against the counter for a moment. Suspended in air by the sleek black, steel holder, from smallest to largest, hung five out of six ceramic knives. The second-to-largest slot, the one I suspected should be holding a butchering knife, was empty.

Frantic, I dialed Douglas's cell phone and hoped I still had enough juice in the batteries of the laptop to complete the call. I felt like I had been using it nonstop all day. I would have used his landline, but most phones display the incoming number, and he would have recognized his home phone right away.

While I prayed for him to answer, I poured a glass of water from the tap and drank it down. Now and then I felt a little woozy from the whack on the head I got the previous night, and this was one of those times.

"Hello?" said Douglas on the fifth ring.

"Douglas, it's Lee," I said, relieved at hearing his voice.

"Darling girl!" he yelped. "I was just talking about you to Stefano. We're heading into dinner in a moment. What a day we've had. We must have bought six cases of wine. And listen, my pet, he feels so bad about asking for that—"

"You mean Stefano is with you?"

"Of course. We're at the Schramsberg Winery sampling some deliciously wicked champagne and toasting you, dear heart. Right at this moment. This must be mental telepathy. I was just telling Stefano—"

"Let me get this straight," I demanded, interrupting again. "You are saying Stefano is with you right now at a winery in Napa and has been all day?"

"It sounds like you've had too much to drink, darling, and not me. I've said it a couple of times. And why do you sound so strange? Are you all right, Lee?"

I heard another man's voice become dominant in the background, a man with a Spanish accent, who was having an intense conversation with Douglas.

"Douglas," I said, trying to get his attention back. "Douglas, never mind. I've got something wrong. I've got to hang up, Douglas. I'll talk to you soon."

"But I…" I heard him say before I disconnected.

I slumped down on one of the counter stools and looked up again at the empty knife slot. I was right about some things but wrong about others. None of the pieces were fitting together the way I'd thought they would. I was riding a runaway locomotive but had no idea where we were headed.

Rinsing the glass, I put it away, looking around me for anything else I might have touched or altered. There was no point in letting Douglas or Stefano know someone was in the apartment. I went to the door, locked it, and returned the keys over the sconce. I knew two things for sure. One, I would have to tell Frank my suspicions about the ceramic knife, and two, the man in San Miguel was not Stefano. Back to the drawing board, big time.

Getting back into the cab that had been waiting for me, I gave the driver my home address and leaned back in the seat. I thought about Mom, opened up the laptop, noticed I had another forty minutes of battery power, and looked for a message from her. *Strange*, I thought, *she said she was going to let me know when she boarded the plane*. I looked at my watch. It was nearly nine o'clock. That would be eleven, Mexico time. Surely, she'd have gotten a flight out of Mexico City by now. I punched in Richard's number, and he answered on the third ring. I could hear Richard's favorite mariachi CD and chatter in the background as he said hello.

"Richard, have you heard from Mom?"

"No, I haven't. I've been leaving her messages, too, for about the last three or four hours."

"I don't like this, Richard."

"Maybe she's on a plane right now and was so rushed she couldn't take the time to call us," he said.

"Can you track her?"

"Not unless she puts the signal on."

"I thought you had a way of getting into someone's cell phone and finding out where they are? You've done it to me. Can't you do that with the sat phone?"

"Not this model, Lee. I've built a resistor into it, so if you don't want to be located, you can't be. Just a minute," he called out to his wife. "I'll be right there, honey. Lee, I've got to go. Vicki is throwing her yearly bash for her employees from the Obsessive Chapeau, and I'm the bartender."

"Okay," I said. "I guess it isn't time to panic yet."

"Let's see what another hour brings, okay? I'll talk to you then." He hung up as we pulled up to the curb in front of the family house. I paid the cab fare, dragged myself up the walkway, and rang the bell. I was exhausted but wanted Tío to know I was home. He answered the door and hugged me.

"Where is your mama?" he said, breaking from the embrace and looking behind me.

"Oh, she's flying in on another plane from Mexico City," I said, not wanting to worry my uncle.

"Lila's in *de Efe? Por Que*?"

"Why? She went to visit someone to extract a little information. She should be back soon," I said and then changed the subject. "Is Mira up?"

"No," he said, shaking his head. "She is sleeping. Today she went out for a walk and then insisted on helping with dinner."

"So she overdid it a little?"

"*Si*, but that is a good thing. She is becoming normal again."

"That's good," I agreed, secretly glad I didn't have to see the look in her eyes when I told her any hope of finding the dog statue just blew up in my face. Time enough for the bad news tomorrow.

"Okay, Tio, I think I'll go home now…" I began.

"What is wrong, *mi sobrina*?" he said, pulling me inside and shutting the door. "Something is wrong. *Que paso*?" he demanded.

"I don't have the strength to go into it now. I need to do some tall thinking. Plus, when Mom gets back, we should know more. Maybe."

He pulled me into another big bear hug, saying nothing.

"Thanks, Tio," I said, leaning into his shoulder. "I sure needed that."

"Trying to make things right can be a burden," he said, breaking free and looking at me.

"And heavy is the head that wears the tiara," I quipped. He smiled at me with worried eyes. "I need to go home. I'll let you know when I hear from Mom. It should be any minute." I turned to leave.

"Are you not forgetting something?" he asked. I looked at him questioningly. *Su gato*?" he said.

"My cat?" I answered. "Tugger! *Dios mio*. Where is my head? And where is my cat?" I went farther into the foyer and looked around.

"In the family room. He lies sleeping on the sofa. Wait, I will get his halter and leash," Tío offered, heading for the closet while I went into the family room. I stroked Tugger whose nose began to twitch, and upon opening his eyes, he licked my hand, purring. Who says a girl's best friend isn't her cat? When Tío returned with his halter and leash, I put them on the sleepy feline. Gathering up a puddle of purr in my arms, I went out the back door, across the lawn, and toward the garage.

I was deep in thought nearing the front steps of the apartment when I heard a voice call, "Pssssst!" from somewhere in the darkness. I wheeled around, nearly dropping Tugger.

"Who said that?" I asked, setting the cat on the ground. "Who said that?" I said louder, wrapping Tugger's leash around the railing at the bottom of the stairs. "Show yourself," I demanded.

Something moved in the shadows, coming within range of the garage night-lights. I went into the classic, karate defense position and waited.

"All right, I'm coming. Please don't hurt me," the voice whined.

"Robby Weinblatt! What the hell are you doing here again?"

"I-I..." he stuttered and then froze, gaping at me. I grabbed him by the front of yet another oversized T-shirt and pulled him toward me. "Don't rip my shirt off of me," he begged. "It's the only one I got left. And please don't hit me."

I put my face into his. "You've got two seconds to tell me why you're here, and then I'm going to take all the frustrations of the past few days out on your sorry butt." I was in a Raymond Chandler mood.

"I came to apologize. I came to apologize," he cried out. "My mom said I had to apologize for the way I treated you, or I couldn't come home. I told her that Lenny was going to throw me in jail, and I've been hiding ever since he found out, but she's a born-again Christian. She says I have to make atonement first!" He ran out of breath and began to sob.

Okay, I was thrown. I didn't know what he was talking about, but he was getting loud, and I didn't want his voice to bring Tío out into the backyard. "Okay, okay," I said, releasing him. "Lower your voice and come upstairs." I bent down and picked up Tugger who had been standing perfectly still and staring wide eyed up at the kid.

I started up the stairs, followed by Robby, who sniveled, "I like your cat."

I stopped climbing the stairs and turned around, scrutinizing his face under the porch lights. He stumbled up the next stair and stared up at me, a look of terror returning to his features.

"Easy, boy," I said. "You don't have any scratches on your face or your shoulders, do you?" I stated more than asked him.

"Scratches?" he answered, puzzled.

I wheeled around and continued up the stairs. "Never mind. Just one more thing I got wrong." I unlocked the door, put the cat down, and turned off the alarm.

"Come on in, Robby, and let's sort this out." He followed me across the living room and into the kitchen, both of us trailed by a cat dragging a leash.

"Wow. Nice digs," Robby said, looking around and wiping his nose with the bottom of his T-shirt. "I don't have anything nearly this nice."

"But you would have," I said, putting water to heat in the microwave, "once you got all that money from Silo Junction."

"Oh, that," he said, looking down and shuffling his feet. "That wasn't for me."

"Sit down," I said, studying his face. He looked even younger than I remembered. "You want some coffee or milk? How old are you, anyway?"

"I'm nineteen. Last month," he retorted, regaining a little spirit. He sagged again. "I'll take some milk. I'm kind of hungry."

Scooping coffee into a cone and placing it atop a carafe, I said, "There's some peanut butter on the shelf over the counter. Silverware's in the drawer below. Milk, bread, and jam are in the fridge. Wash your hands first then help yourself."

"Thank you, Miss Alvarez," he murmured, getting up, and going to the sink. I watched him carefully wash his hands then cross to the fridge.

"You're awfully polite now for someone who was a former scumbag," I remarked, hearing the beep of the mic and pouring the boiling water over the ground coffee.

"I had to! I had to try to make you go away," he said, having the grace to hang his head as he came back to the kitchen table with milk and the supplies for a sandwich. "I'm really not much of a scumbag."

"Could have fooled me."

"Thanks, but it's just an act." A small smile flashed across a face filled with heaviness and fatigue. "I've watched reruns of *The Sopranos*."

I hid my laughter. "Make one for me, would you?" I said, setting a clean glass in front of him. I sat down at the other end of the table and watched him slather peanut butter on another slice of bread. "So who was the money for, if not you?"

227

He gulped and looked up at me with wet eyes. "It was for Mom. I swear. It wasn't right that Lenny cut her out like that. She needed the money and I—"

"Wait a minute," I interrupted. "What has your mother got to do with Leonard Fogel?"

He stared up at me, an incredulous look on his face. "Well, she's our mom! Why shouldn't he help out? Why should she have to pay all the bills by herself? With Lily being sick, she can't work. He never even sent her—"

"Hold the phone. Time out," I interrupted. "Leonard Fogel is your brother? And who's this Lily?"

"You didn't know that? He's my half brother, actually. I thought you knew everything," he said, shaking his head.

"How come you two have different last names?"

"Well, duh," he said, taking a big bite out of his sandwich. "Different fathers."

I slapped my forehead just as Tugger jumped into my lap. "I think you'd better tell me the whole story," I said, removing Tugger's halter and throwing it into a corner.

Robby chewed for a moment, swallowed milk, and began to talk. "Lenny's dad was Mom's first husband and—"

"First?" I interrupted again. "How many did she have?"

"Three. That's before she got saved. Now she doesn't have any. She and Bruce Fogel got divorced when Lenny was three. Now Lenny's dad lives in

228

San Diego with his second wife and four kids. Mom married my dad, Aaron Weinblatt, about two years after their divorce."

"Where does your dad live?"

"My dad died in the Gulf War. He was a marine."

"I'm sorry," I said, taken up short.

"Thank you. Mom says he was the love of her life. That used to piss Lenny off when she'd say things like that. That's why five years ago, when his dad said Lenny could live with him in San Diego and go to school there, Lenny did. He never came back to see Mom, not once. That really hurt her." By now, he'd finished his peanut butter sandwich and was eyeing mine.

"Help yourself," I said, pushing my plate over to him. "I really just want coffee." I pushed Tugger off my lap, got up, and went to the counter. Removing the cone from the pot, I poured myself a large cup of black coffee. I suspected I would be needing it. Tugger, meanwhile, sauntered over to Robby and hopped onto his lap. The kid held his second sandwich with one hand and stroked the cat with the other. Purring, Tugger made himself comfortable on what must have been a pretty scrawny lap.

"That still doesn't explain the money," I said, sitting down again.

Robby stopped eating and put the sandwich down. "When Lenny started his new business, he said I could come up and work for him. It wasn't until I got here that I saw all the money he was making. Like a gazillion dollars or more. He wasn't

229

sending any back home to help out. Mom was on food stamps and Lily's doctor bills —"

"Again, who's this Lily?"

"Our little sister. She's seven. She's got cerebral palsy and even with social services, Mom can't do it. It's bad enough that when her dad found out about the palsy he took off but —"

"That's husband number three?"

"Jake," he spat out, much as I used to do when I said Robby's name. "And Mom can't work because she's got to take care of Lily, and I send back all the money I can, but Lenny won't give her a dime." He broke off and covered his face, crying into his hands. Tugger looked up at him, I swear, with sympathetic eyes. "Oh God, I'm so tired."

"So you decided to take matters into your own hands and sell out your brother in order to have some money for Lily and your mom?" He snuffled into his hands, nodding his agreement.

"Okay. But how did I fit into this? Why were you so mean to the hired help?"

He lowered his hands and wiped his eyes, this time on a paper napkin. "Oh, I knew from the first week you weren't who you were pretending to be. I suspected that Lenny hired you to find me out. Before you did, I was hoping I could scare you into quitting." He snorted. "No way."

"But how?" I pressed. *After all, I was quite a good actress,* I thought, *really getting into the part and all that.*

"Your underwear, for one thing."

"Excuse me," I said, nearly spilling coffee down the front of my blouse.

"Oh sure. One day you bent over in front of me and those baggy, black pants you were wearing came down below your… ah… panty line and I saw the La Perla logo. They're all over the internet."

"You saw the La Perla label on my underwear?" I managed to get out.

"Sure. Those things cost about fifty bucks each. That's all that JLo wears." He went on, warming up to the subject. "Now a real down-and-out woman with children in East Palo Alto would be more like my mom, wearing something from Walmart." He looked at me. "Wouldn't she?"

I looked back at him, speechless.

"Then I started paying attention to the way Lenny wasn't talking to you. He'd talk to everybody else but not you, and I wondered why. So then I decided to follow you home on my moped and saw you get off the bus at that shopping mall, get into that really neat car, and drive here."

"I think the wrong person is the PI here," I said, getting up for a second cup of coffee.

"That's why when Lenny told me to wait in the car that night I got to thinking I got found out."

"So you traced his steps, saw the Discretionary Inquiries sign, and ran. That was two days ago. Where have you been ever since?"

"I've been hiding out in the public library during the day and spending the nights at Bingo Bango when everybody left. I haven't been getting much sleep."

"You look pretty wrung out. Why did you come here night before last?"

"I was hoping I could talk to you. Maybe you'd convince Lenny not to put me in jail."

"But I scared the bejesus out of you, and you took off."

He inhaled a jagged breath, nodded, and reached for his sandwich again, absently stroking the purring cat with his free hand. I had a feeling Tugger was a better judge of character than I was. "By the way, your other shirt is in the back of my car."

"Thanks," he said. "When I'd called home and told Mom about what I did to Lenny, she said I couldn't come home until I made up for it. She said I had to give the money back I took, apologize to Lenny for stealing the codes, and then to you for being so nasty. It was the only Christian thing to do. I've been waiting for you ever since, so I can go home. That's before I go to jail, I guess."

"Leonard's not pressing charges, but this does explain the strange voice mail message I got the other night, where he sounded more guilty than angry."

"He's not going to send me to jail?" Robby said. "What a relief. Maybe the fact I'm his half brother means something."

"I should have guessed. You two do resemble each other," I said, shaking my head. "I remember once I looked at the back of Leonard and thought it was you, only—" I stopped myself and stared forward. "*Dios mio.*" I set down the half-empty cup and stood up, banging the palm of my hand against my forehead. "Stupid, stupid, stupid."

"What is it?" Robby said, dropping the sandwich. "You're not going to become violent again, are you?"

My phone rang, and I reached for it, looking at the number of the incoming call. "Richard," I blasted. "Why didn't you tell me that Leonard Fogel and Robby Weinblatt were half brothers?"

"What? How can that be?"

"Oh, it can be," I retorted. "I'm sitting here with Robby right now, and he told me the story of their lives. He and Leonard have the same mother but different fathers."

"Well, that partially explains it, although it doesn't justify the slipup on our part," he said. "I'm sorry, Lee, but we were given specific instructions by Lila to check only so far back on the backgrounds of each employee. I remember that Len was in San Diego living with his father before moving here a year ago, and Weinblatt's been in Bakersfield until about six months ago. I did notice their mothers had the same first name, but 'Mary' is such a common name. Lee, I'm so sorry," he repeated. "We weren't really looking for that type of connection. You'd think Len would have been forthcoming with that."

"You'd think," I said. "Moving on, have you heard from Lila?"

"No, but I just got in some information on this Ramírez de Arroyo character."

"I thought you were bartending tonight."

"I've been reprieved. Vicki knew something was going on, and I've given her the highlights, so I'm doing research instead of playing host."

"That woman's a saint, Richard, in a custom-made hat."

"Don't I know it, but back to Stefano Ramírez de Arroyo. I managed to get all the birth records for the past fifty years for anyone with that name in both Spain and Mexico—"

"What you can coax out of a supercomputer," I interjected.

"It's a program."

"It's a gift."

"Anyway," Richard said dismissively, "he isn't from Barcelona as he claims. He just went to college there. He was born and raised in Guanajuato and Julio de Arroyo Mendez, the co-owner of Mesoamerican Galleries is his—"

"Brother," I interrupted.

"Cousin," Richard corrected.

"Close enough. This is all making sense to me now. I'm pretty sure I know where that missing truck is heading, and I'm on my way over there right now to look for it. Listen, call Frank, and tell him I think I've located the owner of the ceramic knife, and—"

"Wait a minute, where are you going?"

"Hey, what about Tex?" I asked, not answering his question. "Maybe Tex knows where Mom is."

"She doesn't pick up at either the rancho or on cell phone."

"Hmmm, call *Señor* Lopez. Maybe he can tell you something."

"I'll do that."

"Meanwhile, I've got to run. Keep me posted."

"Lee, tell me where you're going."

"Why don't we keep this on a need-to-know-only basis?"

"Tell me, or I swear, I'll track you down and come and get you. You know I can do it."

"Okay, okay. Calm down," I said. "Mesoamerican Galleries. I'm going to check out a few things. Maybe I'll just sit and wait and see what happens."

"Wait? For what? You're not going to try to get inside, are you? That's breaking and entering!"

"Richard," I said, "during this whole fiasco I've made every wrong choice I could possibly make. I'm not going to be doing anything like that again, so don't worry about it. That truck's had over a twenty-four-hour start on us. In a few hours, I think it's going to come barreling up University Avenue heading straight for the gallery. I would like to be there to greet it."

I hung up before he could say another word. My phone started ringing again almost immediately, and one glance told me it was Richard again. Brothers can be such a pain.

I turned the phone off and looked at the kid cooing in my cat's face. "Robby, everything's going to be all right, at least for you. Try not to worry. We can talk about this more in the morning. I've got something else I need to deal with right now." I hustled my bustle to the inside door that goes down to the garage and my car.

"I'll go with you. Maybe I can help," he offered, about to stand.

"Thanks but no thanks. Why don't you call your mother; tell her you've done the Christian thing, and you're going to be home sometime tomorrow? Meanwhile, the linen for the pullout couch is in the closet over there. Likewise for the towels," I said, pointing. "You're free to stay here for the night, if you'd like. You look like you could use some sleep."

His face lit up like a soccer stadium. "Wow, dude, thanks. Can I play with your cat while you're gone? What's his name?"

"Tugger, and he's an indoor kitty, so don't let him out. He's got food in the fridge, and he could use some fresh water." I opened the door and hit the lights, looking down at the garage steps. Turning back to Robby, I added, "This door self-locks behind me. I don't know when I'll be back, so don't wait up." I slammed the door shut, took the stairs two at a time, and got into my car.

The first thing I did was to unlock the glove compartment and check for the nylon holster housing my new snub nose. I would have preferred the one I'm used to, the detective special, but that was under the floorboards in the living room, and I couldn't chance that Robby might see me take it. Nothing scares people like a loaded gun, and he looked scared enough already.

Regarding the Colt Royal Blue residing in my glove compartment, I got carried away at a gun show. It was pretty. It matched the car. It was on sale. I named it Lady Blue and had only used it three times on the practice range. At that point, I'd never aimed a gun at anyone, much less shot them.

I checked to make sure it was loaded. There was extra ammunition in the glove compartment, and I knew I was set. As I was backing out of the driveway, I turned the phone on for an instant to give Tío the news about my houseguest. Knowing my uncle, he'd walk over with a tray of his homemade soup for Robby.

Just as I was hanging up from Tío, I heard the signal that someone was trying to reach me on my other line. It was Richard; I turned off the phone again without answering it. I didn't need any lectures about what I was doing. In my gut, I knew everything was tied to that gallery. Like that truck rushing up the highway, I had a rendezvous with Quetzalcoatl, the plumed serpent god of the Toltecs and Aztecs. Nothing was going to get in my way.

Chapter Thirteen

A Sleigh of the Hand

The annual Palo Alto Wine and Food Fair was scheduled to begin the following day and run through Sunday night. From eight in the morning to eleven o'clock at night, all the merchants on University Avenue hawk their wares on sidewalks in between booths of participating California vintners and well-known restaurants selling delectables. Local artists demonstrate their talents, and musicians perform, while strolling patrons drink wine and nibble on high-caloric goodies.

For those seventy-two hours, sidewalks promised to be jammed with foot traffic spilling out into the roadway, including families pushing baby carriages or attached to large dogs. Roads are blocked off and local buses and trucks rerouted, so happy shoppers won't find themselves under the wheels of passing vehicles. Palo Alto becomes a town in full swing twenty-four hours a day for those three days.

If a truck being sought by two countries wanted to unload its contraband in an alley behind a gallery, it would have to arrive the night before all the madness began. Otherwise, there would be a three-day wait, risking detection. I was sure the driver had an open throttle to get here in time.

At 10:30 p.m., I parked on University. I found a space by a pizza parlor down the street from the gallery and leapt out of the car. I was wearing dark green slacks, good, but a white blouse, bad. I keep a multipocketed black jacket in the trunk of the car, along with other staples. Opening the trunk, I threw the cotton jacket on and buttoned it to the top. I also grabbed a small screwdriver, pencil flashlight, can of mace, and an old, thick credit card that had gotten me into more places in the middle of the night than my fake ID and a low-cut blouse.

Getting back in the car on the passenger's side, I surreptitiously shoved the holstered snub nose into one of the jacket pockets, spare ammo into another, and the phone into a third before I got out of the car again and locked it.

I figured I couldn't get into the gallery itself, odds on it having a sophisticated alarm system, but I could wait in the back alley. This way I would be on hand for whatever arrived in the dead of night, like a truck zipping up from Mexico loaded down with smuggled goods. Beforehand, I wanted to case the front of the building, Phillip Marlowe style.

Shops had locked their doors and gone home but chic restaurants and designer bars were open as usual. Everything looked calm before the three-day marathon began in pursuit of the almighty dollar.

239

Groups of people sauntered by, oblivious to a lone woman strolling toward a three-story building called Mesoamerican Galleries in the middle of the block.

A tall, hatted man, draped in shining chains, hurried down the sidewalk heading in my direction. Race! I scooted into the shallow entrance of the closest store, scrunching myself into the dark doorway. Heavy boots on the sidewalk echoed within my small chamber as he strode by. I emerged and watched his retreating figure. Had he come from his own nearby gallery or had he come from Mesoamerican's? I continued on to the gallery but looked back over my shoulder from time to time. Race had vanished into the night.

Closing in on my prey, I pressed my nose to the plate glass that shimmied all the way up the front three floors of the building. Inside, about twenty feet back from the glass, were two white walls, two stories high, reaching up to the open-air balcony of the third floor. A hallway ran through the middle of the walls to the back of the gallery. Spotlighted paintings and art pieces, strategically displayed, climbed up each wall to the pale-oak-trimmed railing of the top level. On the bottom floor and to the right, a red-carpeted, circular staircase with an oak banister led up to the third floor. I noticed it was roped off at the top. That floor probably functioned as storage, and the rope was to discourage visitors, which didn't work on me.

While I pondered if there was any way of getting inside without setting off the alarm, a shadow moved across a light source from

240

somewhere in the back, on the other side of the great white walls. Was I lucky enough to find someone still inside? I pushed at one of the double glass doors, fully expecting it to be locked. Wonder of wonders, the door swung noiselessly open, followed by a *ding-dong* sound overhead. I stepped inside, hoping I'd come up with a plausible reason to be there.

A young Latino man, beautifully dressed in a black silk shirt, white tie, and very tight black slacks hurried down the hallway. He smoothed back the sides of his pompadour with a manicured hand while extending the other one in my direction. I would have pegged him for a ballroom dancer rather than an art dealer.

"I am so sorry," he fawned with a slight accent, "but we are closed. I was only finishing up some paperwork at my desk and am about to leave."

"Oh, that's too bad," I said, "because my client insists that I buy those three items right up there." I pointed vaguely. "I'm an interior designer; perhaps you've heard of me? Chloe Leviticus?"

He hesitated and then said, "Of course. Miss Leviticus. I am José. If you will come back tomor—"

"Oh no!" I said, grabbing the sides of my head as if it was all too much to absorb. I gave my best Sarah Bernhardt sigh. "This is terrible, just terrible. My client, Mr. Paul Bunyan, wanted me to purchase them today. Well, I know it's my fault for coming so late, but I didn't know what else to do. You see, I was on the horns of a dilemma. My daughter belongs to a Girl Scout group, and the

241

meeting ran late..." I trailed off, trying to look desperate but appealing.

"You have a daughter so old? That is not possible," he said, grabbing my hand and planting a very wet kiss on it. "Which ones did you say?" I took the opportunity to wipe my hand off on the back of my pants when he stretched his neck to look up to where I'd pointed.

"Those big three, on the wall up there. The... ah... picture, the glass vase, and... ah... the other thing right below it. Oh, and possibly a fourth. That one, over there." I pointed in another direction.

"Well, I..." he began. With perfect timing, a ringing phone from the back area stopped him further. He turned to me. "Excuse me one moment, miss, and then I'll see what I can do for you."

"Thank you so very much," I said and almost curtseyed. I watched him dash to catch the phone, and then I made a beeline for the double doors. Hoping it would click in place if it was opened wide enough, I pulled one of the doors open. It did. Then I made with some dashing myself, up the stairs, over the rope, and into the darkness of the third floor.

From the shadows, I watched him return a moment later, saying, "I am so sorry, miss, for leaving you..." He froze when he saw the lack of me, looked around, and then spotted the open door.

"*Hijo de perro*," I heard him mutter. After making sure I hadn't taken anything, he shut the door, locked it and the other one, checking them both carefully. Part of me was afraid he would come upstairs, but he never did. A minute or two went by and the light downstairs went off.

I heard the faint musical notes as he punched in numbers setting the alarm, then the opening, closing, and locking of the door at the back of the building. I burned it on my brain that when I opened the back door to leave, the alarm was going to go off, sending for a bevy of police. I hoped to be long gone.

The streetlights provided ample illumination through the front glass wall, and pivoting around, I gave the floor my complete attention. Everywhere I looked, I saw boxes. Large, small, opened, sealed, they were stacked everywhere. I chose one of the open boxes, threw back the flaps, and feeling through the layered packing paper, found a small terracotta statue of a fertility god and goddess united in passion. I took it close to the banister for better light.

A happy couple passed by outside on the sidewalk. Mindful that if they looked up they might be able to spot me, I stepped back into the gloom until they were gone. Safe, I come forward again, turned over the statue, and searched for a mark indicating it was a replica. Not surprised, I found it and returned the statue to the box. They would have to sell some models and replicas as a front, if nothing else.

I pulled the flashlight from my pocket, switched it on, and headed toward the back. It became darker with every step. I walked through a tight path flanked on both sides by more boxes. Another thirty feet, and the stacked boxes blocked out the light from the street completely. All was murkiness, save for the small shaft of light moving back and forth in front of me. Soon I arrived at an area that was about fifteen feet or so of open space. Sitting on top of an industrial-gray, rectangular rug was a long, empty worktable, file cabinets, and a modern desk with a chair, all in matching pale oak. Behind the furniture was another three-foot-high, banistered balcony, and like the front, it was set in from the outside wall by about twenty feet. To the right was a duplicate staircase to the one in the front, leading down to the back of the first floor. Careful not to trip over a stray box here and there, I made my way to the work area and sat down in the chair behind the desk.

I swiveled around in the chair, reached out, and grabbed the handle of the top file drawer. Locked. With the flashlight between my teeth to free up both hands, I took out the small screwdriver and began to pry the drawer open. It gave in an instant. *When are people going to learn to invest in file cabinets with a good locking system?* I clucked to myself.

I rummaged through standard, letter-sized manila folders, neatly labeled and alphabetized, then grabbed a handful. Twirling back to the desk, I started pouring through them. Receipts and bills of sale, names and addresses, all looking very normal. Did I have it wrong again?

Whoa, Nellie. None of the receipts had the name Mesoamerican Galleries as a heading. In fact, there was no logo or heading on any of them. Even though each purchaser's name was different, the receipts were signed by Julio de Arroyo Mendez,

Stefano's cousin. Some of the amounts were astronomical, too, ranging from fifty thousand to several hundred thousand dollars. One receipt, merely marked "Toltec idol," was for 1.5 million dollars. It was the only one with no buyer's name or address.

I returned the files to the drawer and got up, about to tackle more boxes. That's when there was a noise below, at the back door. Someone was jimmying the lock. I switched off my flashlight and hid behind a stack of boxes.

The door opened, and light from the back alley streamed in, gone with the closing of the door. The *beep beep* warning of the alarm pierced the air, followed by a scratching, clipped sound. Then silence. I waited, knowing that whoever it was, they had no more right to be here than I did. That didn't make me feel any better.

Rustling and the sounds of someone's footfalls on the soft padding of the rug of the stairs filled the air, coming ever closer. I jammed the flashlight in my pants and went into attack stance. Not time yet for the snub nose heavy in my jacket, but I reached in and undid the snap holding it firm inside the holster. My heart thudded in my chest.

I sensed rather than saw someone at the head of the stairs. Instinctively, I knew he was searching for me. I leaned into the boxes and waited. Quiet movement, almost undetectable, brushed by me in the dark. Then an intake of air. The sound of that breath was my guidepost. I knew the approximate height of the man and his distance from me. I lunged and grabbed him from behind, both arms around his neck in a headlock. I yanked him back toward me, while jabbing a hard knee into his kidneys. There was an "Oomph," and he crashed to the floor.

I turned to run, but my feet were knocked out from under me. I went down too. This guy knew what he was doing.

The man tried to throw himself on top of me, but I'd rolled on my back with knees against my chest and catapulted him backward with my feet. He smashed into a section of boxes, toppling them on top of him. Sounds of shattering pottery and breaking wood mixed with his grunts pierced the black void. I let out a yowl of satisfaction.

From somewhere under the rubble, I heard him call my name out in the darkness. "Lee? Is that you?" I also thought I recognized the voice.

"Gurn?" I snatched at my flashlight and switched it on. I got to my feet and pulled the revolver out of my pocket. I pointed both in his direction. "Get up, you scumbag, and if you make one wrong move, your kneecaps will never be the same."

I shone the light in his direction, and he surfaced from underneath the pile. The beam of light partially blinded him, but he could see well enough to tell I was holding a revolver.

"Lee! Rich sent me."

"What?"

"I'm a friend of Richard's, I swear. You can call him."

"What are you talking about?" I said, still hesitant to lower the gun. "You've got thirty seconds to explain yourself, and then I won't be responsible," I threatened.

"That's what I'm doing," he said in a more reprimanding tone than I would have used in his position. "Your brother and I go back to the navy reserves. I was his commanding officer, and we became friends."

"So you're not a certified public accountant?"

"Yes, I am. I'm both. That's the point of being a reservist," he replied and a might huffily too.

"Wait a minute, what's your name? Not the Gurn part, what they used to call you, the nickname."

"Huckster. I'm Huckster."

"Go on," I said, lowering the revolver.

"Rich is the one who turned me on to Mexico. He knew I was going back and forth between San Francisco and San Miguel, so he asked me to keep an eye on you."

"Oh, he did, did he?" I ground my teeth together, bringing the revolver back up again.

"I agreed because he's a good guy, and I wanted to help out. That was before I met you. He only told me you were his sister, he didn't tell me about the rest of you," he said, stepping forward.

"Don't move," I said in clipped words. I held the revolver at arm's length. He stepped back. "But keep talking."

"After the fiasco on the plane, I didn't think I could suave my way into your life, so I decided the stealth approach might be better."

"So it was you behind us from the airport to the rancho."

247

"I wanted to make sure you got there."

"You didn't follow me on horseback the same day, did you?"

"I don't ride horses. Never did. When Rich told me you spotted the plates on my car and got a partial number, I switched to my motorcycle. I staked out the front gates. Saw the police arrive the next morning and take you into town. I followed. I was going to stage an accidental meeting with you in San Miguel, but your friend nearly got hit by that car, so I didn't have to. The rest you know."

"Not quite. How did you get here from San Miguel?" I asked.

"When I dropped you off at the Leon Airport, I filed flight plans, fueled up, and flew directly here. I got here a little while ago. I spoke with Rich, and he told me where you were. I promised I would find you."

"That's a lot of work to do just for a pal," I remarked.

"I didn't do it entirely for him. I did it for me. I like the girl even if the girl doesn't like me."

I placed the flashlight on top of a box with it aimed at his face, dug out my phone, turned it on, and hit the speed dial. Lady Blue was still pointed at his right kneecap, so the man in front of me remained motionless.

"Richard," I crooned when he answered. "It's your sister."

"Liana! Did Huckster find you? I've been frantic."

Finger off the trigger and safety back on, I pointed the revolver to the ceiling. Laying it next to the flashlight on the top of the box, I said, "You miserable rat, how dare you?"

"Well, if you'd answer your phone," came his indignant reply, "you would have known. You think I'm going to let you and Mom go off by yourselves when there are dead bodies everywhere? I tried to tell you!"

Mr. Gorgeous Gin Guy, aka Gurn, aka Huckster, came over and took the phone out of my hand, saying, "Rich, don't worry. I've got her now, and we're leaving."

"You've got me? It's looks to me as if it was the other way around." I snatched the phone away from him. "Richard, if you ever do anything like this again I'll—" I was interrupted by the sound of a key in the back door. "Gotta go," I whispered into the phone and turned it off.

Gurn reached up for the flashlight and killed it. I picked up the revolver. Together, we scurried behind some boxes.

The downstairs back door opened. Light flooded the bottom and upper floors. I heard the musical notes of the alarm keypad being tapped by a person who had no way of knowing Gurn had already disabled it.

Indistinguishable talk, shuffling, and then what sounded like a gaggle of people ascended the staircase. Gurn looked at me, and I put my forefinger to my mouth. He gave me a look that said, "You state the obvious." We backed into the shadows. I would have been content to stay there, listening to the proceedings, if only.

"You'll never get away with this, you mangy coyote," Tex said. I was so shocked when I heard her voice, I jumped. The next voice almost caused me to drop the gun.

"Now, Virginia, there's no *point* in *aggravating* the gentleman. He'll see the *futility* of his actions soon enough," said Lila, stressing enough words for me to tell that while her voice sounded cool, she wasn't feeling that way.

Gurn grabbed my shoulders to hold me back. I shrugged him off and went to the other side of a box where I could have a view, obstructed though it was. The silver-haired man who'd disappeared from the shop in San Miguel was now pointing a lethal-looking Smith and Wesson pistol at Tex and my mother, their hands bound in front of them with duct tape.

"*Silencio*," Stefano's cousin ordered, so angry his body shook with it. He gyrated around the center of the work area while Mom and Tex stood near the desk. Stationed at the top of the stairs, two nasty-looking men held their arms by their sides and shifted their weight from one foot to the other, caught up in Julio's rage. The shorter one's face was covered with scratches and several looked infected. Score one for Tugger.

I raised my revolver and tried to ready myself, unsure of whether to aim at his head or his heart. He was less than twenty feet away. Even with a snub nose, it would be an accurate shot.

"You think you can ruin my life's work and that of the entire de Arroyo Mendez family and get away with it? Now we have to make new plans, find a new place to store our heritage, start over." He walked closer to Mom and aimed the pistol in her face. "You two will pay," Julio Mendez threatened, his voice filling the room, "and so will your family."

"Your heritage?" Tex came back. "You're stealing from the Mexican people."

Julio shifted the aim of his pistol over to Tex and backed up a few steps, waving the pistol back and forth between the two of them. With mounting fury, he said, "For forty-five years, ever since my grandfather found the hiding place of the Toltec priests through his years of searching, those trinkets have been our salvation. This is the way we feed our children, clothe them, send them to good schools, give them a better life. Do you think we are going to pay attention to what the government says or what you do?" Julio sneered, lowering his voice but never his gun. He spat. "I spit at your feet, *mujeres*. Both of you."

Tex glared at him but backed up. Lila, to her credit, remained still and stone faced.

Fighting the urge to fire then and there, I knew I had to wait until he took his sights off the two women. I'd read about shooters pulling the trigger as a reflex action on their way down. I didn't need my mother or Tex to be standing in the way of a bullet.

"That's a long time to keep such a secret," Lila said evenly, undercutting his emotions. "How many of you are there? How did you and your family manage to do it?" Julio shifted the pistol, again aiming it at my mother.

251

Gurn tapped me on the shoulder and gestured he was going to move nearer to where the two henchmen had been drawn in by Julio's ravings. They now stood side by side, several feet in from the head of the stairs, with their backs to a stack of boxes. I dug out the can of mace and handed it over.

Giving me a thumbs-up sign, Gurn moved away. I watched him get into position. When the time came and he pushed the stack of boxes, I was sure Julio would be momentarily distracted. Then I'd make my move. I had just been waiting for him to swing the pistol away from either woman's face for just an instant. Then I was going to drop him.

"It was not easy," Julio said. I focused full attention on him again. He seemed to be calmed somewhat by Mom's ladylike demeanor. "My grandfather was a great man, a great man, an inspiration to us all. As a poor youth, he had been fortunate enough to work on a dig in Mexico City and paid attention to what the *jefes* would say, always learning. He'd heard of a legend telling somewhere far north of the Yucatàn was a hidden treasure, where the last of the Toltec priests had fled from their Aztec pursuers, taking with them their accumulated wealth of silver, gold, and idols of worship. He spent the early part of his life seeking this treasure.

"When he finally found the cave on the other side of the mine's entrance, he knew what he had. The gold and silver had either been sold off or looted centuries before, but what remained had great value. He knew that. He called a family meeting, deciding to tell no one but his own. He

252

went to work for the man who owned the rancho before this woman's husband," Julio said, pointing the pistol at Tex, "to keep an eye on things and to keep strangers away." He brought the pistol back into Mom's face again.

I could do nothing but wait. I sensed Gurn didn't want to do anything, either, not with my mother staring down the barrel of this angry man's gun. I looked in Gurn's direction but couldn't see him. Whatever he did and whenever he did it, I would be ready.

"You mean no outsiders, no one except your family members knew? For all those years?" Mom asked.

Following my mother's lead, Tex added, "It's remarkable so many people could keep a secret like that for so long."

That's it, I thought, *keep him talking, ladies. Sooner or later, he'll move the gun away. Then he's mine.* A bead of sweat trickled down my nose.

Julio droned on. "*Si*, it is, and we were not greedy. No, never. You did not know the foreman and his wife, Eduardo and Eva, were sent there to keep an eye on things, to keep you and the *vaqueros* away from the cave. We did not know they would betray us, steal from their own family. They are the ones who started all this trouble by taking and losing the statue your son found."

My right hand began to shake with the tension of holding the revolver taut for so long, finger on the trigger. I switched to my left hand. My breathing came fast and shallow.

"For generations, the family would vote on what pieces to sell and only as we needed them. For this wedding, for that business. Never having too much money to earn the authorities' interest but enough to keep the family thriving. Soon we became more educated; we became people of importance in important places. A commissioner here, a judge there, a customs agent..."

"An assistant curator at a museum," Mom added.

"*Exactamente*. We are everywhere," he bragged.

I saw the glint of a diamond stud in his left ear. I made my decision. The head.

"Over sixty of us, all in important, strategic places. We are educated men of the world. I myself have a degree in archaeology from Cornell University. I own this place, along with another family member who is not as trustworthy as I would like," he said, looking around him, his anger picking up momentum again. "This was the perfect place to find buyers who do not care how a piece arrives to them, so long as they get it. Private collectors, wealthy and eager."

"I'm impressed," Mom said, nodding. Tex nodded, too, but clearly wasn't.

"Are you?" Julio asked my mother. "That is good because I would hate for you to die not agreeing with the reason. Now you will tell me where that daughter of yours is, and I will make your deaths easier for you." He moved closer, the pistol at my mother's heart.

I aimed and cocked the hammer.

The back door burst open, and there was the thumping of feet running up the stairs. Everyone turned toward the noise except for Julio. He'd been startled but kept the pistol pointed at Mom.

I stepped out from behind the box and waited for any slight change in the positioning of his firearm before I took what would probably be my one and only shot.

No one even looked in my direction; all attention was on the stairs. What happened next went by like the speed of light. In other ways, it was the slowest ten seconds of my life.

"Julio!" Stefano's voice came from what sounded like midway up the stairs. "Stop! Do not do it. No more killing," he begged, waving his arms and breathing hard, pausing at the head of the stairs.

Julio said nothing but swung his armed hand around. A gunshot rang out, and Stefano collapsed into Douglas, who was three steps behind him.

"Oh my God," screamed Douglas. "You shot him. You shot him!"

As Julio's extended arm began in its arc back toward my mother, I fired. Within a nanosecond of reasoning, I changed my mind. I didn't shoot to kill. But Lady Blue got him where I intended, the right thigh.

With a look of surprise and pain, Julio dropped down, wrapping himself around his bleeding leg. I ran forward, revolver to his head, and snatched the pistol out of his limp hand. I shoved it into one of my many pockets. Boxes toppled over, followed by scuffling, grunting, and the pffffft of an aerosol spray. I knew Gurn was subduing the two other men, but I never faltered my focus on either Julio or on the revolver pointed at his head.

"You okay over there, Gurn?" I hollered after a moment of silence.

"Under control. I'm just tying these guys' hands together with their own belts."

"Mom," I said, without looking at her. "Are you okay?"

"Yes, yes," she said, coming to my side. "Virginia?"

"I'm fine. I'm fine," Tex replied. "We'd better call an ambulance, though, for these others."

I temporarily took my eyes off the moaning Julio and glanced over to a silent Stefano, chest covered with blood, cradled in Douglas's arms. "Mom, find the phone in one of my pockets and call nine-one-one. I can't remember now which one it's in."

She looked at me and gestured with her bound hands. "That would be difficult, Liana."

"Here, then," I said, putting Lady Blue in her bound hands. "If he makes one move, Mom, shoot him right between the eyes."

"Let's not sink to *clichés*, Liana," she said. "I can handle him." Her voice was calm, but blanched fingers stood out against the dark steel of the weapon.

Tex crossed to the desk, grabbed a pair of scissors, and brought them over to me, waiting until I found the phone. "Cut this damned tape off me, will you?" she begged after I punched in three numbers. "Then I'll get your mother."

"Don't worry about me," Lila said over her shoulder, "I can get the tape off later. For now, I don't want to distract myself."

The tape came off Tex's wrist in one snip. She did the rest. I threw the scissors on the desk as 9-1-1 answered. While giving the police a quick rundown, I hurried to Douglas's side, watching his contorted face. I will never forget the expression, a combination of loss, sorrow, surprise, and helplessness. I had nothing to offer him, but help was on the way if it wasn't too late.

I touched his arm. Douglas looked up, saying to no one in particular, "None of this was his fault. He told me about his family on the way here. He couldn't break free. He tried and now he's been shot. He may die. I thought he was a good guy. How could I have been so wrong?" Douglas began to sob.

"He may still be a good guy, Douglas. We don't know everything yet," I said, crouching down and putting my arm around him.

"He's a traitor. That's why I shot him," shrieked Julio. "He never cared about any of us. Always pretending he was too good for the family, running away to Spain. I hope he's dead!"

"*Señor!* I would advise you to be quiet," Mom thundered, louder than I've ever heard her speak. Julio turned his attention to her and the revolver she was holding. "My hands are getting tired from holding this gun in such an awkward way."

A tearing sound made both Douglas and me look up. Tex ripped at her slip. "Here," she said, folding the material. "Try to staunch your friend's bleeding with this." Douglas took the fabric, unsure of what to do with it. "Press it down on the wound as hard as you can. Like this, see?" She took it back and demonstrated. "The ambulance should be here soon."

Meanwhile, Gurn crossed over to Mom. "I've got this now, Mrs. Alvarez," he said, reaching for the revolver.

"Who are you again?" Mom asked, before releasing her hold on the weapon.

"Gurn Hanson, Richard's friend."

"Oh," she said, handing the revolver over. "Well, Mr. Hanson, are you sure you have dealt with the other two?"

"Yes, ma'am. They're going to need a little attention from the medics, but they're down for the moment," he answered. "Your daughter carries mace."

We heard sirens in the distance. I got up and went to my mother. She was standing rigid, staring at nothing. I called her name, and she looked at me. I led her over to the desk, reached for the scissors, and cut the tape off her wrists as gently as I could. Free, she wrapped her arms around me and squeezed hard. I squeezed back.

"I don't know where you came from or how you got here, but I didn't think I would ever see you again," she murmured with a catch in her throat. I bit my lower lip until it bled.

Chapter Fourteen

Le Dénouement

Two minutes later, the police arrived along with the paramedics. The medics took Stefano and Julio away in separate ambulances once they learned Julio was the one who shot Stefano. Then all hell broke loose. Everyone who could talk started running off at the mouth at the same time.

The two nameless men were pointing to us and jabbering away in Spanish. Douglas was going from cop to cop, begging to be allowed to go to Stefano. Tex, looking peculiar in her ten-gallon hat and fancy snakeskin boots, insisted on speaking in a foreign language, "Texan." Gurn kept trying to take charge, as if we were part of a squadron. Mom attempted to run the proceedings like one of her board meetings. I was trying to persuade somebody, anybody, to get ahold of Frank Thompson. Bedlam.

Finally, the police had had it. They lined us up against a wall and told us to shut up, or we would be charged with resisting arrest on top of everything else. With two people shot, two found weapons, and breaking-and-entering charges, the cops were on the other side of cooperative. With more order, they called each of us over to the desk one at a time and started taking our statements.

It was in the middle of this that Frank barreled in wearing his uniform sans tie and socks. Richard had called Frank at home, getting him out of bed. Frank, in turn, phoned his men and told them to hold us there until he arrived. He didn't look happy.

He strutted up and down. "I see one or two of the usual suspects," he said, stopping in front of me, "plus some new additions. Who wants to go first?" We all started talking at once, drowned out by Douglas's wails. Frank held up his hands and turned to me.

"Okay, Miss Alvarez, let's hear it. When the phone started ringing in the middle of the night, I knew right inside here," he said, banging on his chest like it was a drum, "right here, the call would involve you."

"You told me to get involved," I said, "so here I am, involved."

"That did not include breaking and entering or shooting somebody," he shouted and, lowering his voice, turned to Mom. "I am shocked, Lila, to see you in on a B and E. You and Tex should know better than to—"

"Hold your horses, Frankie," Tex interrupted, stepping forward. "We were rustled right off the plane and dragged here, roped and hog-tied, sure as shooting. Tell him, Lila," she ordered. Gene Autry couldn't have said it better.

Before Mom could respond, I saw the look on Douglas's face. I took over.

"Frank, I know you have a lot of questions for us, but do you think we can continue this at the hospital? Douglas wants to be there to see what's going on with Stefano. Besides, we've already given statements. Can't you read them or something while we're at the hospital?"

Douglas jumped in, pleading, "Please, Chief Thompson, please. We won't give you any trouble. I just need to be near my friend."

Frank hesitated for a moment. "Very well. But everyone will have to go there in police cars and with my men, understood?" He turned to me. "You! Don't do or say anything without checking with me first."

"Right. I won't," I said. "But just one thing, Frank."

"What is the matter with you?" he bellowed. "Do you know how many charges may be leveled against you? I don't think you can count that high."

"Right, but hear me out. Within the next few hours, a truck is going to arrive here carrying millions of dollars worth of stolen Mexican artifacts. This all ties in with that murdered thief. I swear," I added. Frank's eyebrows waggled, but he was silent. "Listen, it would be a good idea for you to turn off these lights; make everything look normal, but have your men staked out here, waiting."

"Oh, it would, would it?" he said in a sarcastic tone.

"Yes," Mom answered before I could. "The truck should be here *quite* soon. It's about a thirty-six-hour drive straight through."

"I see," Frank said. I could tell Lila's words gave my story more validation. He turned back to me. "Well, you've been busy," he said.

"Only doing what you told…"

"Shut up."

"Right."

We were herded by gender into two separate police cars, Mom, Tex and I in the back seat of one, and Douglas and Gurn in the other. Frank trailed us in his own car, and we were at the Stanford Hospital within minutes.

During the ride, Mom tried to say something to me but was shushed by the younger officer in the front seat, a brown-eyed cop with bad acne. I looked at her, and she looked back at me, with exasperation in her eyes. I knew we both wanted to know from the other how each of us got to the gallery.

When we arrived at the hospital, Mom turned to him and said, "I would like to call my son and let him know we're all right. He must be frantic with worry about us."

Officer Bad Acne opened his mouth to reply when the automatic doors of the emergency room opened, and we heard, "Mom! Liana!"

Richard came running out, followed by Vicki, his wife. They embraced both of us at the same time, talking a mile a minute.

"Thank God! Frank phoned us and said you were on your way here. He promised you were all right." Richard turned from one to the other, with anxious eyes.

"We're all right," Mom said, shivering. "It's a little chilly, that's all." Vicki removed her cape and threw it around Lila's shoulders.

"Thank you, my dear," Mom said, wrapping the cape closer to her.

"Are you sure you're okay?" asked Vicki, looking both of us up and down. We nodded. "Thank God! When Richard finally told me what was going on, I broke up the party and sent everyone home."

"I didn't want to burden you with this, Vicki," he replied. "I knew this was a big shindig you were throwing and I didn't—"

"Oh, piffle," Vicki interrupted. She uses words like that all the time; it adds to her Alice in Wonderland charm. "As if anything was more important than the family's welfare!" she scolded with a smile. "I'm just grateful you're both all right."

I smiled back at one of the sweetest women on earth, knowing our family was lucky to have her as a recent addition.

"Neither of you have told Tío any of this, have you?" I said, looking from one to the other. "He doesn't need to be upset in the middle of the night."

"No, no! Vicki and I are the only ones who know," Richard said and then spied Tex on the other side of the police car. "Tex! You too? Is everybody here? Are you okay?"

She came around the car and nodded. "I'm fine, hon, but this has been one helluva trip back to the States. I'd rather be pulling up the rear of a roundup."

"Okay," Officer BA said. "That's enough talking. We'd better get inside like the chief said."

Obediently, we shut up and followed the officers into the emergency waiting room, where a brief chat with admitting told us the two injured men had been moved upstairs to the third-floor operating rooms. We were hustled into an elevator and found ourselves exiting into a waiting area set up like a large living room. Douglas and Gurn were already seated in two faded wingback chairs. They stood up when they saw us.

"We wondered what happened to you three," Gurn said and then spotted Richard. "Rich, good to see you." The two men shook hands.

Richard was about to introduce Gurn to Vicki when this obnoxious officer took over again. Obviously, he felt personally responsible for keeping us quiet.

"That's enough talking. The chief says you are to remain silent. You five" — he gestured to us — "sit over there." He pointed to a section of the room complete with a faded floral sofa, matching easy chair, and several end tables strewn with magazines several years old.

Tex, Mom, and I sat on the uncomfortable but large sofa, and Richard took the chair, Vicki on his lap. None of us was allowed to speak to each other for upward of an hour. Just as we had leafed through every magazine covering the Brad Pitt and

Jennifer Aniston divorce way back when, Frank came out of one of the inner doors. He squatted down in front of Douglas and whispered in his ear. Patting him reassuringly on the shoulder, Frank stood up, coming over to our small group.

"Glad to see you made it here, Richard, Victoria." He looked at all of us. "I was just telling Douglas the doctors are still operating on his friend, but so far, the good news is the bullet missed the lungs and a main artery. He's lost a lot of blood, though, so we still don't know if he's going to make it."

"What about Julio?" I asked. "He's going to be all right, isn't he?"

"He doesn't have life-threatening injuries, but his leg looks none too good."

I started to ask him for more details, when he was signaled by one of his officers coming down the hall.

"Excuse me," Frank said, leaving us and crossing over to him. We watched him talk with the man, nodding repeatedly. Then he returned.

"A dark blue, 1994 box truck with Mexican license plates drove into the back alley about twenty minutes ago. When my men approached the driver and his companion, they bolted. They caught one of them about a block away." He turned to Richard. "That youngster you sent me the picture of inside the cave. The other one got away for the moment," he said. "When my men took the keys and unlocked the back doors of the chassis, they found dozens of what look like pre-Columbian figurines, all different sizes and types."

"I knew they were on their way here, and by the way, Frank, they're Toltec figurines, not pre-Columbian. You knew they were coming, too, Mom, didn't you?" I said, turning to her.

"Not really." Mom smiled at me. "But *you* believed it, and that was good enough for me."

"Well, you were right," Frank said. "I'm told the truck careened into the alleyway at about sixty miles an hour and ran into the trash cans at the end. After they fled, my men found a handwritten manifest list of everything that was in the back of the truck. Every piece was declared a replica by a customs agent."

"But they're the real thing," I insisted.

"Francis," said Lila, who always calls Frank by his given name. "By Julio's own *admission*, his family has a network of people in very high places, including the customs department at the Mexican border. Dr. Lopez, the head curator at the Museo de Antropologio, has suspected it for months but had no proof."

"I don't think that will be a problem now. We've got the cache and a man's name on all the documents of entry. We'll soon know whether or not they're genuine."

Richard chimed in. "Mira McFadden has given me a list of expert appraisers in the Bay Area, if that helps."

"Thanks. I'll keep that in mind. My men say everything was packed in such a hurry that some of the pieces are wrapped in towels and clothing. Nothing broken, so far."

"Well, hurray for the Mexican government," Tex said, stepping forward. "But what about my boy, Frank? Is there enough evidence to free him?"

"Not yet," Frank said, shaking his head. "So far, we don't have anything linking the suspected illegal contraband from Mexico to the murder of the burglar here in Palo Alto." He looked over in Douglas's direction. "That's another reason I'm hoping this Stefano makes it. Maybe he'll talk and clear Carlos."

"What about Julio?" I asked. "Has he said anything?"

Frank shook his head. "Nothing. He won't say a word. Of course, we've got those two thugs from the gallery and the boy from the truck. Maybe they'll open up." He turned back to Tex. "It's now a waiting game."

She nodded and put a shaking hand to her cheek. "Thanks, Frankie. I know you're doing your best," she added and, with a wan smile, sat down in one of the chairs. Mom followed her, taking Tex's hand from her face and holding it.

"Regarding you, young lady," Frank said to me, "we've got enough statements saying you shot that man in self-defense. We're going to let the B-and-E charge slide, under the circumstances. We'll be keeping your weapon for a few days, plus your PI license, but other than that, I don't see any lasting problems for you. Actually, for any of you," he said louder, drawing Douglas and Gurn into his frame of reference. The two men got up and walked over to us. "I've vouched for Liana, Tex, Lila, and you, Douglas. All of you are released into your own recognizance under the proviso you appear at the police station by ten o'clock tomorrow morning for further questioning.

"As for you, Gurn," he said, turning to the sandy-haired man. "Not only does Richard vouch for you, but I've heard some good things about you from Colonel Packard in DC, when I spoke with him a few minutes ago. I understand that at one time you were of some use to him on a project."

"You've been a busy man, Chief," Gurn said, extending his hand. "But I do appreciate being vindicated."

Frank shook hands with Gurn, then came over to me, saying in my ear, "You could do worse than this one, Lee. I think he's a keeper."

I was so stunned by his words, I couldn't think of a thing to say. I wandered over to a chair on the other side of the room. Mom came to my side, saying, "Liana, we're free to go. Aren't you coming? It's nearly four in the morning."

"Thanks, Mom, but I'll stay a little while with Douglas. I don't want him to be alone. My car's over on University, anyway. I've got to get it before seven. That's when they start ticketing. I'm sure one of the officers will give me a ride back there."

She smiled, touched me on the cheek, and went back to Tex, Richard, and Vicki. They gathered their things, and somewhere in the distance, I heard Richard say he would drive everyone home. Waving to me, my family and Tex left.

My intent was to go to Douglas's side, but I was beyond exhausted. I found myself leaning my head back on the wall and closing my eyes. I heard someone sit down beside me, and I looked toward the sound. Gurn leaned into me. He wasn't smiling. I knew he had something serious on his mind.

I sat erect, evaluating what I knew of this man. Not many would risk their lives for comparative strangers, and yet that's exactly what he'd done. He'd followed me from one country to another, trying to protect me. In the gallery, he'd been right there. I had trusted him completely with my life and the lives of people I loved.

"So what happened back there?" Gurn asked. "Why didn't you shoot to kill? That's what anybody else would have done."

I looked down at the hands in my lap, shaking my head. "I don't know. I couldn't do it. Besides, it was just as easy to shoot him in the leg. Easier." Why was I defending myself to this guy? And yet I felt I had to. I became silent.

He grunted and was also silent. After a minute or two he asked, "You ever shoot anybody, Lee?"

I shook myself and rubbed my forehead, suddenly aggravated, suddenly scared. "That's not what I do, fer cryin' out loud. I'm an intellectual-property operative. I wear designer clothes and high heels. I don't deal with life-and-death situations. If the first bullet hadn't brought him down, the next one would have been to the heart or head. I do know that." I faltered, feeling naked, and somehow lacking.

"You're lucky it went down the way it went down. He could have kept on going, even with the bullet in his leg, and taken your mother out before you could do anything about it."

I took in a sharp breath but said nothing. He patted me on the knee and stood up looking down at me gaping up at him.

"Think about what I've said if you're ever in a similar situation. You broke every rule when you played it that way even though it turned out all right. Remember that." Then he smiled at me, eyes and all.

Gurn drifted back to Douglas, said his goodbyes, and left me sitting there. A few minutes later, I hauled myself up and went over to Douglas. We were the only ones remaining in the waiting room. I sat down, grabbing at his hand. He clutched mine, and neither of us would let go. We fell asleep leaning against one another. We were awakened by the whooshing sound of the door opening and saw a doctor dressed in blue standing in the doorway. We both stood up, waiting for what he was going to say.

"One of you the significant other of the man we just operated on?" He looked from me to Douglas and back again. He wasn't sure which one of us he should be addressing.

"Are you talking about the man called Stefano?" I clarified. "The one with the bullet in his chest?"

Now thinking I was the significant other, he turned to me and said, "It was touch and go for a while, but he's going to be all right." He smiled, and the fatigue dropped from his face like magic. "He lost a lot of blood, but we got everything fixed up. He's going to be okay."

"Oh, thank God," Douglas said, covering his face with his hands. I grabbed him, helping him to remain standing. Douglas's reaction made the doctor rethink which one of us he should be talking to.

"You can see him when he gets out of recovery," the doctor said to Douglas. "But that won't be for a couple of hours. Why don't you go home and get some sleep?"

"I'm not going anywhere," Douglas declared. "Maybe some coffee from the cafeteria. Anybody else want coffee?"

"Not for me, Douglas," I said, turning to the doctor. "What about the other man? How is he doing?"

Frank appeared from nowhere and came to my side, touching my elbow with his hand. The doctor opened his mouth to answer, but Frank spoke first.

"Let's go get your car, Lee. I'll tell you on the way," he said, ushering me into the elevator. We were followed by a relieved and glowing Douglas on his way to the basement cafeteria. The ride in the elevator was silent. We got off at the ground floor, waved goodbye to Douglas, and he continued on to the basement.

Frank and I didn't speak even as we went out the hospital doors and walked through the parking lot. Arriving at his car, he went to the passenger's side and opened the door for me, a first. My heart was racing because I knew whatever Frank had to say it wasn't going to be good. I got in and waited for him to get into the driver's seat.

Starting up the car, he looked both ways and pulled out. "Lee, they had to amputate the leg. The bone was damaged beyond repair."

I pressed the fingers of both hands against my mouth to keep from crying out. I fought to keep sobs from replacing my labored breathing.

Frank glanced over at me, concern written all over his face. "You want to know how I look at it, Lee?" Frank asked, pulling out into the light traffic of El Camino Real. "You were facing down a killer. At any moment, he was going to shoot your mother and Tex. He'd just shot his own cousin. That's after murdering three other people that we know about. I think he's damned lucky to be alive. That's what I think."

I sucked in breath before finding my voice. "He lost his leg because of me."

"You could look at it that way. Here's another. If anybody else had been in your shoes, like me, he'd be dead." Frank pulled over to the side of the road and turned off the engine. He leaned against the side of his door with his right arm over the top of the seat, looking over at me.

"Liana, you are the child of my best friend, a man whose loss I will mourn until the day I die. Don't you think I know what you're going through? What you are facing now is the main reason I never wanted you to be a PI and fought you every step of the way. I knew that in your line of work, you'd have to carry a gun, and someday you might have to use it on somebody. Someday you might have to maim or kill. Well, that day is here.

"I've had to accept the fact this is what you do, what you're good at doing, so I guess you'll have to accept it too. You want a confession?" he asked, studying a speck of something on the steering wheel. "Sometimes after a really rough day, I get home, and I don't even want to talk to Abby. I take the longest shower I can take, hoping it will wash some of it away, all the while knowing the next day, I'm going right back out there again. Understand?"

I nodded and leaned against the car door. "I do understand, Frank. I do. I just haven't made peace with it yet."

"Well, you work on that," he said. "When you make peace with it, you get back to me, and tell me how you did it." He looked over at me and smiled, starting the car again.

I threw my head back into the neck rest and tried not to think about the moral dilemmas that had forced their way into my life. Besides, there were questions buzzing around in my mind. How did Julio get hold of Mom and Tex, for one thing? I asked Frank and got an earful.

Julio had recognized me in San Miguel from the Christmas photo he saw at Douglas's apartment, when he helped Stefano move in. He panicked, thinking I had followed him to Mexico, where he had gone to "handle" the situation with Eduardo and Eva. Seeing me, he ran into a nearby store, owned by another one of his blasted cousins, hoping to get away. Then he'd turned the tables, trailing Tex and me through the streets. When I took off with Gurn, he didn't have time to get to his car, so he stuck with Tex, hoping she would lead him to me. The bastard followed Tex all the way to Mexico City where she picked up Lila from the museo and then to the airport. His goal was to shut up anyone who could do any more damage to him and his family. He almost succeeded.

We stopped at a red light, and Frank looked over at me. "You know why he took your mother and Tex to the gallery?" I shook my head. "His wife, kids, and parents were at his Bay Area home. He told Lila and Tex he didn't want to kill them around his family. He needed some place quiet, like the gallery. Nice guy, huh?"

"Not so very," I replied, feeling my face flush. "Turn around and let me go back and shoot his other leg," I joked and then was sorry I'd said it. "That's not funny. That's sick," I said, hitting my forehead with my fist. "When I'm tired, I'm tasteless or I have no taste. Which is it?"

"Probably both." He laughed and so did I. "Actually, you become more macabre than usual, but your father was like that."

We arrived at my parked car and he pulled alongside it, putting his own car in neutral. "Remember to show up at the station around ten. I'll call you if anything breaks before then. I'm hoping one of the men in custody will talk soon."

"Promise?"

"I said I would, didn't I?" he growled and then winked at me. "When I get tired, I get cranky."

I laughed and looked at my watch. It was close to seven. Douglas and I must have been asleep for a couple of hours. I don't think Frank had closed his eyes since he was awakened around midnight, and here he was going off to the station with a full day's work ahead of him.

"Frank, thanks," I said, opening the door, getting out. "Thanks for everything."

"Sure." He smiled at me, open and easy. "Today will be a better day. You'll see."

"If it isn't, that's just part of the job."

"Just part of the job," he echoed. I shut the door and watched my father's best friend drive off into the rising sun. A good guy if ever there was one.

I was in my driveway within fifteen minutes and would have driven by the main house if I hadn't seen nearly every light in the joint ablaze. I stopped the car midway down the drive and got out. Banging on the back door, I entered the mudroom and crossed into the kitchen. Lack of sleep, and the knowledge of how close I'd come to losing Tex and my mother, heightened each of the five senses within me.

I paused in the doorway as if for the first time, glancing around the twenty-by-thirty room. It still wore the original clapboard walls and cabinet doors from when the house was built in the '20s. The kitchen had been recently painted crocus yellow, Mom's favorite color, with green and white accents. Even though the appliances were modern stainless steel, the kitchen had an ageless, Old World feeling about it.

Mom and Tío hadn't heard me come in. I stood and watched them with their backs to me fussing over platters piled high with food. I listened to the chorizo frying in the pan, the ticking of the wall clock, Tío humming, and the clicking of my mother's heels on the terracotta tiles. Each sound filled me with an overwhelming sense of relief and love. This was what it was like when fate gave you another chance to be alive.

I cleared my throat.

"Liana!" Mom said, wheeling around, holding on to a steaming platter of 'Tío's sweet breakfast tamales. "We were *hoping* you'd make it back in time for breakfast."

"*Mija*," said Tío, putting down his spatula. He left the heavenly smelling chorizo on the stove to wrap me in one of his famous bear hugs. "*Estas bien?*"

"*Bien.* Yes, I'm fine," I said, hugging him back. "What a night. Mom can tell you."

"She has been doing that," Tío said, going back to the stove to tend to the chorizo. "You must rest today," he said, pointing the spatula at me. "You have been on the whirlwind."

"Come into the dining room," Mom said, standing at the swinging door before heading in herself. "Everyone's inside: Richard, Victoria, Mira, Virginia, and even that sweet Robby Weinblatt," she said. "He told me that is his real name, not Robert, as I'd started calling him. How you could *ever* refer to him as a bad-natured, evil young man, I will never know. He did what he did for his mother."

"I know, Mom." I grinned. "It's really Leonard who turned out to be the lowlife scumbag," I said, grabbing a plate of scrambled eggs, tortillas, and a bowl of homemade salsa. Mom paused in the doorway about to call me on my language when I jumped in: "I know. Watch my mouth. Will do."

I pushed her through the door and followed her into the dining room. I had just set the plates down on the table, listening to greetings from everyone, when my cell phone rang.

A hush fell over the room, and everyone looked at me, stopping whatever they were doing. We all knew, whether it was instinctively or due to the early hour, that this was an important call.

"Hello?" I said and listened. "Okay, Frank. I'm with you. Go on." Everyone paid attention to the one-way conversation, not moving, not making a sound. I responded to Frank with clipped phrases in between long pauses of listening. "Yes. Yes. For sure? He did? They will? When? Tomorrow? I see. Thanks, Frank. I'll tell everyone. Oh, Frank," I said, suddenly remembering. "Could you or one of your men notify Chief Miguel Ortiz of the San Miguel Police Department that he's wrapped everything up, and he should put in for that promotion? Great. I appreciate it."

I hung up and turned to Mira and Tex, sitting next to one another, gripping each other's hands. "One of the two men in custody admitted he overheard the robber trying to extort money from Carlos for the return of the statue and phoned his boss, Julio. Julio stole the knife from Douglas's kitchen and used it on the thief right before Carlos arrived at the garage."

"Does this mean it's over?" asked Mira.

"My son will go free?" Tex asked.

"It's all over but the shouting," I said. "Frank says once the paperwork is done, Julio will be officially charged, and Carlos will be released. He's phoning Mr. Talbot now. Maybe Carlos will be free as early as tomorrow. For sure the next day." There was a moment of silence. Then a whoop went up from everyone around the table, including Lila.

"I don't know what's going on," said Robby, looking around, "but it's a good thing. Right?"

"It is, *joven*," laughed Tio, handing him a plate filled with food. "A very good thing. Now eat something. You look like a plucked chicken. We have to fatten you up before we send you back to your mama."

Chapter Fifteen

Lives Intertwined

The full-length mirror in the ladies' room at Allied Arts reflected back the same hideous figure I'd seen at home. Even Tugger had hidden under the bed when he heard me swish by in my green taffeta meringue. The one I felt the sorriest for out of all of us was Jennifer. At five foot one, and a full-figured gal, she got stuck with the Orange Julius job that made her look like something out of the Macy's Thanksgiving Day parade. She was talking a witness-protection program.

An hour earlier, the harp and oboe had begun to play, marking the start of the procession. Four bridesmaids and I had rustled down the aisle together sounding like a runaway helicopter trapped inside a covered bridge. We'd even drowned out the music. It was the noisiest fifty-foot trek of my life. We arrived to stand beside a speechless preacher and a giggling groom and best man. The music petered out, and our gowns went into an enforced silence.

Fortunately, the organist began to play "Here Comes the Bride." The congregation sobered, stood, and watched the most beautiful bride I've ever seen in my life glide silently down the aisle, toward the man she loved.

Reminiscent of a classical Greek dress, the gown was in the palest of ivories. Sheer, silk organza floated over a bias-cut slip, plain and unadorned, save for a long cord of seed pearls. The cord journeyed from under her bust, crisscrossing in the front and back, then wrapped around her slender waist in a girdle effect. As the bride walked holding a small bouquet of gardenias, red-gold curls peeked out from under a diaphanous veil that billowed behind her, catching rays of sun flooding in through stained glass windows. The veil was held in place by a crown cluster of seed pearls, her only form of jewelry. Mira's look was luminous, otherworldly, and breathtaking.

Those of us who knew her well held our breaths and wondered if she was going make it to the altar without some sort of ensuing disaster. Luckily, that day Mira was perfection in every way and steady on her feet.

The reception was now in full swing, and I felt I could relax a little. Everything was going as planned. The bride and groom had danced their first dance; the groom's mother had officially handed over the deed to the four-thousand-acre rancho, and the mariachi band, much to my mother's and Victoria's joy, had asked Richard to play a solo on his guitar, mesmerizing us with his musical talent. All was right with the world.

If only I didn't have to leave the ladies' room and go back out there in this getup, I thought, glancing in the mirror again. I let out a deep sigh, asked myself how Barbara Stanwyck would handle herself in my place, opened the door, and ran into my mother.

"Ah, here you are. Did you know Mr. Hanson has been looking for you?"

"Crap. Sorry, Mom," I said, looking at the expression on her face. "Really. I'll try to be better about my language. Honest."

"Thank you, Liana. I find it *most* disconcerting."

I wanted to say I found it most disconcerting to have someone around who talks straight out of Jane Austen's *Pride and Prejudice* but let it go.

"You seem to be hiding, dear. I would have thought you would want to mingle among the guests after all you've done to make this event happen."

"Yeah, well. I'm sort of keeping a low profile or trying to."

"You can't avoid Mr. Hanson forever."

I nodded, thinking frantically of how to change the subject. "So, Mom, heard from Robby Weinblatt yet? Or Leonard Fogel? Take your pick." I pulled her over to the side of the door, letting two women pass on their way into the ladies' room.

"Funny you should ask. Mateo and I got a letter just today from Robby. Such a sweet boy to send a handwritten letter in this day and age. You can tell he's been brought up well."

"Oh yes," I said, thinking she was conveniently forgetting the treachery and larceny part of the equation.

Mom went on. "It seems his mother has finally gotten a visit from Leonard after all these years, and it went quite well. Leonard's going to start contributing money to the household on a regular basis. Isn't that lovely?"

I nodded. In truth, I had received a letter myself the day before yesterday outlining the same things. Robby had said he was going to write Tío and Mom as well, and I had thought to use it to get off the subject of Gurn Hanson.

"Robby's going to go back to school. He wants to be a detective," I laughed. "Can you imagine?"

"How did you know that, dear?"

"Huh?"

"How did you know that Robby wanted to go back to school? He wrote it in the letter, but I hadn't had a chance to mention it yet."

"Oh, I think I heard it somewhere," I answered vaguely. "Mom, you're right. I should mingle with the other guests, just like you said. I'll go do that now. How do I look?" I saw the expression on her face. "Oh, never mind."

"Try not to *think* about it, Liana, and hold your head up high, *regardless*," she said as I scurried down the hall.

Going back into the main banquet room, I could see everyone was having a great time. I waved to Mr. Talbot, who was doing a very classy version of the calypso with Mrs. Talbot, and searched for Douglas. I found him sitting alone and took the opportunity to plop myself down by his side. He'd heard the sounds of me coming over the trumpets of the band and turned to me, smiling. That's the beauty of taffeta: you never have to announce your arrival.

"Lee," he said, resting an arm on my shoulder. "There you are. I've been waiting for you to have some free time to talk to me. Tell me," he said with a straight face. "Does the manager of the Orange Bowl parade know you're here? He's going to be pretty upset when he finds one of his floats missing."

"Oh, hush up," I answered. I looked down at myself and watched the overskirt settling down around me much like a slow-leaking balloon. "Well, when this shindig is over, I can burn the dress in effigy for every bridesmaid who's had to wear something like this. I suspect the other bridesmaids will join me. I see big bonfires in our future." We both laughed. "You know it's not so much the color—"

"Yes it is," he interrupted.

"I think it's really the volume," I continued.

"It's both, darling. You need to face it. Be brave. Be strong. I've seen more sedate costumes in a drag queen show."

When it comes to quips, I can never top Douglas, so I gave up. I turned to him, studying his face. Between the wedding and dealing with every level of bureaucracy known to man on both sides of the border, we hadn't had much of a chance to converse since the night at the hospital.

"How are you doing? How's Stefano? Care to talk about it?" I asked.

His smile wavered a little before he said, "He's being released from rehab next week."

"That's a good thing," I encouraged.

"Yes. There's been a little permanent nerve damage to the shoulder. With continued therapy, he should regain full use of his arm."

"Another good thing."

"He's managed to scrape together the bail—he wouldn't take any money from me—so he can come home until the trial."

"You're trying to work things out with him?"

"I think so. We'll have to see how it goes," he said, looking down for the moment. "Stefano didn't know about a lot of it, being in Europe most of the time. I mean, of course, he knew about the cave and the antiquities from when he was a child, but he always tried to stay on the fringes of it. He looked the other way, I guess. He said he came back from Spain hoping things had changed or the stash had been played out. He thought he was going to run the gallery legit." Douglas stopped for a moment, staring out, deep in his own thoughts. Turning back to me, he said, "It's funny the things we tell ourselves just so we can get through the day, isn't it?"

I nodded, and we sat in silence for another moment. The mariachi band was playing "Cielito Lindo" in the background and people were talking, dancing, and laughing. Douglas took a deep breath and went on. "To his credit, when you called me in Napa, and he heard you asking me if he had been with me all day, Stefano knew what had happened. You saw Julio in San Miguel and thought it was him.

"Then he confessed to me that Julio had seen your picture in the apartment several days before. He knew you were the one I'd given the necklace to. It had accidentally gotten into a box of replicas, and he wanted it back. When Julio recognized you on the street in San Miguel, he phoned Stefano, demanding to know everything about you. He was convinced you were out to destroy the family legacy."

"I guess I was, even though I hadn't put it together yet."

"The man had a real vendetta against you that Stefano says he couldn't talk him out of. Then he'd learned Julio killed their other cousin and his wife the day before, execution style, in Mexico. Stefano was terrified Julio would hurt you, so he insisted we go to the gallery and try to stop him. He knew Julio would be there."

"That would be Eduardo and Eva," I explained. "They were pilfering from the Mendez family."

"That's when he realized how far Julio would go. He was telling me this on the drive back from Napa, but I couldn't take in everything he was talking about, you know?" His eyes searched mine. "I was so blind, Lee. Like about the knife. When I was telling it to the police, the words coming out of my mouth sounded so thin. What an imbecile I was."

"No, no you weren't," I said, taking his hand. He looked at me, arching an eyebrow. "Well, maybe a little." We both laughed.

"I noticed the knife was missing the day after Stefano moved in, Lee. I had read the newspaper accounts of the murder in the Sunday *Chronicle*, but I didn't put it together."

"The police never released the information of it being a ceramic knife, Douglas. They just said a knife. They wanted to keep that bit to themselves."

"Ah! I see," he said. "I feel a little better. That Saturday, Julio had been helping us carry in and unload boxes. I remember he'd gotten a phone call right in the middle of everything and took off. That must have been when he took the knife, because later on that day Stefano and I noticed it missing. He phoned Julio, and Julio said he'd dinged it when he was putting things away in a nearby cabinet and threw it away. He offered to replace it. Stefano told him not to bother; we'd get another one. We hadn't gotten around to it yet." He rumpled his hair and let out a sound of exasperation. "Sounds stupid when I say it, doesn't it?"

"Not really," said Frank, who'd sneaked up on us. We both jumped and looked at him. "Mind if I join you?" He sat down beside me, looking quite elegant in his black suit, gray shirt, and gray-and-black, silk tie. I forget sometimes Frank was a clotheshorse in his younger days.

"Julio only had a matter of minutes to get to the meeting place and grabbed the first weapon he could find. At least, that's what we've pieced together."

"That's right," I agreed. "How could anyone possibly have suspected him? I sure wouldn't have."

Douglas took my hand and kissed it, saying, "You're so sweet to say that, Lee, and such a liar."

286

"Excuse me?" I said, drawing myself up to my full height in the chair. Frank laughed and took a sip of his champagne.

"You know and I know you'd have figured it out a lot sooner, if you had been in my place," Douglas said. "But that's you, generous and forgiving to the end. For the record, if it were me, I'd be so annoyed you hadn't put two and two together and had caused me all that trouble, darling."

"You didn't cause any trouble, darling," I said, imitating him. "You were an innocent victim whose only mistake was in believing in the person you loved. I understand Stefano's turning state's evidence in exchange for a lighter sentence. Over fifty people have been indicted so far, both here and in Mexico. Isn't that right, Frank?"

He nodded. "You know the kid in the cave, the one who came up in the truck? He was the son of the two people shot on the Garcia property."

I stared at him. Somehow, knowing I had taken a picture of the youth, and he had lost both his parents in such a way, made this seem all the more horrible. I could tell by Douglas's expression he felt the same.

Frank looked down at the half-filled glass in his hand and swirled the champagne around. "The kid didn't know Julio killed his parents until we told him. The only good part about it was that once he found out, he couldn't talk fast enough. He didn't know much, but he could certainly point us to the right people."

"That poor boy," said Douglas, shaking his head.

"Makes you not so sorry that bastard has to wear a prosthesis on his leg for the rest of his life. With him spending his life in jail, he won't be doing much walking, anyway."

Frank drank the last of his champagne.

"He denies the crushed diamond stud is his, Lee, but we've proven it is. We've got a dozen photos with him wearing one that now seems to be missing. And we found a bill of sale from ten years ago for the purchase of one blue-white diamond ear stud. Exact same description as the diamond at hand. He must have lost it in the struggle with the dead man. At least, that's what the prosecution will go with. And by the way, you shouldn't have held on to evidence like that. But thank you for helping to wrap up the case against him."

"You're welcome," I said. "In the beginning, I didn't know if it had anything to do with the murder or not. After all, I found it fairly far from the crime scene and after your men had been in the area."

"I've reprimanded the team who supposedly did a clean sweep. Oversights will happen. But they better not happen again."

I covered one of his hands with mine, gave him a broad smile, and said with mock sincerity, "That's all right, Frank. You've always got me as your backup."

"That's what I'm afraid of." Frank harrumphed, then turned to Douglas. "What's the latest on Stefano?"

"They're talking about eighteen months jail time, maybe less," said Douglas. "Then we're going to see where he and I are."

"Good. Maybe it will work out for you." Frank gave him a friendly pat on the shoulder and got up. "I've got to go and find Abby. They're playing a salsa. That's her favorite dance." He waved goodbye and was lost in the crowd.

"I thought I'd found my knight in shining armor," my friend said quietly after a moment.

"Don't give up hope, Douglas. Maybe he just needs a little polishing." I grabbed his arm and stood up, trying to shake the mood. "Let's forget about all of it and dance. I do a wicked salsa," I said, grinning at him.

We took to the floor and were making some great moves until a woman put her heel through one of the folds of my hem, nearly pulling me over. Secretly delighted, I flitted into the kitchen looking for the poultry shears I'd noticed earlier when I was checking on the caterers. Now that this ha-ha creation had been damaged, I figured it was open to all kinds of changes. I grabbed the scissors, went into a nearby restroom and locked the door.

I pulled the dress off over my head, stood it up in a corner, and squirmed out of the stiff crinoline petticoat. One brief glance at the small trash can under the sink convinced me to open the overhead window and shove the ghastly thing through a little at a time. I did. It fell noisily to the ground, and I could only hope it didn't take out a passing dog.

Armed with the shears and grim determination, I turned to the gown. I whacked at the overskirt near the waistband. Within seconds, it was relieved of its behemoth outer layer. Out the window that went, too, sounding like a flock of geese flapping over a waterway. Being environmentally conscious, I vowed to deal with the disposal of the ex-glad rags after the party. When no one was looking.

I put the dress back on, reached behind me, grabbed the hem of the underskirt, pulled it up and began to wrap it around my body. Finally, I tucked the tip end underneath the belt and voila! I had an almost passable knee-length sheath. I applied more hot-pink lipstick, hoping the color helped to equalize the greenish hue that currently lived upon my cheeks, and exited the bathroom. I dropped the shears on the kitchen table and reached out for the kitchen door. It swung open, and there stood Gurn and his lopsided smile. I should have held on to the scissors.

Rats, I thought. I'd been avoiding him since the night at the gallery, but he just wouldn't go away.

"Hey, Lee." He smiled, coming at me. "You've been avoiding me, haven't you?"

"I have not! What an ego," I said, taking on my mother's tone of condemnation. "I've been very busy."

How did he get an invitation, anyway, I wondered as I was backing up from him. I guess in a fit of goodwill, Mira, Carlos, and Tex felt it was the appropriate thing to do. After all, he was partially responsible for the happy ending, although I think I could have handled those two goons by myself, given the opportunity.

"I've left three messages for you during the past two weeks, at home and at your office, and you haven't returned a one." He grinned, putting his arm around my waist.

"Look," I said, extricating myself. "Between the American consulate, the Mexican consulate, the local authorities, the Mexican authorities, the customs departments of both countries, and all the grateful museums across the continent, I haven't had much time to do stuff like return calls."

"No?"

"No."

"What about today?"

"I'm the maid of honor and the wedding planner. I have things to do." I tried to pass him and go back into the reception area.

"Not anymore. It's done." He grabbed me by the hand and pulled at me. "Dance with me. Right here, right now. I promise not to spill anything on you."

"Stop that," I said, slapping at his hand. "Boy, you can be one obnoxious pain in the butt, you know that?"

"No I'm not, and you know it," he answered. "I think we could have something special, you and I, if you'd give it half a chance."

"Hold it right there," I said, raising my arm with the palm of my hand toward him. "I just got out of a relationship, and I'm not anxious to start another one."

"You got dumped, huh?" His eyes twinkled at me.

"I didn't get dumped," I sputtered. "Well, maybe a little... All right, I got dumped." He moved closer and put both arms around me, backing me into the wall. I continued blathering. "I'm very happy by myself. I don't want anybody in my life. I don't need anybody in my life. Just me, my work, and my cat." I could feel his lips brushing my forehead and then his warm breath on the side of my face. He leaned down and nibbled on my ear. "Oh, jeesh," I groaned.

"Say you'll go out with me. At least once, tonight, after the reception's over," he whispered.

"On one condition," I whispered back. He grunted ascent; I kept talking, and he nibbled away. "Tell me how you disabled the alarm at the gallery."

He stopped, drew back, and looked at me. "You're kidding." I shook my head. "You're not kidding?"

I leaned back against the wall. "That's it. That's the deal. Tell me how you did it, and I'll go out with you." Gurn started to laugh, hands on his hips, his head thrown back to the ceiling. "Well, I didn't think it was that funny," I said, crossing my arms and looking at him as severely as I could.

"Lee, I can't tell you that."

"What do you mean you can't—"

"Here's what I can tell you. It resembles a PalmPilot, only it uses a magnetic signal based on what the computerized sensors perceive to be the size and electrical output of the alarm. To simplify what it does, it's able to lock a system into place for several seconds so it becomes incapacitated."

"Incapacitated," I repeated.

"Exactly. During that time, you can get inside. Then the system resumes as if nothing has happened. You use it again when you want to get out."

"But the system doesn't send out a signal that it's been messed with?" I asked.

"No," he said, shaking his head. "It can't. It's just been frozen in time. Neat, huh?"

"Okay, this begs two questions."

"Only two?"

I ignored him. "One, how did you get hold of such a thing? And two, how come you had it with you?"

"The second question is easy to answer. I had been following you, and just in case I needed to get into some place with an alarm system, I brought it with me."

"Go on."

"The first question I can't answer. Sorry. National security and all that."

I was stunned. "I don't get this. You keep telling me you're an accountant."

"I am, but I'm also a lieutenant commander in the naval reserves. What I do when I'm there, I can't tell you." He leaned into me.

I pushed against his chest with both my hands as hard as I could and turned to the door. "I don't need someone like you in my life," I yelled. "It's complicated enough."

He grabbed my arm, spun me around, and kissed me. Warm, soft, fiery, and hard, all or nothing. *Oh jeesh*, I said to myself again, *I'm done for*. I kissed him back, damning myself the entire time.

When we broke free, I looked at him and said, "You'd better like cats."

"I love cats. Got one of my own."

I was pushing through the door to the main dining room when I heard a voice boom. "And there she is!" A spotlight flashed in my face, and I froze in my tracks, while every eye in the room turned toward me. Mira stood at the other end of the great room with the microphone in her hand. She continued speaking with a bright smile on her face. "I don't know how many of you are aware that this wedding wouldn't have taken place without our wonderful friend, Liana Alvarez."

Carlos jumped up, grabbed the mic from Mira and said, "Come on down here, Lee, so we can thank you properly!"

Feeling like I had just won a slot on *The Price is Right*, I looked around me and shook my head, slinking back inside the kitchen. Gurn grabbed at my waist and pushed me into the room in front of him. Then he came to the front of me, dragging me across the dance floor and toward the bride and groom's table, which was facing the assembled guests. On my way around to the back of the long table, we passed Warren McFadden, who looked me up and down with shocked eyes. I gave him one of those "I don't know what happened to my dress either" looks and joined the newly married, standing in between Mira and Carlos. Both put an arm around me. I felt like an Oreo cookie about to go into a glass of milk.

"Ladies and gentlemen," said Mira, taking back the mic from Carlos. "I don't think Liana Alvarez needs any introduction to most of you, but for those of you who don't know, Lee is the best friend a person could ever have. I owe my wedding and my entire future to her."

"Mine too," chimed in Carlos.

"Well, let's not be dramatic," I muttered, waving it all away and trying to escape. They held fast.

"And that's why, Lee, Carlos and I want to give you this," she finished and handed me a silver box tied with a silver-and-white bow.

"You didn't have to give me any —" I started to protest.

"Shush, Lee," Mira ordered. "Just open it."

I undid the ribbon and pulled off the top, sweeping aside white tissue paper. I lifted out a small, blue earthenware statue of a dog, about six inches tall, with an upturned tail and laughing face. Staring at it, I said, "This can't... Is this?"

"Yes, it is," said Mira.

"The statue that started the whole thing," added Carlos.

I looked from one to the other. "How can this be?" I asked.

"Oh, it can be," shouted Richard sitting to the other side of the standing Carlos.

"But how? If this is real..." I began.

"It is real," said Mira. "Very real, so be careful with it. It took us a lot of time and paperwork to get

295

the Mexican government to let us hand this to you, if only temporarily. It's the way all of us wanted to say thank you for the work you did, not just Carlos and me, but an appreciative Mexican nation."

"Thank you, I think," I said, confused. "You're letting me hold this, but you're not giving it to me?" I looked at both of them.

Carlos came forward laughing, and took it out of my hands, cautiously setting it on the table. "That's right. It's not ours to give," he said. "It has to go back. See those two guards over there?" He pointed to a couple of serious-looking men standing close by. I had taken them earlier to be watching over the wedding gifts.

"Those two men are here from the Museo de Antropologia to guard this little dog. *Señor* Manual Lopez, head curator of the museum, is watching out for it too. Take a bow, *señor*." A rotund man from one of the tables in the back stood up briefly and waved.

What's going on? I thought. It looked like everybody was in on it too. I saw Mom, Richard, and Tío grinning from ear to ear as if they, too, knew. "Is everybody in on this but me? What's the deal?" I asked, starting to laugh.

"The deal is," responded Carlos, "the Mexican government is allowing this artifact of the Toltec civilization to stay in this country, thanks to you. It will travel from museum to museum across the United States as a symbol of our two countries' friendship. Here is what Mira and I are really giving you. It's in fourteen-karat gold, so you'd better appreciate it," he pseudo-whispered, holding up a plaque.

The audience began to applaud, and Carlos turned to them, waiting for the applause to die down before saying, "I don't think many of you know this. Because of Lee, an international familial organization, systematically stealing centuries-old artifacts from Mexico and selling them, in the United States and abroad, to private collectors, has now been apprehended. Fortunately, through the record-keeping of this infamous family, the authorities have been able to initiate the return of the majority of these irreplaceable treasures to the Mexican people."

He held the plaque in the air, saying, "This plaque will travel with the statue wherever it goes. Let me read out loud the inscription that the president of Mexico himself has written." Carlos cleared his throat before going on: "'*This Toltec statue of a dog, created during the tenth century by a long-gone but mighty civilization, is on permanent exhibit to the people of the United States of America, courtesy of a grateful Mexican nation and in honor of Miss Liana Alvarez.*'"

Everyone started to applaud again, but Carlos held up his hands. He was on a roll. A natural orator, that guy.

"On a very personal note, if it hadn't been for Lee, I would have spent the rest of my life in jail, paying for a crime I did not commit. I will be grateful to her till the day I die."

Mira leaned into the mic, adding, "We both will."

297

I reached for the mic. "Thank you Mira, Carlos, all of you. I'm so taken aback, I don't know what to say." I nervously moved the shiny plaque back and forth in my hand. "Except, I didn't do this alone. I couldn't have. I had a lot of help. Not just friends." I gestured to Gurn, who winked at me. "But mostly, it couldn't have been done without my family. Richard Alvarez, my brother, who comes up with the most astonishing apparatuses to get you through any crisis you may run into in the field. And Tío Alvarez, who keeps our family centered and loved." I looked toward my uncle and said, "'They also serve who only stand and wait,' Tio. And to Lila Alvarez," I said, turning to my mother, who stared at me, her hand to her breast, "we like to think of Mom as being the brains behind DI, but she's also its heart. She's the one who makes everything go smoothly. Or as smoothly as things are going to go with me around." Everyone laughed, including Mom.

"And, of course, to Dad, Roberto Alvarez, who is with us in spirit every day of our lives. So I will accept this honor only if the last three words on the plaque can be changed. Instead of 'in honor of Miss Liana Alvarez,' it should read 'in honor of the Alvarez Family.'"

≈

Read on for the first
chapter of Book Three of
the
Alvarez Family Murder
Mysteries

Death Runs in the Family!

Death Runs in the Family

Book Three

In

The Alvarez Family

Murder Mystery Series

Heather Haven

Chapter One
Another Mrs. Papadopoulos?

I threw back the covers and staggered to my front door, commanded by the insistent ringing of the doorbell. Ordinarily, after the night I'd had, and it being eight o'clock in the morning, on a Sunday no less, I would have just let it ring; hoping whoever it was would go away or fall into a sinkhole. But this ringer wouldn't stop, and the bell sounded more and more like an air raid siren to my hung-over eardrums.

My name is Liana Alvarez. Everyone calls me Lee except my mother and the less said about that the better. My email reads Lee.Alvarez.PI@DI.com, but I don't always respond in a timely fashion, especially when I'm in the middle of a case. DI stands for Discretionary Inquiries, the family-owned investigative service, and everybody knows what a PI is. I'm thirty-four-years-old, five foot eight, 135 pounds on a good day, with thick, brown/black hair. The love of my life, the gorgeous Gurn Hanson, says my eyes are the color of twilight. At the moment, however, they mostly resembled a beady-eyed hippo's.

The previous night, Lila Hamilton-Alvarez, mother and CEO, fobbed off a last-minute job on me, one not so good for my California lifestyle. Due to our close relationship, my designer-clad mom knows she can do this. So, instead of being at home playing with my cat and sucking down a mango-orange-guava yogurt shake, I was imbibing huge amounts of Tequila Slammers. This slamming was in an effort to get the tipsy girlfriend of a software thief to reveal where he'd gotten to. Said girlfriend dished, but my liver will never be the same.

Me being about as hardboiled as a two-minute egg, the following morning found me sleep deprived, alcohol poisoned, and feeling enormously sorry for myself. But I still remembered to look out the peephole instead of throwing open the door because L.H. Alvarez did not raise a stupid child. Not seeing anyone, I leaned against the framework in a hangover-induced quandary. Was someone there or not?

But the ringing continued, so shrill and loud that it had to be an affirmative unless my front door's electrical system had gone wiggy. I squinted into the little round circle of glass again, strained my eyeball downward, and spied what looked like the back of a curly, platinum blonde, female head. I left the chain on when I opened the door, because my mother did not raise...never mind.

Facing away from me, the blonde female continued to lean into my doorbell for all she was worth, oblivious to my presence. A serious shrimp, she wore a pair of fire engine red spike heels and still didn't clear much over five foot two. Looking pretty harmless unless she came at me with one of those six-inch spikes, I undid the chain and opened the door.

"All right, all right. I'm here. Get off the bell."

Startled, red stilettos wheeled around and faced me. "Hi," she said in a voice with no bottom to it, reminiscent of Marilyn Monroe, but not nearly as sexy. "I was beginning to think you weren't here."

As self-confident as her body language had been earlier, she seemed to become unsure of herself, shy almost. Although how anyone could pull off shyness in that getup I'll never know. The killer heels were a perfect complement to the red satin miniskirt, scanter than a Dallas cheerleader's costume, and the plunging neckline of the yellow and green floral blouse emphasized cleavage aplenty. A thin, black polyester sweater, way too small, was buttoned haphazardly below her breasts. Clanking gewgaws hung from her ears, neck, wrists, and fingers. She looked like a walking display case of gaudy jewelry. Before me stood a young lady who could send any self-respecting fashionista screaming into the night.

"You're Lee, right?" she said in a barely audible voice.

"That's me," I croaked, and I tried to clear my throat, which didn't do much good. "And you are?"

"Why, I'm Kelli, with an 'i.'" The name was pronounced as if it should mean something to me.

She waited a beat, expectantly.

I was clueless.

"Kelli with an 'i'?" Although in my condition, it came out more like "Kawawaya?'"

"Yes, Kelli. With an 'i.'"

There was the damn pause again.

She stared at me, as if me not knowing whom she was made me too stupid to live. I stared back in complete agreement. I think I hiccuped.

"Nick's wife," she said, in a manner reserved for the slow of mind.

"Nick's wife?" I stuttered.

I only knew one Nick, and that was a Nick I'd divorced four years prior with joy in my heart and a gun in my hand. "When you say, 'Nick's wife,' you don't mean, Nick Papadopoulos, as in my Nick or rather my ex-Nick, by way of being my ex-husband, Nick? You're talking about someone else, right? Another Nick I can't quite place..."

My voice trailed off because she was nodding in the affirmative every time I said his name.

"You're Nick's wife?"

She nodded again just as Tugger, my adolescent orange-and-white cat, came out of the bedroom and trotted down the hallway followed by my boyfriend's gray and white Persian mix, Baba Ganoush, named for the eggplant dish. My boyfriend, Gurn, was in Washington DC, and I was cat sitting this darling, little green-eyed girl until his return.

Baba entered quietly, but Tugger caterwauled the entire time, obviously complaining about being awoken at such an ungodly hour of the morning. He sauntered over, sat down in front of me, stared up at this Kewpie doll of an intruder, and gave a long, wide mouthed yawn. My sentiments exactly.

Kelli looked down. "What a beautiful cat," she exclaimed, not seeing Baba who was hiding discreetly behind my legs. Then the girl/woman extended both arms out to Tugger.

Without further ado, my traitorous feline leapt into her open arms, snuggled in, and began to purr almost as loudly as he yowls. There was nothing left for me to do. I opened the door wider and stood aside.

"All rightie. You'd better come in, Kelli, and bring the cat with you. He's not allowed outside." I bent down and picked up Baba, who rewarded me with her own yawn.

"What's his name?"

"Rum Tum Tugger, but we call him Tugger. This one is Baba. She's a friend's cat."

"What a darling cat," she cooed, walking over the threshold and into my home. "And I just love your name, Tugger," she said, rubbing noses with my little guy.

"Go straight down the hallway and turn to the right. That's the kitchen."

"What an awesome place. Who would have thought such a hot apartment would be over a garage?" Kelli tottered down the hall chatting away, while I bent over to pick up the morning paper. Barely able to straighten up, I set Baba down, afraid I'd drop her. I needed coffee bad.

"And whose house is in front? Or should I say, mansion?"

"My mother and uncle live there. Back in the thirties, this apartment was for the chauffeur. I've done it over."

"Lucky you."

"Yup, lucky me."

With a throbbing head, I traipsed behind Kelli, my eyes riveted on her foot action in those heels. It was nothing short of remarkable. Even Baba seemed impressed.

"I like your kitchen." Continuing the review of my two-bedroom, one bath digs, she scrutinized the backsplash. "Those tiles French? I know they use a lot of yellow and blue in France. I read it once in a book."

I wasn't going to touch that statement with a ten-foot pole. "No, Talavera from Mexico. I hauled them back on one of my trips to Dolores Hidalgo."

"Neat," she murmured, now looking up at my ceiling. "What's that?" Kelli slowly spun in place studying the large inverse teacup-shaped dome set in the center of the terracotta ceiling.

"It's called a cupola."

"What's it for?"

"See the series of small glass windows at the top? Not only do you get extra light, but you can open them with this pole for fresh air." I pointed to an eight-foot pole languishing in a nearby corner, while I wondered which kitchen cabinet held the Aspirin.

"Cool." Kelli focused again on Tugger, rocking him back and forth in her arms and cooing in a bilious tone of voice.

With the *House and Garden* tour over, I slipped around her, threw the paper on the counter, and reached for the coffeepot with a not-too-steady hand. I poured water into it and counted out scoops, suddenly aware the cooing had changed to sobs.

I turned, scoop in hand, and saw Kelli crying into Tugger's lustrous fur, something I've been known to do myself. Tugger reached out and caressed her face with a soft paw, purring his head off. A true gentleman, my Tugger. Even Baba sat at Kelli's feet looking up, emerald eyes large with concern.

I clicked the coffeepot on and let it do its thing while I did mine.

"Sit down, Kelli, and tell me what's wrong." I put my arm around a shoulder and guided her to one of the cobalt blue chairs gathered around my kitchen table.

Kelli snuffled and wiped at her runny nose with the hand that wasn't wrapped around a cat. I slapped a paper napkin from the holder into said hand and chucked Tugger under the chin. He was a good boy.

Kelli blew her nose and started talking. I couldn't hear or understand a word.

"Kelli, you'll have to speak up and not just a little."

Whether she was embarrassed, or something else was on her mind, she started playing with Tugger's tail, something he can't stand, so I took her hand, shook it, and made her look up at me.

"What is it?"

Kelli snuffled again, and a large tear ran down a painted cheek. "He told me if I was in trouble, and he wasn't around, I was to come to you."

"Who told you that?"

"Nick."

"Nick said that?"

She nodded. I was shocked but tried not to show it. This was the ex-marine who started cheating on me soon after the honeymoon and who beat me up when I finally confronted him. He was the main reason I got a black belt in karate, to protect myself from his unwanted attentions before

and after the divorce. When I flattened him one day, he got the message and left me alone. But I still breathed a sigh of relief when I found out he'd moved to Las Vegas and married someone else, someone currently sitting in my kitchen blowing her nose into one of my paper napkins.

"So where is Nick?"

Her voice nearly gave out on this one. "I don't know." She cleared her throat and began to speak louder. "He's been missing for a week. That's why I'm here."

"Forgive me, Kelli. I'm not quite getting this." I smelled the coffee, got up, poured some into a mug, and took a good, scalding gulp before I turned back to her.

"Coffee?" I offered. She shook her head and wiped another tear away. "If he's missing in Las Vegas, why are you here in Palo Alto?" I started opening cabinet doors, searching for the errant bottle of Aspirin.

"Because last night I found this on the doorstep." She reached inside her blouse—I didn't think anything else could fit in there—and pulled out a crumpled envelope. "I got into the car and drove most of the night to get here. I've been waiting in your driveway since around five thirty this morning." She thrust the packet at me.

I stopped my search for Aspirin, sat down, took the small, square shaped envelope and looked inside. A man's gold wedding ring looked back at me. My PI mind kicked in, albeit if only on one - and-a-half cylinders.

"Is this Nick's?"

She nodded, pursing her lips together.

"Was he wearing it the last time you saw him?"

She nodded again.

"Was there anything else inside the envelope?"

This time she shook her head. I could see this was going to be more or less a one-sided conversation.

"Have you been to the police?"

She looked at me as if I'd suggested we eat the cat she cuddled in her arms.

"I can't go to the cops." This time her voice was loud and clear.

"Why not? It's what they're there for, among other things. We pay them to find missing people. I don't mean to sound like a poster boy, but I am a big believer in using natural resources."

"You don't understand." Her voice became small and childlike again.

"Then enlighten me."

"Nick has been... we've been... there have been some money problems ever since he had to close the office..." She stopped speaking, sobbed, and buried her head again in Tugger. Looking a little soggy and cramped, my boy had apparently had enough and pushed free of her grasp. He hopped down from her lap and sauntered off toward the bedroom with a careless flip of his long, graceful tail. Baba followed, giving a toss of her luxuriant tail for good measure.

Maybe if I'd had a tail, I'd have done the same thing. But I didn't, so I stayed put.

In that instant, I reevaluated Kelli's persona. Once you got past a face looking like it had been drawn upon by the more colorful contents of a crayon box, she was quite pretty, with a gorgeous kind of coloring that takes your breath away. I'd put her hair down to Clairol's finest but knew then it was a natural pale blonde. Her eyes, huge and round, were the bluest blue I've seen outside a Paul Newman movie, even when red-rimmed and surrounded by running black mascara. Barely out of her teens, there was a residual sweetness to her that bad taste had yet to tarnish.

Still, she was absolutely everything my classy, conservative, and well-bred mother would find appalling. Lila Hamilton-Alvarez's idea of bad taste hovers around the lines of an art gallery showcasing Andy Warhol's work. I just had to get Mom and Kelli together one of these days. Then stand back and watch.

"So tell me about Nick," I said, getting up for a second cup of coffee. "He's a real estate agent or something?" I noticed I could move my eyebrows again. Things were looking up.

"He's what they call a broker. And he was good. We had lots of money, even after the recession. He bought me a new Mercedes convertible for my birthday. Yellow. But something happened, and he had to close the office. And oh, I don't know, everything fell apart about six weeks ago."

"How so?" I said, resuming my search for Aspirin.

"Bills were piling up. We got behind in our mortgage payments. We had to sell my car." She shook her head. "He wouldn't let me go back to work, either. I offered, but Nick said no."

"What type of work did you do?" Bingo! I found the Aspirin bottle hiding behind the sugar.

"I was a blackjack dealer at the Royal Flush Casino. That's how I met Nick." A fleeting smile crossed her lips for the first time, I guess at the memory.

"You don't look old enough." I crammed three pills in my mouth, took a slug of coffee, and sat back down.

"I'm twenty-two. I'll be twenty-three in a couple of months." I realized I was the same age when I married Nick. Glad to see I was part of a pattern here.

"Then he went to work for a bank as a courier or something, I could never figure out what, but when I asked him…"

Her voice faded out. Maybe she was talking, maybe she wasn't. I couldn't tell. I waited. She reached out a hand and touched one of mine. Still looking down at the floor, she began to pour her heart out, loud and clear.

"Nick told me you were the best thing that ever happened to him."

I blanched. *What kind of man makes a statement like that to a current wife about his ex?*

"Nick said if anything happened to him, I was to come to you. He said you're the only person in the world he trusts."

I froze. *What the hell is the matter with the man?*

"He also said you were the most beautiful woman he'd ever seen."

Okay, it's official. The man's a bozo.

She looked up at me with appraisal in her eyes. "I guess I can see why he'd think that," she said, her baby voice riddled with doubt.

"Now wait a minute." I checked out my reflection in the stainless steel toaster and ran fast fingers through hair looking like it had been combed with an eggbeater. "I usually look a little better," I said, with a feckless laugh that sounded like the death rattle of a soot-clogged moped. "I've had a tough night. I was up until two thirty knocking back margaritas and tequila shooters with the girlfriend of a missing-in-action software designer, hoping to get her to tell me where the M.I.A. was."

Kelli nodded a little too enthusiastically, as if she were the unwilling caretaker of the town drunk.

"And she must have had a hollow leg," I went on, "or me a hollow head, because at last count, four shooters and three margaritas passed her lips and consequently mine before she uttered the magic words, 'Bruce, South Dakota,' and slid under the table."

Out came another feeble laugh. This one sounded like the sucking noise made by a water buffalo's leg when he pulls it out of a mud hole.

"You see?"

She nodded sagely. "You like to drink."

"No, no! Last night's bout was business. I had to get this 3D program, this little computer gizmo back, understand? It was vital to my client."

"Is it like the 3D they do in the movies, like in the cartoons and stuff?"

She was finally with me. "Yes! But this 3D is on a computer. And being worth about fifteen mil, the client wanted it back *pronto*."

Kelli inhaled a sharp breath at the amount. Money she understood.

"But let's move on," I said, feeling somewhat vindicated, even though I needed to work on my laugh. "What exactly do you want from me?"

"I want you to find Nick."

I must have rolled my eyes or something because she grabbed at my hand this time. "Please, Lee. He once said you were the nicest, smartest person he ever knew."

I'll kill him.

Kelli let go of my hand and looked down at short, black fingernails. Hers, not mine. I don't do nail polish. "Please help me. I don't have anybody but Nick. My family disowned me after...after... Then I moved to Las Vegas, but I don't have any friends, not real friends. None that could or would help." She put those black fingernailed hands up to her face and started blubbering into them.

"Did you two have a fight or words?" She shook her head. "Did he seem unhappy or preoccupied about something?" Another shake.

"He has a cell, doesn't he?" She nodded but continued to blubber. "What happens when you call it?"

A muffled voice spoke through her fingers. "Nothing, it goes into voice mail. I must have left fifty messages, and he's never called back."

"What about friends? Has he been in contact with any?" She gave her head another sad shake. "Credit cards? Have any been used during the time he's been gone?"

"The only one not maxed out is in the bureau drawer. I got the statement yesterday, and there aren't any new charges. None of his clothes are missing, and he didn't take the car. I've got it; it's right outside. But he's got to be hiding somewhere."

"Why do you say that?"

She shrunk into herself. "Oh, maybe he isn't. Maybe he's..." She broke off and suddenly leaned into me with such force, I spilled half my coffee in my lap. "I've been reading the papers looking for unclaimed dead bodies. I even called the morgue once."

"Oh, I'm sure he's not dead." *Only the good die young, sweetie.*

I set the dripping cup down on the table and reached for several paper napkins to blot up the mess.

"And I've been calling the hospitals every day too." She went back to blubbering. I patted one of her shoulders with a limp, coffee-drenched hand, while the other dabbed at my wet, stained robe.

"Maybe he rented a car, took a bus or a plane. There are other ways of getting out of town."

"No, he's around. I can feel." She wiped her eyes with her soggy, make-up stained napkin. I gave her a fresh one, noting to buy more at the rate we were going through them. She blew her nose into it and handed it back to me.

Gee, thanks.

Then Kelli looked up at me and smiled. It was a rather glorious, angelic smile and made you want to like her. Oh, God. I did like her.

I'm doomed.

"Sometimes I think he's watching me." She reflected. "Or somebody's watching me." She actually started to swoon at this point. I thought she was going to pass out and grabbed to steady her.

"When was the last time you slept? Or ate?" She shrugged her shoulders and shook her head in a dismissive manner. "Where are you staying?' She raised the shoulders again, this time dropping them in a sad, waiflike gesture.

"I don't know. The car, I guess. I don't have much money left, only enough for gas, about twenty or thirty dollars. I spent the night in your driveway, because I can't

afford a motel room. There was four thousand dollars in our savings last week, and it's gone. All his stuff is still in the condo, but the money's gone! All I have left is the car and Lady Gaga."

"Beg pardon?"

"Lady Gaga's my goldfish. She's in her tank in the car. I can't leave her out there when the sun comes up; it'll get too hot. I had to keep the heater running in the car last night, so she wouldn't get too cold. They're delicate," she explained, looking into my bloodshot eyes with the sincerity of a true animal lover. "They need a constant temperate temperature in order to maintain optimal health," she said, as if reading from a manual.

She looked at me.

I looked at her.

"All rightie." I stood, resigned to my fate as the world's biggest chump. "Go get Gaga. We'll find somewhere in the apartment where the cats can't get at her. Then we're going to feed you. I can only make scrambled eggs, so if you want something else, you're out of luck. You can crash on the couch for a day or two until I make some phone calls and see what's going on. I'm not promising anything, but I'll do the best I can."

Kelli snatched at my hand and held it to her cheek in an act of gratitude and supplication. If I'd been wearing a ring, I think she might have kissed it. If this is what the pope goes through on a daily basis, you can have it. Wait a minute. It was more like the godfather.

I opened my mouth to speak when the landline rang. Pulling away from Kelli, I grabbed the phone after the first ring. Few people know this number, and each person who does means a lot to me. I'd turned off my cell and given the hour, I knew the call had to be important. I looked at the incoming number. Richard, my brother. He knew better than anybody what I'd been doing the previous night.

"What's wrong?" I said, leaving the kitchen and crossing into the living room for privacy.

He paused and gulped. "I'm on my way over to the Big House. I'll be there in about five minutes. Meet me there."

Since we were kids, the Big House is what he and I have called the large two-story family home, an ode to the American success story, Palo Alto style.

"Where are you now?" I asked.

"DI I just left the office."

"On a Sunday morning? What the hell were you doing there?" Silence. "Richard? What's wrong?"

"Lee, there's some... some news. Vicky just told me it's in this morning's *Chronicle*." Vicky and he have been married less than a year, but she is the finest addition to a family any one could ask. I adore her. My brother's voice cracked as he went on.

"That's why I'm calling you. Mom didn't want to wake you after the night you had. But I don't want you to find out from the papers. I'll be there in five minutes."

"Find out what? Jesus, Richard, you're scaring me. Just tell me."
More silence.

"Richard! The paper's in the kitchen. Should I go read it, or are you going to tell me right now?"

He let out air in a whoosh then said, "It's Stephen. It's about Stephen." He hesitated. "It's bad."

"Stephen?" I tried to flip my mind around from Kelli's mess to Mom's only living relative, outside of us. My heart began to pound. Something happened to Stephen. Stephen, my older second cousin, who taught me how to ride a bike, play Scrabble, who'd stolen my Easter candy when he thought I wasn't looking, who tipped over our canoe on a disastrous but fun river ride — wonderful, gregarious, sweet-natured, joke-telling Stephen. Although he'd moved to Phoenix thirteen years ago, he was still a much loved, integral part of the family. I tried to steel myself.

"When you say 'bad,' how bad is bad?"

His voice broke. "The worst. There's no other way to say it. He's dead, Lee. He's dead." Richard became lost in sobs.

I gasped, drawing air into my lungs so fast it physically hurt. Then I half stumbled, half sank into a nearby wingback chair, glad it was there, glad it caught me.

"*Dios mio!*" I whispered.

Richard gulped. "Sorry, Lee. I didn't mean to break it to you like that. But I didn't know...I couldn't think of any other way to say it. I'm sorry."

"But he was only forty-three," I said, faltering over the words.

"I know."

"Maybe there's a mistake." My voice had an anguished, yet angry tone. "Maybe —"

"No mistake, Lee," Richard interrupted me, his voice low and hoarse. "The medical examiner's off-the-record comment was it probably was a heart attack. He was dead before he hit the ground."

318

My kid brother began to cry full out, while I listened on the other end of the line. I sat still, trying not to breathe, trying not to move, warding off the inevitable rogue waves of emotion heading in my direction. I knew them only too well. They would be like the ones pounding at me when our father died. They would strike again and again, endlessly and without mercy. My mind fought off the oncoming onslaught and hid behind numbness and denial.

"Richard, this can't be. I don't understand. Stephen was in such good health. He had a physical every year. How could this...?"

"I'm searching for the answer to that question, myself. Meanwhile, you need to come."

"Of course, I'll come." My voice broke. "Where are you?"

"About two blocks from home. Meet me in the driveway."

"Why there? Why not inside the house?" More damned silence. "There's something else. Something you're not saying." Fear grabbed me. I didn't know why at the time. Call it premonition or something in Richard's voice.

He took a deep breath, exhaling it in a rush but hesitating over the words. "It might be a lack of sleep, Lee, or shock; I don't know—" He interrupted himself. "No, it's not any of those things. I'd thought, I'd hoped, but facts don't lie. I've been up all night, checking stats, looking into this."

"Looking into what?" I demanded. But the other end of the line went stony silent again. "Richard, are you still there?"

"I'm here," he said. His voice was filled with grief, but there was something else besides the sorrow—something that reached out and clamped down on me as if it were a steel vise. For a moment, all I could hear was my brother's staccato breathing and the sound of my own heart thudding in my ears.

"Oh, God, Richard, you don't think his death was accidental or from natural causes."

"No."

"You think Stephen was murdered."

"Yes."

Books by Heather Haven

The Alvarez Family Murder Mysteries
Murder is a Family Business, Book 1
A Wedding to Die For, Book 2
Death Runs in the Family, Book 3
DEAD...If Only, Book 4
The CEO Came DOA, Book 5
The Culinary Art of Murder, Book 6
Casting Call for a Corpse, Book 7

Love Can Be Murder Novelettes
Honeymoons Can Be Murder, Book 1
Marriage Can Be Murder, Book 2

The Persephone Cole Vintage Mysteries
The Dagger Before Me, Book 1
Iced Diamonds, Book 2
The Chocolate Kiss-Off, Book 3

The Snow Lake Romantic Suspense Novels
Christmas Trifle, Book 1

Docu-fiction/Noir Mystery Stand Alone
Murder under the Big Top

Collection of Short Stories
Corliss and Other Award-Winning Stories

Multi-Author Boxed Sets
Sleuthing Women: 10 First-in-Series Mysteries
Sleuthing Women II: 10 Mystery Novellas

About Heather Haven

After studying drama at the University of Miami in Miami, Florida, Heather went to Manhattan to pursue a career. There she wrote short stories, novels, comedy acts, television treatments, ad copy, commercials, and two one-act plays, produced at several places, such as Playwrights Horizon. Once she even ghostwrote a book on how to run an employment agency. She was unemployed at the time.

One of her first paying jobs was writing a love story for a book published by Bantam called *Moments of Love*. She had a deadline of one week but promptly came down with the flu. Heather wrote "The Sands of Time" with a raging temperature, and delivered some pretty hot stuff because of it. Her stint at New York City's No Soap Radio - where she wrote comedic ad copy – help develop her longtime love affair with comedy.

She has won many awards for the humorous Alvarez Family Murder Mysteries. The Persephone Cole Vintage Mysteries and *Corliss and Other Award Winning Stories* have garnered several, as well.

However, her proudest achievement is winning the Independent Publisher Book Awards (IPPY) 2014 Silver Medal for her stand-alone noir mystery, **Murder under the Big Top**. As the real-life daughter of Ringling Brothers and Barnum and Bailey circus folk, she was inspired by stories told throughout her childhood by her mother, a trapeze artist and performer. The book cover even has a picture of her mother sitting atop an elephant from that time. Her father trained the elephants. Heather brings the daily existence of the Big Top to life during World War II, embellished by her own murderous imagination.

Connect with Heather at the following sites:

Website: www.heatherhavenstories.com
Heather's Blog:
 http://heatherhavenstories.com/blog/
https://www.facebook.com/HeatherHavenStories
https://www.twitter.com/Twitter@HeatherHaven

Sign up for Heather's newsletter at:
http://heatherhavenstories.com/subscribe-via-email/

Email: heather@heatherhavenstories.com.

She'd love to hear from you. Thanks so much!

The Wives of Bath Press

The Wife of Bath was a woman of a certain age, with opinions, who was on a journey. Publisher Heather Haven is a modern day Wife of Bath.

www.heatherhavenstories.com

Made in the USA
Middletown, DE
01 October 2021